Pathways for Ecumenical and Interreligious Dialogue

Series Editor
Mark Chapman
Ripon College
University of Oxford
Oxford, UK

Building on the important work of the Ecclesiological Investigations International Research Network to promote ecumenical and inter-faith encounters and dialogue, the Pathways for Ecumenical and Interreligious Dialogue series publishes scholarship on such engagement in relation to the past, present, and future. It gathers together a richly diverse array of voices in monographs and edited collections that speak to the challenges, aspirations, and elements of ecumenical and interfaith conversation. Through its publications, the series allows for the exploration of new ways, means, and methods of advancing the wider ecumenical cause with renewed energy for the twenty-first century.

Raimundo C. Barreto • Vladimir Latinovic
Editors

Decolonial Horizons

Reimagining Theology, Ecumenism and Sacramental Praxis

Editors
Raimundo C. Barreto
Princeton, NJ, USA

Vladimir Latinovic
Tübingen, Germany

ISSN 2634-6591   ISSN 2634-6605   (electronic)
Pathways for Ecumenical and Interreligious Dialogue
ISBN 978-3-031-44838-6   ISBN 978-3-031-44839-3   (eBook)
https://doi.org/10.1007/978-3-031-44839-3

© The Editor(s) (if applicable) and The Author(s), under exclusive licence to Springer Nature Switzerland AG 2023
This work is subject to copyright. All rights are solely and exclusively licensed by the Publisher, whether the whole or part of the material is concerned, specifically the rights of translation, reprinting, reuse of illustrations, recitation, broadcasting, reproduction on microfilms or in any other physical way, and transmission or information storage and retrieval, electronic adaptation, computer software, or by similar or dissimilar methodology now known or hereafter developed.
The use of general descriptive names, registered names, trademarks, service marks, etc. in this publication does not imply, even in the absence of a specific statement, that such names are exempt from the relevant protective laws and regulations and therefore free for general use.
The publisher, the authors, and the editors are safe to assume that the advice and information in this book are believed to be true and accurate at the date of publication. Neither the publisher nor the authors or the editors give a warranty, expressed or implied, with respect to the material contained herein or for any errors or omissions that may have been made. The publisher remains neutral with regard to jurisdictional claims in published maps and institutional affiliations.

This Palgrave Macmillan imprint is published by the registered company Springer Nature Switzerland AG.
The registered company address is: Gewerbestrasse 11, 6330 Cham, Switzerland

Paper in this product is recyclable.

Dedicated to Dale Irvin in recognition of his leadership in organizing this conference and his exceptional scholarship.

Contents

1 Decolonial Horizons: An Introduction   1
Vladimir Latinovic and Raimundo C. Barreto

Part I   Migration, Diaspora and Decolonization   17

2 Coloniality, Diaspora, and Decolonial Resistance   19
Luis N. Rivera-Pagán

3 Immigration, Immunity, Community, and the Church: Roberto Esposito's Biopolitical Immunitary Paradigm   37
Craig A. Phillips

4 Decolonizing Among Filipin@ Migrant-Settlers   55
Cristina Lledo Gomez

Part II   Decolonizing Dialogue   77

5 "A World in Which Many Worlds Fit": Ecumenism and Pluriversal Ontologies   79
Raimundo C. Barreto

6 Colonization, Proselytism and Conversion: Can Interfaith Dialogue Be the Answer? Pope Francis' Contribution   101
Roberto Catalano

7 Decolonial Options for World Christianity: Thinking and Acting with Santa Teresa Urrea and Prophet Garrick Sokari Braide   121
Ryan T. Ramsey

Part III   Decolonizing History and Theological Education   141

8 Decolonizing the Reformation: Centering Ethiopian Christianity, Decentering the Eurocentric Narrative   143
David Douglas Daniels III

9 Race, Theology, and the Church: A Transatlantic Conversation, and a Model for a Church in Productive Tension   163
R. Ward Holder and Cynthia Holder Rich

10 Nuevo Mundo Theology as a Latinx Decolonial Response to the Global Crisis in Theological Education   183
Oscar García-Johnson

Part IV   Worship, Rite and Sacrament as Decolonial Events   203

11 Toward a Decolonial Liturgical Theology   205
Laurel Marshall Potter

12 Toward Decolonizing Penitential Rites: A Diasporic and Ecumenical Exploration of Worship on (Still) Colonized Land   227
Kristine Suna-Koro

13 Decolonizing Churches and the Right to the Sacrament   247
Dale T. Irvin

Index   265

Notes on Contributors

Raimundo C. Barreto is Associate Professor of World Christianity at Princeton Theological Seminary. He holds a PhD in Religion and Society from the same school and holds degrees from Mercer University and Seminário Teológico Batista do Norte do Brasil. His most recent publications include *Protesting Poverty: Protestants, Social Ethics and the Poor in Brazil*. Baylor University Press, 2023), and the co-edited volumes *Alterity and the Evasion of Justice in World Christianity* (Fortress Press, 2023), *World Christianity, Urbanization, and Identity* (Fortress Press, 2021), and *Decolonial Christianities: Latin American and Latinx Perspectives* (Palgrave/McMillan, 2019). Barreto is the co-editor of the *Journal of World Christianity* and one of the conveners of the Princeton World Christianity Conference.

Roberto Catalano, born in Turin, Italy, holds a doctorate in Missiology from Urbaniana University in Rome. From 1980 to 2008, he lived in India, where he was Cultural Officer at the Consulate General of Italy in Mumbai and taught Italian language in different institutions. Since 1996 he has been actively involved in interreligious dialogue. From 2008 to 2021, he was co-director of the International Office for Interreligious Dialogue of the Focolare Movement. In and from Rome he organized events of dialogue with Hindus, Muslims, Buddhists, Hindus, and Jews. At present, he teaches theology and praxis of interfaith dialogue and theoretics of dialogue at the University Institute Sophia, Loppiano-Firenze (Italy). He authored articles for journals and magazines and published five books.

David Douglas Daniels III is the Henry Winters Luce Professor of World Christianity at McCormick Theological Seminary where he joined the faculty in 1987 and the Professor Extraordinarius at the Institute for Gender Studies, University of South Africa. Daniels serves as an associate editor of the *Journal of World Christianity*. He holds a PhD from Union Theological Seminary-NYC. He publishes on topics related to the Black Church and Global Pentecostalism in addition to African Christians in sixteenth-century Europe. He has served on research projects funded by the Lilly Endowment and other foundations as well as participated in funded research projects in Germany and Norway. He has delivered public lectures in the United States and other countries.

Oscar García-Johnson (PhD, Fuller Theological Seminary) is Professor of Theology and Latinx Studies at Fuller Seminary. He is an ordained American Baptist minister, was a regional minister with ABCLA; has planted four churches, and loves cycling, cooking, woodworking, and socializing. He uses decolonial theories in the fields of theology, religion, ministry, and cultural studies to reimagine Christian identity, doctrine, and praxis in the global space. His writings include *Spirit Outside the Gate* (2019), *Conversaciones Teológicas del Sur Global Americano*, ed. (2016), *Theology Without Borders* (2015), *The Mestizo/a Community of the Spirit* (2009), and the seven-volume work, *Teología del Nuevo Mundo* (Editorial CLIE, 2022).

Cristina Lledo Gomez is a native Filipina living on the traditional lands of the Darug and Guringai peoples. She is a Presentation Sisters Theology Lecturer at BBI-The Australian Institute of Theological Education and Research Fellow for Charles Sturt University's Public and Contextual Theology Centre. Lledo Gomez is the author of *The Church as Woman and Mother* (2018) and co-editing *God of Interruption: Mothering and Theology* with Julia Brumbaugh and *500 Years of Christianity in the Philippines: Postcolonial Perspectives* with Agnes Brazal and Ma. Marilou Ibita. Other forthcoming publications include chapters in the *Oxford Companion to Asian Theologies* (on ecclesiology) and *SCM Companion to Feminist Theologies* (on Mariology).

R. Ward Holder is a historical and political theologian and holds a joint appointment as Professor of Theology and Politics at Saint Anselm College in Manchester, New Hampshire. He writes on the manner in which religious convictions shape both theological and political convictions. Among other works, he has co-authored with Peter B. Josephson, *The Irony of Barack Obama: Barack Obama, Reinhold Niebuhr, and the Problem of Christian Statecraft*, Ashgate, 2012; and *Reinhold Niebuhr in Theory and Practice: Christian Realism and Democracy in America in the Twenty-First Century*, Lexington, 2019. Most recently, he published *Calvin and the Christian Tradition: Scripture, Memory, and the Western Mind*, Cambridge, 2022.

Dale T. Irvin is Professor of World Christianity at the New School of Biblical Theology. He is also chair of Ecclesiological Investigations International Research Network and a founding co-editor of the *Journal of World Christianity*. He previously served on the faculty of New York Theological Seminary for 31 years, the last 13 of those as President. A graduate of Princeton Theological Seminary (MDiv) and Union Theological Seminary in New York (PhD), he is the author and editor of several books, including *History of the World Christian Movement*, a three-volume project with Scott W. Sunquist. Over the past several decades, his articles have appeared in a number of journals and edited volumes. He has held visiting or adjunct appointments at a number of theological schools and universities and has lectured throughout the world. An ordained minister in the American Baptist Churches USA, he is a member of The Riverside Church in New York City.

Vladimir Latinovic graduated from the Faculty of Orthodox Theology at the University of Belgrade and holds his PhD from the Faculty of Catholic Theology at the University of Tübingen. He is writing his habilitation (second doctoral thesis) at the Protestant Theological Faculty of the University of Heidelberg. He also works at the Ecumenical Institute in Tübingen, where he teaches dogmatics, ecumenism, and orthodox theology. He is a coordinating board member of the International Research Network Ecclesiological Investigations (EIIRN) and the founder and co-chair of the Orthodox Eastern Catholic Dialogue Group (OECD). He published three volumes on *Christology and Communion* (Ashendorff, 2018–2022) and edited six books on ecumenical and interreligious dialogue (Palgrave).

Craig A. Phillips is a retired Episcopal Priest and Lecturer in Theology at Saint Anselm College in Manchester, New Hampshire. He is a former assistant professor at Temple University. Craig has also taught at Georgetown University, Virginia Theological Seminary, and Rosemont

College. He holds a doctorate in Theology and Ethics from Duke University, an M.Div. from Harvard University, and an A.B. in Religious Studies and Classics from Brown University. His research focuses on the intersections of literary theory, philosophy, postcolonial and critical theory, and political and contemporary theology. Craig is an active member of the American Academy of Religion and the Society of Biblical Literature.

Laurel Marshall Potter is Assistant Professor of Liberation Theologies at the University of St. Thomas in St. Paul, Minnesota, with interests including decolonial thought and praxis, Latin American theologies, and questions of theological method. She is co-author of *Re-membering the Reign of God: The Decolonial Witness of El Salvador's Church of the Poor* (Lexington, 2022), and her writing has appeared in *Ecclesiology*, the *NACLA Report*, and the edited volume *Valuing Lives, Healing Earth: Religion, Gender, and Life on Earth* (Peeters, 2021). Laurel enjoys over a decade of personal and professional relationship with ecclesial base communities in El Salvador, and her current project compares receptions of Vatican II–era liturgical theology and practices of liturgical in(ter)culturation in NuestrAmerica today.

Ryan T. Ramsey is a PhD candidate in Religion at Baylor University. His dissertation examines the life and religion of Mexican folk saint Teresa Urrea using the lenses of World Christianity and decolonial thought. He also researches, presents, and publishes on the history of Pentecostal and charismatic movements. He is a fellow with Baylor University's Academy for Teaching and Learning and a scholar with the Graymoor Ecumenical and Interreligious Institute. He holds a Master of Arts in Religion from Yale Divinity School (2019) and a BA from Lee University (2014).

Cynthia Holder Rich (MDiv, MCE, PhD) serves on the Faculty of Theology of Tumaini University Makumira near Arusha, Tanzania, and at Trinity Lutheran Seminary at Capital University, Columbus, Ohio, USA. She has also served in theological education in Madagascar and Michigan. She is the author of *Indigenous Christianity: The Power to Heal in Community* (Peter Lang, 2011) and the editor of *The Fifohazana: Madagascar's Indigenous Christian Movement* (Cambria Press, 2008) and *Christian Zionism in Africa* (Fortress Academic, 2021). She has published extensively on the impact and operation of race and gender in the church, missiology, confessional Christianity, and faith-based justice efforts. She is an ordained clergyperson in the Presbyterian Church (USA).

Luis N. Rivera-Pagán is the Henry Winters Luce Professor of Ecumenics and Mission Emeritus at Princeton Theological Seminary. He is the author of several books, among them: *A la sombra del armagedón: reflexiones críticas sobre el desafío nuclear* (1988), *A Violent Evangelism: The Political and Religious Conquest of the Americas* (1992), *Los sueños del ciervo: Perspectivas teológicas desde el Caribe* (1995), *Entre el oro y la fe: El dilema de América* (1995), *Teología y cultura en América Latina* (2009), *Ensayos teológicos desde el Caribe* (2013), *Essays from the Margins* (2014), *Voz profética y teología liberadora* (2017), *Evocaciones literarias y sociales* (2018), and *Historia de la conquista de América: Evangelización y violencia* (2021).

Rev. Dr. Kristine Suna-Koro is Professor of Theology at Xavier University, Cincinnati, OH, USA. She is a diasporic Latvian-American Lutheran theologian working at the intersections of sacramental and liturgical theology, postcolonial, and decolonial thought as well as diasporic studies and migration discourses. She is the author of *In Counterpoint: Postcoloniality, Diaspora, and Sacramental Theology* (2017). She is serving as Co-Editor in Chief of Dialog: *A Journal of Theology* (Wiley) and Co-Chair of Religions, Borders, and Immigration seminar at the American Academy of Religion.

CHAPTER 1

Decolonial Horizons: An Introduction

Vladimir Latinovic and Raimundo C. Barreto

This collection of essays, the first of two volumes, emerged from the Decolonizing Churches Conference organized by the Ecclesiological Investigations International Research Network on June 22–25, 2022, in San Juan, Puerto Rico. The conference took place at the Metropolitan Campus of the Universidad Interamericana de Puerto Rico (UIPR) in San Juan with the support and participation of the Seminario Evangélico de Puerto Rico, Universidad Interamericana de Puerto Rico, and other regional institutions. Due to the ongoing global uncertainties caused by COVID-19, the conference was held in hybrid mode.

We invited proposals for papers addressing the need and rationale for decolonizing churches and theology in the Caribbean, Latin America, and their diaspora. We also welcomed papers dealing with the topic of colonization/decolonization in other global contexts. Intrinsically related to the

---

V. Latinovic (✉)
University of Tübingen, Tübingen, Germany
e-mail: vladimir.latinovic@uni-tuebingen.de

R. C. Barreto
Princeton Theological Seminary, Princeton, NJ, USA
e-mail: raimundo.barreto@ptsem.edu

© The Author(s), under exclusive license to Springer Nature Switzerland AG 2023
R. C. Barreto, V. Latinovic (eds.), *Decolonial Horizons*, Pathways for Ecumenical and Interreligious Dialogue,
https://doi.org/10.1007/978-3-031-44839-3_1

idea of decolonizing theologies, papers presented at this conference included topics addressing oppressions based on gender, racial, and ethnic identities; economic inequality; social vulnerabilities; climate change; and global challenges such as pandemics, neoliberalism, and the role of information technology in modern society. As Ecclesiological Investigations seeks to foster interdisciplinary and transdisciplinary scholarship, we invited proposals for papers from historical, dogmatic, social scientific, and practical disciplines. The conference welcomed paper proposals reflecting perspectives from all major Christian traditions. Some papers focused on specific case studies while others dealt with comparative ecclesiologies or theologies. Fostering what S. Wesley Ariarajah has coined as "wider ecumenism,"[1] we also welcomed proposals dealing with the need to decolonize interfaith relations and which addressed challenges and promises of pluralistic contexts.

Papers were presented in English, Spanish, and Portuguese. Non-English papers were translated in advance into English and submitted to the conference planning committee so that they could be posted prior to the beginning of the conference, facilitating the participation in discussion sessions of those who do not speak these languages. Plenary sessions that were conducted in Spanish or Portuguese were translated simultaneously. While these two volumes do not exhaust the wealth and thoroughness of the conversations held during the conference, the select essays chosen for each volume offer a good insight into the main concerns and the diversity of contexts, (inter)disciplinary approaches, and language that informed those conversations. Some of the essays the reader will access in English in these two volumes were translated, since this publication is aimed at the anglophone academia. The editors are aware of the paradox involved in the prioritization of English readers in a work meant to advance the cause of decoloniality. We accept the risks of such an enterprise, though, convinced of the need to help those operating in anglophone bubbles to engage the important scholarly production emerging, particularly on this important theme, in languages such as Spanish and Portuguese. Furthermore, as it has been the case with other publications with which the editors have been involved in the past several years, we operate in the

---

[1] See, for instance, chapter 6, titled "Wider Ecumenism: A Promise or a Threat?," in S. Wesley Ariarajah, *Strangers or Co-Pilgrims? The Impact of Interfaith Dialogue on Christian Faith and Practice* (Minneapolis, MN: Fortress Press, 2017), 105–113.

hope that at some point this material can be translated and published in other languages.[2]

The question these coupled volumes seek to answer is that of the pertinence of the engagement of decolonial thought and practice in the study of religion and theology, turning the reader's attention, however, to a decolonial approach to research on ecclesiology. As such, these volumes cross disciplinary, geographical, and cultural borders, addressing questions such as: Why is it important to decolonize our understandings of church? What does the task of decolonizing church entail? Which are its potential consequences? What does one envision when one thinks about decolonized or decolonial churches? Which are the differences between the two? And, finally, perhaps the most complex one: Is it even possible to decolonize church?

In fact, those attending the "Decolonizing Church" Conference last year in San Juan were confronted with that last question, when a group of local Native Americans entered the room unannounced. During the Q&A session, they addressed some of the very issues that these two volumes seek to analyze, such as models of interpreting the decolonization of the church, and the possibility and legitimacy of a role for the churches in these processes, given that they were key players in the colonial enterprise that led to the invasion and occupation of colonized territories. The issue of returning these lands to their original owners was also raised by these visitors as they interpellated conference organizers and participants.[3]

---

[2] A similar paradox was present, for instance, in the publication of the book *Decolonial Christianities: Latinx and Latin American Perspectives*, edited by Raimundo Barreto and Roberto Sirvent (New York, NY: Palgrave Macmillan, 2019), which also had some chapters translated from Spanish. Four years later, the whole volume has been translated into Portuguese. See Raimundo Barreto and Roberto Sirvent (eds.). *Cristianismos Decoloniais: Perspectivas Latinx e Latino Americanas. Novas Abordagens à Religião e Poder* (São Paulo: Editora Recriar/Editora Unida, 2023).

[3] The initial moment of this eye-opening experience is narrated in the second volume by Elaine Padilla, as she was in the midst of her presentation when these distinguished guests entered the room. They stayed with us for a couple of hours after that session, talking individually with several of us. While their initial questions rightfully used some irony to proof our intents, they were truly interested to understand what was the proposal of the conference. While the organizers of the conference had made attempts to identify local Indigenous leaders to invite to the conference, the limits of our efforts and our failure to accomplish that goal were blatant. While many important Puerto Rican voices were part of the conception and planning of the conference, we must acknowledge that we failed to secure the presence and participation of Native Americans in the organizing committee.

Research concerning the task of decolonizing church and ecclesiology remains critical. Over the past 500 years, Christians and churches throughout the world have been on both ends of the modern colonial enterprise. The fact that Christians have participated in acts of resistance to colonialism and engaged in liberating praxis, though, does not atone Christianity from the major role it has played and continues to play in the fostering and expansion of global colonial designs. And that is exactly the difference. While we can enumerate instances in which Christian individuals and communities have stood on the side of justice and have contributed with efforts to reverse the impact of colonialism and coloniality in the contemporary world, when we speak of the Church's participation on the other end of this spectrum, we are not talking about isolated individuals or communities and their stories but mainly also about modern Christianity's role and participation in the production of a racialized "global hierarchy of superiority and inferiority along the line of the human [...] politically, culturally and economically produced and reproduced [institutionally] for centuries."[4]

The understanding of what Enrique Dussel called "the myth of modernity" and "the invention of the Americas" demanded "the eclipse of the other,"[5] the Indigenous other, the African other, and all non-European others in the creation of world system, which, having Europe as its self-proclaimed center, when not managing to erase the non-Christian, non-European, subsumed them into a hierarchized world order in which all other civilizations and peoples were lacking when compared to the European romanticized history of progress. Europe did not become a united self-proclaimed world center merely due to internal circumstances as narratives with an emphasis on the renaissance and the enlightenment seem to convey. Europe would not be modern without the riches extracted from invaded lands and exploitation of their genocided peoples, nor would

---

[4] Ramon Grosfoguel names the conglomerate of institutions that created such a globalized hierarchical (racist) order as "the institutions of the 'capitalist/patriarchal western-centric/Christian-centric modern/colonial world-system.'" Ramon Grosfoguel, "What is Racism?" *Journal of World-System Research* 22/1 (2016): 9–15 (10).

[5] These three sentences represent different parts of the title of a book in which Dussel advances his theory of transmodernity, showing that modernity cannot, in fact, be seen as a European phenomenon since it emerges from the European encounter, as invaders, conquerors, and colonizers, of territories which they would later rename as America. See Enrique Dussel, *The Invention of the Americas: Eclipse of "the Other" and the Myth of Modernity* (New York, NY: Continuum, 1995).

it become the economic center of the world without the labor of enslaved Africans and other enslaved nations and persons—keep in mind that Indigenous peoples in the Americas, when not fully enslaved, were commonly placed under conditions analogous to slavery through the creation of legal and theological fantasies such as the *encomiendas* or *repartimientos*.[6]

The rise of independent Latin American states after three centuries of European colonialism ended the colonial conditions created both in Latin America and in the ordering of the world. Eurocentric theological, scientific, and cultural universalisms advanced totalizing frames that continued to inform the hierarchical ordering of the world—perpetuated in modern Eurocentric legacies and Western geopolitics of knowledge—which determined what is acceptable or not as knowledge, who validates it, and what is universally valid and what is not.[7] This perpetuation of colonial hierarchies even after colonial administrations are gone is what Latin American and Latinx thinkers have called coloniality—or the colonial matrix of power.[8]

Decoloniality, on the other hand, is, as Catherine Walsh rightly underscores, a praxis otherwise, composed by "(trans)local struggles, movements, and actions to resist and refuse the legacies and ongoing relations and patterns of power established by external and internal colonialism [...] and the global designs of the modern/colonial world."[9] Such a praxis is not new. It has existed for as long as colonialism has been installed as

---

[6] Ibid., 120. *Encomiendas* were estates given by the Spanish crown to *encomienderos* (usually rewarded soldiers) with good Christian reputation who were also "granted the labor of the defeated foes," for whom, though, they are responsible and supposed to treat well, protect, and Christianize/Europeanize them. Indigenous labor was used without limits in the *encomiendas* for farming and mining. Many were worked to death. The Spaniards did not care, since the *encomienda* gave them an infinite supply of cheap laborers. As Justo and Ondina González put it, "in reality, the encomienda was slavery." Justo González; Ondina E. González, Ondina. *Christianity in Latin America: A History* (New York, NY: Cambridge University Press, 2008), 29.

[7] Walter D. Mignolo and Catherine E. Walsh. *On Decoloniality: Concepts, Analytics, Praxis* (Durham: Duke University Press, 2018), 2.

[8] It is important to keep in mind, though, that colonialism itself has not ended, as many of the Puerto Ricans attending the conference pointed out. After all, as Luis N. Rivera-Pagán has pointed out, Puerto is the oldest colony on earth today. Luis N. Rivera-Pagán, "Listening and Engaging the Voices from the Margins: Postcolonial Observations from the Caribbean," in *Essays from the Margins* (Eugene, Oregon: Cascade Books, 2014), 44–62.

[9] Mignolo and Walsh, op. cit., 16.

praxis of resistance, resilience, and survival. It exists side-by-side with colonialism and coloniality, denouncing, resisting, adapting, negotiating, persisting, surviving, and not being erased at the end of the day. Decolonial praxis thus combines elements of resistance, criticism, and creativity. It is not only about denouncing and dismantling colonial praxis and lingering power matrices, but also about overcoming challenges, reimagining and reinventing ways of being and knowing, of living in the interstices, constantly crossing borders, which sometimes exist within a person's body.[10] In other words, decoloniality is critical thinking, as it sheds light on ontological and epistemic injustices that deep down are meant to erase memories and ways of being and knowing of formerly subjugated subjects. However, its approach focuses primarily on those silenced subjects, seeking to revitalize what was lost, recreate and restore tentatively erased subjectivities and silenced or repressed subjects—their voices, their knowledge, their ways of being and knowing. As Nelson Maldonado-Torres puts it, "The Decolonial Turn is about making visible the invisible and about analyzing the mechanisms that produce such invisibility or distorted visibility in light of a large stock of ideas that must necessarily include the critical reflections of the 'invisible' people themselves."[11] Walsh and Mignolo add to that the elements of relationality and complementarity, considering the ways as

> [D]ifferent local histories and embodied conceptions and practices of decoloniality, including our own, can enter into conversations and build understandings that both cross geopolitical locations and colonial differences, and contest the totalizing claims and political-epistemic violence of modernity.[12]

---

[10] As Gloria Anzaldúa teaches us, the borderland is not simply a geographical space but an open wound where two worlds merge forming a third space, a border culture. In the book that made her widely known, *Borderlands/La Frotera: The New Mestiza*, she states, "A borderland is a vague and undetermined place created by the emotional residue of an unnatural boundary. It is a constant state of transition." Going further, she adds elsewhere, "But I, like other queer people, am two in one body, both male and female. I am the embodiment of the *hieros gamos*: the coming together of opposite qualities within." The border is not a physical space outside ourselves only, but also something that perpasses, *atravessa* our own bodies. Gloria Anzaldúa, *Borderlands/La Frontera: The New Mestiza*. The Critical Edition (San Francisco, CA: Aunt Lute Books, 2021), 57, 76.

[11] Nelson Maldonado-Torres, "On the Coloniality of Being: Contributions to the Development of a Concept," *Cultural Studies* 21/2–3 (2007): 240–270 (262).

[12] Mignolo and Walsh, op. cit., 1.

All these elements are included in this collection of essays in the complexity—sometimes impetuosity—that is characteristic of the rise of what has been suppressed. Considering the variety of voices represented in these two volumes, it is important for the reader to keep in mind that they come from different contexts and disciplinary conversations, having sometimes distinct conversational partners and approaches to the theme of decolonization/decoloniality. For instance, not all authors are deeply acquainted with the distinctions between decolonization and decoloniality assumed in this introduction, which has been mainly developed by decolonial scholars such as Anibal Quijano, Walter D. Mignolo, Catherine Walsh, Nelson Maldonado-Torres, Ramon Grosfoguel, Arturo Escobar, Gloria Anzaldúa, Josef Estermann, and Sylvia Wynter, to cite a few. Those less engaged with recent theoretical developments on decoloniality and border thinking in the Americas might engage decolonizing approaches developed through the political decolonizing movements of the second half of the twentieth century, which gave birth to this entire conversation through the genius of a generation of thinkers such as Frantz Fannon, Amilcar Cabral, and Aimé Césaire, among others. A third set of theoretical and methodological references that are often engaged in this sort of conversation are postcolonial thinkers like Homi K. Bhabha, Edward Said, Gayatri C. Spivak, Betty Russel, and Boaventura de Souza Santos, to name some.

Depending on where a given author is situated geographically and disciplinarily, and what kind of conversations they are more regularly engaged with, their theoretical references and conversation partners may vary, sometimes coming from one of these three distinct sets of theoretical differences, other times combining them in different ways. The editors of these volumes embrace such a theoretical and methodological variety as representativity of the "pluriversal decoloniality" and "decolonial pluriversality" that Mignolo and Walsh refer to as "being thought and constructed outside and in the borders and fissures of the North Atlantic Western world."[13] While these multiple approaches enlighten and enrich each other, sometimes they remain in tension with one another, and still are allowed to coexist. This is a characteristic of decoloniality, which advances a paradigm marked by *vincularidad* (binding, connectedness, independence), "the awareness of the integral relation and interdependence amongst all living organisms (in which humans are only a part) with territory or land and the cosmos," which, by its turn, "unsettles the

[13] Ibid., 2.

singular authoritativeness and universal character typically assumed and portrayed in academic thought."[14]

The main commonality among the authors included in these two volumes is that they agree about the importance of decolonizing theology and ecclesiology. Such a process of decolonization is, above all, epistemic, seeking, as Enrique Dussel points out, to invert the inversions the early messianic Christianity represented in the Jesus movement. The first inversion, starting in the fourth century, reaches its apex when the emperor of the newly formed Holy Roman Germanic empire is crowned by the Pope, turning what he describes as an early messianic Christianity into a triumphant one, which ceased to be critical of empire, becoming, instead, its supporter and legitimator. The paradox is unavoidable:

> The Messiah crucified by the soldiers of the Roman Empire was now acclaimed as the Christ: the Christ who had lost Isaiah's image of "suffering servant" in order to be Pantokrator: the all-powerful [God] of the Byzantine basilicas. Christ is now the name of the God who founded the Empire, in whose name the Roman armies confront slaves, the Germanics, the barbarians, the rebellious farmers, and the slaves that pretend to be free.[15]

This is the inception of the Christendom, which from that point on will reshape the view of Christianity, associating it with empire, and becoming, as Dussel rightly points out, "a new hegemonic culture."[16]

The second inversion takes place with the transformation of Christendom into a world system, a self-proclaimed center of an incipient global geopolitics, a radical change in geopolitics that would relocate Europe from its peripheral status to the center of global commerce and politics. Through this second inversion, Christendom becomes imperial Christendom as it expands its reach to dominate "oppressed colonies in the name of gospel of the Crucified one."[17]

The epistemological decolonization of Christianity Dussel proposes demands the dislodging of the Eurocentric apparatus of modern/colonial

---

[14] Ibid., 1–2.

[15] Enrique Dussel, "Epistemological Decolonization of Theology," in *Decolonial Christianities: Latinx and Latin American Perspectives*. Edited by Raimundo Barreto and Roberto Sirvent (Cham, Switzerland: Palgrave Macmillan, 2019), 25–42 (27).

[16] Ibid., 28.

[17] Ibid., 32. As Dussel puts it, Imperial Christendom manifested its contradiction as it "crucified the indigenous in the name of the one that was crucified."

Christianity and the relocation of its theological epicenter from imperial Christendom to the experience of the subaltern, those whose lands, cultures, and ways of being and knowing the world have been colonized. What these two volumes add to that quest is the question about what does this process mean for our ecclesiological understandings and practical church experiences today.

This first volume starts this important conversation, focusing on four major areas. Its first part, "Migration, Diaspora and Decolonization," acknowledges that empire, colonialism, and coloniality are also at the root of experiences of migration and diaspora. More recently, the globalization of capital (including the power imbalances and environmental crises it has created) and significant developments in transport and communication have contributed in unique ways to intensify migration flows worldwide.[18] According to the 2022 World Migration Report, around 281 million people live today in a country different from that they were born,[19] including both editors of these two volumes. If they all lived in the same territory, that would be the fourth most populous country in the world, just behind India, China, and the United States. However, migration is not only a contemporary phenomenon. It has existed since immemorial times. The prominence of migration in today's globalized world, however, makes it crucial to examine human conflicts and identity through the lenses of transnational communities and networks formed through multiple migration flows. This first part is comprised of three chapters.

The second chapter is authored by Luis N. Rivera-Pagán and focuses on the relation between two key processes in modern history: imperial colonialism—including slavery—and the struggle for decolonization and liberation. Paradoxically, both activities were carried out in the name of God and Christianity. The realization of the conference "Decolonizing Churches" in Puerto Rico, which has been referred to as the oldest colony in the world, becomes itself an evidence of such paradox. Additionally, diaspora, migration, and liberation theology are discussed, with a particular focus on the advance of a critical decolonial theology.

---

[18] Afe Adogame, Raimundo Barreto, and Wanderley Pereira da Rosa, "Introduction: Migration and Public Discourse in World Christianity," in *Migration and Public Discourse in World Christianity* (Minneapolis, MN: Fortress Press, 2019), 24.

[19] IOM – UN Migration, "World Migration Report 2022," available at https://worldmigrationreport.iom.int/wmr-2022-interactive/. Accessed on July 20, 2023.

This is followed by a contribution from Craig Phillips in which he reflects theologically on immigration and the status of refugees and asylum seekers in contemporary political discourse in the United States. This chapter analyzes the theological themes of immunity, community, and sanctuary found in current debates, relating Roberto Esposito's biopolitics to postcolonial theories of decolonization. Phillips argues that racism is implicit in current immigration practices and that the church should confront this racism by setting an example of radical hospitality and welcome, suggesting some practical ways to make that happen.

In the fourth chapter, Cristina Lledo Gomez explores decolonizing practices among Filipin@s living outside of the Philippines, interpreting the concept of decolonization as a means to address and overcome what she describes as a colonial mentality and internalized oppression. The Centre for Babaylan Studies (CfBS) has engaged in such a process of decolonization for many years. Lledo shares her experiences leading an online decolonizing group from Australia in connection with the CfBS. She then examines how churches can consider taking up decolonial practices to address colonial mentality among Filipin@s. Overall, she suggests that decolonization is an important tool for creating an equitable and just society.

The second part of the book, also comprised by three chapters, focuses on the idea of "decolonizing Christianity as thinking otherwise," pointing to the importance of revisiting concepts, events, and stories in Christian life and history through new historiographical and epistemological lenses.

In Chap. 5, Raimundo C. Barreto examines some Latin American contributions that might help us expand the understanding of "the ecumenical" with particular attention to neglected memories and marginalized histories, engaging ecumenics through a methodological and theoretical lens informed by the burgeoning field of World Christianity. Drawing on ideas such as the Zapatista's adage "a world in which many worlds fit" and Arturo Escobar's concepts of the pluriverse, the making of worlds, and knowledges otherwise, this chapter revisits the modern/colonial origins of the modern ecumenical movement, examining the impact of ecumenical collaboration involving Asian, African, and Latin American Christians on broader ecumenical praxis in the past few decades. A decolonial exploration of Western knowledge and thought is conducted in order to advance an ecumenical perspective which focuses on emerging consciousness from in-between spaces, wherein Ecumenism values interconnectedness over universalizing unity.

Roberto Catalano in the chapter that follows discusses how the Church has gone through a crucial change of paradigm since Vatican Council, paying particular attention to the magisterium and witnesses of recent popes, in particular Pope Francis, who according to Catalano is playing a decisive role in contributing to decolonizing the Church both at its center and in the peripheries. His attitude of openness toward all cultures and other faiths encourages constructive dialogue and is potentially creating a new image of Christianity in the world, which moves away from the image of Christianity as a proselytizing religion that was created by centuries of Catholic missions spreading in the shadow of colonialism.

The seventh chapter authored by Ryan T. Ramsey examines Mexican folk-saint Teresa Urrea and Niger Delta prophet-healer Garrick Braide as models of indigenous Christian leaders who resisted coloniality. It looks at historiographical and sociohistorical methods developed by thinkers Boaventura de Sousa Santos and Enrique Dussel to demonstrate how Urrea and Braide seamlessly integrated local religious knowledge with the Christian gospel. Using a terminology that resembles the one seen in the previous chapter, Ramsey suggests that they should be seen as examples of "artisanal knowledges" and "thinking otherwise" in the face of oppression. Furthermore, the essay challenges World Christianity to understand decolonial insights and use them to resist coloniality. It also looks to Urrea and Braide as examples of decolonial Christian leaders that sought to restore indigenous epistemologies and the most messianic impulses of Christianity.

The third part of the book expands the concern with the need for decolonial historiographies. Under the heading "Decolonizing History and Theological Education," the next three chapters challenge eurocentric reductionism in history, pedagogy, and the production of theological knowledge, advancing dialogical models that not only reveal the epistemic crisis Western theological education faces but also point the way forward for the use of more expansive and polycentric narratives and pedagogies.

David D. Daniels opens this third part by arguing that to prevent the entanglement of the Reformation narrative in a matrix of coloniality, it can be expanded to include Ethiopian Christians and their texts, since they played a role in the Reformation. The chapter brings to the fore, in particular, the encounters between Ethiopian and European Christians, which revealed that leading European Catholics and Protestants learned from Ethiopian Christianity. Furthermore, it also explores how Ethiopian-European exchange served as an alternative to the European colonizing model, as it was a collaborative model that promoted peership between Ethiopian and European Christians. Daniels' analysis reveals how coloniality can be challenged when non-European Christians are included in the narrative of the Reformation. By highlighting the role of Ethiopian Christians in the Reformation movement, this chapter expands and enriches the Reformation narrative, offering an alternative to still dominant Eurocentric and colonial approaches.

Looking in a similar direction, although focusing on a contemporary experience, Chap. 9, jointly authored by R. Ward Holder and Cynthia Holder Rich, explores the collaboration between an American college and a theological college in Tanzania in 2021. This collaboration aimed to explore the impact of racism and colonialism on theology and ecclesiology. Students from both countries concomitantly studied significant theorists on this topic, also engaging in dialogue with five scholars working at the intersect of these constructs and with each other. Traditional pedagogical models were drastically reimagined as the result of this effort. The researchers also realized that this dialogic model can significantly contribute to expand ecclesiological considerations in churches on the whole spectrum of the oppressor-oppressed dyad. This chapter suggests, therefore, that intentional dialogues between historically oppressing and colonized contexts have enormous potential to reimagine and revive churches and their transnational relations.

The last chapter in this third part is contribution by Oscar García-Johnson, who argues that a crisis he sees happening in global theological education is rooted in Western theological education's epistemic crisis. He uses the American Global South as a case study, meaning the various Americas constructed across colonial project to reimagine the concept of Nuevo Mundo as a biblical-theological horizon for retheologizing the Americas before and beyond the imperial logic of colonial modernity. García-Johnson proposes an autochthonous decolonial theologizing as a response to the global crisis in theological education through his project Teología del Nuevo Mundo. He argues that this project can be used to transform the situation in the Global South and to contribute toward a just and equitable form of theological education, claiming that this project has the potential to create new forms of knowledge production and new understandings of theological education, which could lead to a more equitable form of educational practices.

The fourth and final part of this first volume gathers essays which seek to reimagine "worship, rite and sacrament as decolonial events." Chapter

11, written by Laurel M. Potter, considers the liturgical practices of El Salvador's ecclesial base communities (CEBs). These CEBs, which do not enjoy the regular accompaniment of an ordained priest, end up being freer to work beyond the normative rubrics of the Roman Catholic Church to celebrate Christian liturgy. Potter deploys critical qualitative methods to describe the CEBs' liturgical art, altars, and music, which point toward possibilities of a liturgical liberation theology, which while still underdeveloped is very promising. Potter argues that the CEBs resist colonial control of subjectivity, which is the legacy of the colonial Church. By bringing Indigenous wisdom traditions into their liturgical acts, they affirm memories that challenge official histories and celebrate a God who stands with the poor and oppressed.

In Chap. 12, Kristine Suna-Koro examines Lutheran, Roman Catholic, and Episcopalian Penitential rites in public communal worship to understand how they can help advance decolonial transformation. In particular, the author examines the challenges these rites pose for decolonizing Penitential rites in the context of Indigenous land dispossession in North America. Suna-Koro suggests that Penitential rites can potentially open the door to decolonizing liturgy. Yet, the fulfillment of such a possibility requires an intentional delinking from the philosophies of colonial conquest. Such a task calls for contextual rescripting of these rites and adaptive ritual performances.

In the final chapter of this volume, Dale T. Irvin reimagines churches as places of freedom, as interstitial experiences manifesting what Homi K. Bhabha calls "third space." Building on the work of Kristine Suna-Koro, Edward Soja, Henri Lefebvre, and Letty Russell, Irvin proposes the reconfiguration of the Eucharist as a "semiotic event," open to all, advancing a decolonized sacramental imaginary that is "oikocentric," not "ecclesiocentric." This chapter, therefore, argues for "the right to the sacrament" to be extended beyond the ecclesia, based on the fact that the Eucharist, as a hybrid sacramental mystery of divine, human, and nonhuman agencies, can be a transformative manifestation of the third space.

As with any publication of this sort, this volume is the result of the collective work of a number of people without whom neither the conference nor this publication would be possible. Considering that the conference itself was in the making for more than two years and involved local and international collaboration, it is nearly impossible to name all those who contributed for this volume to exist. There are some, however, whom we wish to mention by name. We would like to thank the Cathedral at

Gathering Place in Rochester, New York, which is part of the Union of Charismatic Orthodox Churches, which acted as our financial agent leading up to the conference. Special thanks to Bishop Emilio Alvarez Jr., then leader of the Union of Charismatic Orthodox Churches, one of the cosponsors of the conference and Associate Provost of Asbury Theological Seminary since July 1, 2022, to Rev. Mother Gaye Coston, who is currently interim rector of the Cathedral, manages the finances of the conference as the direct administrator of the church, and is now Treasurer of the new EIIRN Board. The Church made the San Juan Conference an official part of its missionary budget. They accepted donations and registrations and distributed funds for us.

Our deepest gratitude goes to the Recinto Metropolitano de la Universidad Interamericana de Puerto Rico for hosting the conference and to its Dean Dr. Oscar Cruz Cuevas, whose tremendous energy and patience helped immensely to make this conference successful. We would also like to thank all other conference sponsors including Dormition of the Virgin Mary Greek Orthodox Church, New York, Dr. William Lee and Dr. Hwain Chang Lee for the Friday evening banquet in memory of David SUH Kwang-Sun (1931–2022), Georgetown University Department of Theology & Religious Studies, Graymoor Ecumenical & Interreligious Institute, La Universidad Interamericana de Puerto Rico, Mark D. Hostetter and Alexander N. Habib Foundation, Patrick Grace and the Sarita Kenedy East Foundation Inc., Seminario Evangélico de Puerto Rico, and The Union of Charismatic Orthodox Churches.

We would also like to give our gratitude to the organizing committee of this conference, which included, in addition to the two editors of these volumes, Angel L. Vélez Oyola (Director of the Department of Theology and Professor of Theology and History, UIPR), Brian Flanagan (Marymount University, Arlington, Virginia), Cristina Lledo Gomez (BBI-The Australian Institute of Theological Education), Danielle Northup (Georgetown University Student Research Assistant), Elaine Padilla (Associate Professor of Philosophy and Religion, Latinx/Latin American Studies, University of La Verne), Emilio Alvarez (Bishop, The Cathedral at The Gathering Place, Rochester, New York), Jason Welle (Pontifical Institute for Arabic and Islamic Studies, Rome), Luis N. Rivera-Pagán (Henry Winters Luce Professor of Ecumenics Emeritus, Princeton Theological Seminary), Mark Chapman (Ripon College Cuddesdon and Oxford University), Miriam Haar (Institute for Ecumenical Studies and Research, Bensheim), Oscar Cruz Cuevas (Decano, UIPR), O'Meara

Riley (Georgetown University Student Research Assistant), Palmira N. Ríos González (Retired Dean, Seminario Evangélico de Puerto Rico, Former Dean, University of Puerto Rico Río Piedras), Peter C. Phan (Ignacio Ellacuria Chair of Catholic Social Thought, Georgetown University), and Peter de Mey (KU Leuven, Belgium).

Finally, we would like to express our special thanks to Dale Irvin for his leadership in organizing this conference and for taking over the coordination of the Ecclesiological Investigations Network after the passing of our dear colleague and first Network Chair Gerard Mannion in 2019. Ecclesiological Investigations brings together high-quality research and inspiring debate on ecclesiology worldwide through a network of international scholars, research centers, and projects in the field. The purpose of the network is to promote study, research, dialogue, and collaboration in ecclesiology across the spectrum of the Christian tradition. Therefore, the task is to promote a truly collaborative ecclesiology in national, international, intra-ecclesial, and ecumenical contexts. This volume is just one of many that this extraordinary network has brought out.[20]

As a collection of essays derivative from a conference, these two volumes are representative of both the diversity and the limits of the conference. On the bright side, the editors are thrilled to make available for a broader readership the diversity of rich conversations, which took place not only in the rooms where the authors were then presenting their initial work to the conference participants, but also over meals and during the breaks in more informal fashion, which certainly enriched the already excellent quality of papers engaging this important topic from the perspective of six continents and numerous ecclesial perspectives. For instance, taking only into account those essays coming from within the Roman Catholic tradition, one finds conversations that focus on popular Catholicism, the Church's hierarchy, the Vatican II, Pope Francis' teaching, the Church's views on ecumenical and interfaith relations, and liberation theology, more specifically the Ecclesial Base Communities (CEBs). This is just an example of how, even when considered from the perspective of one tradition only, the decolonizing task is always about the *vincularidad* between the many and the one. When one adds other Christian traditions also represented in this volume, geographical diversity, the multiplicity of disciplinary approaches included in it, and the variety of ways of engaging the theme of decolonization/

---

[20] More about the network and these publications can be found on their website: https://ei-research.net.

decoloniality discussed above, it becomes clearer how valuable the contributions collected in this volume and the conversations among them—which will become evident to the readers as they see the regularity with which the contributors to this volume refer to one another—are to a conversation, which is still at its start, even though it has been going on for a few decades now. The conversation on decolonization/decoloniality is evolving not only through the development of new theoretical lenses but also through the integration of already existing ones as this volume also exemplifies. While the terms of the conversation do not intend to produce universally valid truth claims—to mention Orlando Espin—it advances a dialogical and intercultural approach to concepts and ideas, which, constructed from below and in conversation with one another, display the aspiration of universal relevance.[21]

The themes discussed in these two volumes demand epistemic humility. This two-volume project, therefore, does not intend to offer any overarching conclusion. Instead, it highlights lived experiences of decolonial transformation, while engaging them to point to possible futures which can only result from sustained conversations and practices such as those represented in several chapters of this volume. Along the same lines, the editors acknowledge the limits of the voices represented here. While, as highlighted above, we celebrate the diverse backgrounds and experiences present in these chapters, we recognize that the Ecclesiological Investigations Network, in particular, and theological education, more broadly, are still selective spaces in need of further decolonizing. Thus, the conference that generated these volumes still mirrors the academia more broadly and the disproportional representativity of some groups at the expense of others. While lamenting the limitations in representativeness, and confessing our own roles in it, we are confident that the conversations these twin volumes advance are critical to effect the kind of change decolonial thinkers entail. While an increasing number of theologians and religious scholars are engaging these conversations, they still remain marginal in many of our campuses—including those the two editors of these volumes work. We offer this volume as a contribution to expand and deepen those crucial and transformative conversations.

---

[21] Orlando O. Espin, *Idol and Grace: Traditioning and Subversive Hope* (Maryknoll, NY: Orbis Books, 2014).

PART I

Migration, Diaspora and Decolonization

CHAPTER 2

Coloniality, Diaspora, and Decolonial Resistance

Luis N. Rivera-Pagán

> *The Bible... unlike the books of other ancient peoples, was... the literature of a minor, remote people – and not the literature of its rulers, but of its critics... The prophets of Jerusalem refused to accept the world as it was. They invented the literature of political dissent and, with it, the literature of hope.*
> —Amos Elon *(Amos Elon,* Jerusalem: Battlegrounds of Memory *(New York: Kodansha International, 1995), 19)*

L. N. Rivera-Pagán (✉)
Princeton Theological Seminary, Princeton, NJ, USA
e-mail: luis.rivera-pagan@ptsem.edu

© The Author(s), under exclusive license to Springer Nature Switzerland AG 2023
R. C. Barreto, V. Latinovic (eds.), *Decolonial Horizons,* Pathways for Ecumenical and Interreligious Dialogue,
https://doi.org/10.1007/978-3-031-44839-3_2

Introduction

I originate from Puerto Rico, a Caribbean island that has been aptly described by a foremost juridical scholar as "the oldest colony of the world."[1] Christopher Columbus claimed possession of the island for the crown of Castile in 1493, and it remained part of the Spanish empire till 1898, when it was conquered and possessed by the United States.

The transfer of imperial sovereignty from Madrid to Washington was accomplished through the two classical ways of solving conflicts among powerful nations: war and diplomacy. War was perpetrated in the tropical Caribbean and the Philippines; diplomacy was negotiated later in elegant and cosmopolitan Paris.[2] No need to consult the Puerto Rican natives. Washington, Madrid, and Paris were the sites of privileged historical agency. In early 1898, Puerto Rico was a Spanish colony; at the end of that fateful year, it had become a colony of the United States.

This event marked the end of the Spanish imperial saga and the initial stages of imperial *pax americana*.[3] It was part and parcel of the Age of Empire, so aptly named by the British historian Eric Hobsbawm.[4] From the Philippines, Guam, and Hawaii, in the Pacific, to Cuba and Puerto Rico, in the Caribbean, the American ideology of manifest destiny, with its vigorous religious undertones, aggressive military perspectives, and strong commercial interests, was transgressing national boundaries.[5] The military conquest of those Pacific and Caribbean nations, according to the then president of the United States, William McKinley, took place "under the providence of God and in the name of human progress and civilization."[6]

---

[1] José Trías Monge, *Puerto Rico: The Trials of the Oldest Colony in the World* (New Haven: Yale University Press, 1997).

[2] The war between the United States and Spain concluded with the Treaty of Paris, signed December 10, 1898. Spain, militarily defeated, was forced to relinquish its dominion over the Philippines, Cuba, Guam, and Puerto Rico to the new American colossus. Alfonso García Martínez, ed., *Libro rojo/Tratado de París: Documentos presentados a las cortes en la legislatura de 1898 por el ministro de Estado* (Río Piedras, Puerto Rico: Editorial de la Universidad de Puerto Rico, 1988).

[3] Stephen Kinzer, The True Flag: Theodore Roosevelt, Mark Twain, and the Birth of American Empire (New York, NY: Henry Holt, 2017).

[4] Eric J. Hobsbawm, *The Age of Empire, 1875–1914* (New York: Pantheon Books, 1987).

[5] A classic exposition of the North American ideological mythological construct of "manifest destiny" is Albert K. Weinberg, *Manifest Destiny: A Study of Nationalist Expansionism in American History* (Baltimore: The John Hopkins Press, 1935).

[6] Quoted in Kinzer, *The True Flag*, 132.

We have learned much from Edward Said, Homi Bhabha, Gayatri Spivak, and Walter Mignolo about *colonial discourse* and postcolonial critique.[7] Even before these four distinguished émigrés, there were the crucial analyses of colonial ideology and mentality drafted by Frantz Fanon and Albert Memmi.[8] Also, the critical examination of the strategies of coloniality—military power, economic domination, racial hierarchy, cultural arrogance—by the Peruvian Aníbal Quijano.[9] The colonized subjects providing theoretical paradigms to their colonizers? Dislocated, "out of place"[10] Third World intellectuals giving lessons to the masters of the world and challenging their epistemic dominion? Quite a paradox of these postcolonial times!

Imperial power comprises at least three interrelated domains: political subordination, material appropriation, and ideological justification. Colonial discourse mystifies imperial dominion. It diffuses and affirms imperial ideological hegemony. It crafts by persuasion what the mechanisms of coercion are unable to achieve: the fine-tuned consent and admiration of the colonized subjects. "Rulers who aspire to hegemony... must make out an ideological case that they rule.... on behalf of their subjects."[11] Its greatest creation is what V. S. Naipaul has named *mimic men*.[12]

In 1493, the Spaniards came to Puerto Rico with the proclaimed purpose of converting its idolatrous inhabitants to the one and only true religion, Christianity; to teach them how to live according to the European ethical norms of a civil and ordered society; and, as concurrent objective,

---

[7] Edward Said, *Culture and Imperialism* (New York: Knopf, 1993); Homi Bhabha, *The Location of Culture* (London and New York: Routledge, 2001); Gayatri C. Spivak, *In Other Worlds: Essays in Cultural Politics* (New York and London: Routledge, 1998); Walter D. Mignolo, *The Darker Side of the Renaissance: Literacy, Territoriality, & Colonization* (Ann Arbor, MI: The University of Michigan Press, 1995).

[8] Frantz Fanon, *The Wretched of the Earth* (New York: Grove Press, 1968); Albert Memmi, *The Colonizer and the Colonized* (Boston: Beacon Press, 1965).

[9] Aníbal Quijano, "Colonialidad del poder, cultura y conocimiento en América Latina," *Anuario Mariateguiano*, 9, núm. 9, 1998, 113–121; "The Colonial Nature of Power and Latin America's Cultural Experience," en R. Briceño & H. R. Sonntag, *Sociology in Latin America (Social Knowledge: Heritage, Challenges, Perspectives)*, Proceedings of the Regional Conference of the International Association of Sociology (Caracas, 1998), 27–38; "Coloniality of Power, Eurocentrism, and Latin America," *Nepantla*, No. 3, 2000, 533–580.

[10] Edward Said, *Out of Place: A Memoir* (New York: Knopf, 1999).

[11] James C. Scott, *Domination and the Arts of Resistance: Hidden Transcripts* (New Haven, CT: Yale University Press, 1990), 18.

[12] V. S. Naipaul, *The Mimic Men* (New York, Macmillan, 1967).

to reap substantial material benefits for the imperial purveyors of those spiritual goods.[13] As Christopher Columbus wrote in his 1493 report of his transoceanic exploration: "All Christendom ought to feel joyful and make celebrations and give solemn thanks to the Holy Trinity with many fervent prayers for the turning of so many peoples to our holy faith... and afterwards for material benefits, since [...] all Christians will hence have refreshment and profit."[14]

In 1898, the Americans came to allegedly impart upon those they considered to be the poor tropical barbarians the blessings of liberty, justice, humanity, and enlightened civilization. To crown their generosity, in 1917, without consulting "the Inhabitants of *Porto Rico*" (again, who cares about the views and feelings of colonized subjects?), Washington bestowed upon us the gift of American citizenship. That citizenship has allowed Puerto Rican people to participate in the military adventures of Washington aimed to extend its so-called empire of freedom, from the First World War trenches to the fields of Vietnam and the streets of Kabul and Baghdad. As an added bonus, they were set free from messing with any of the crucial decisions regarding their political condition and fate. They could rest assured that those, usually very important decisions on democratic sovereignty, are well taken care by the wisdom and benevolence of the powers that dwell in Washington. How fortunately colonial Puerto Ricans have been!

Maybe this is another occasion to reiterate Gayatri Spivak's famous query, "can the subaltern speak?" A question that Edward Said dared to answer affirmatively: "Indeed, the subaltern *can* speak, as the history of liberation movements in the twentieth century eloquently attests."[15]

---

[13] Enrique Dussel, *1492: el encubrimiento del Otro* (Santafé de Bogotá: Ediciones Antropos, 1992).

[14] Christopher Columbus, *A New and Fresh English Translation of the Letter of Columbus Announcing the Discovery of America*, translated and edited by Samuel Eliot Morison (Madrid: Gráficas Yagües, 1959), 15.

[15] Gayatri Chakravorty Spivak, "Can the subaltern speak?," *Marxism and the Interpretation of Culture*, edited by Cary Nelson and Lawrence Grossberg (Urbana and Chicago: University of Illinois Press, 1988), 271–313. Edward W. Said, *Orientalism* (25th anniversary edition) (New York: Random House, 2003), 335.

Coloniality, Migration, and Diaspora

To the ambivalence of a postcolonial colony whose residents as citizens of the empire can claim in the courts the civil liberties of their citizenship but not its political rights, we should add the crucial fact that more than half of the Puerto Rican population resides in mainland United States.[16] Legally, those Puerto Ricans are not migrants. Psychologically and culturally, they are. They belong to the history of modern diasporas. And diasporas are the source of the bewildering multiculturalism of the postmodern mega cities.

Migration and diaspora are crucial elements of human history.[17] They constitute an experience shared by many former and present colonial peoples all over the world. Nowadays, they have also become important themes of conversation in postcolonial cultural studies.[18] But, as Homi Bhabha has stressed, diaspora is an important object of critical analysis because it is the sociohistorical existential context of many displaced Third World peoples: "For the demography of the new internationalism is the history of postcolonial migration, the narratives of cultural and political diaspora [...] the poetics of exile [...]."[19]

Diaspora entails dislocation, displacement, but also a painful and complex process of forging new strategies to articulate cultural differences and identifications.[20] In the Western cosmopolis, with its heterogeneous and frequently conflicting ethnocultural minorities that belie the mythical *e pluribus unum*, the émigré exists in ambivalent tension. More than half a century ago, Frantz Fanon brilliantly described the peculiar gaze of so many white French people at the growing presence of Black Africans and

---

[16] Angelo Falcón, *Atlas of Stateside Puerto Ricans* (Washington, DC: Puerto Rico Federal Affairs Administration, 2004); Edgardo Meléndez, *Sponsored Migration: The State and Puerto Rican Postwar Migration to the United States* (Columbus, Ohio: Ohio State University Press, 2017).

[17] As Princeton University professor Arcadio Díaz-Quiñones has beautifully shown, in his book *El arte de bregar: ensayos* (San Juan: Ediciones Callejón, 2000), Puerto Rican culture cannot be genuinely assessed if the creativity of its diaspora community is neglected or its significance diminished.

[18] Elazar Barkan and Marie-Denise Shelton, eds., *Borders, Exiles, Diasporas* (Stanford: Stanford University Press, 1998).

[19] Bhabha, The Location of Culture, 5.

[20] Luis N. Rivera-Pagán, *Essays from the Diaspora* (México, D. F.: Centro Luterano de Formación Teológica, Publicaciones El Faro, Lutheran School of Theology at Chicago, Centro Basilea de Investigación, 2002).

Caribbeans in their national midst.[21] Scorn and fear were entwined in that stare. The diasporic person frequently feels, alas, "like a man without a passport who is turned away from every harbour," the anguished dread that haunts the persecuted whisky priest of Graham Greene's magnificent novel, *The Power and the Glory*.[22]

Frequently, nostalgia grips his or her soul, in the beautiful words of a painful biblical lamentation:

> By the rivers of Babylon –there we sat down and there we wept when we remembered Zion.
> How could we sing the Lord's song in a foreign land? (Psalm 137:1,4, NRSV)

Often, however, and sometimes simultaneously, the displacement of migration creates a new space of liberation from the atavistic constraints and bondages of the native cultural community and opens new vistas, perspectives, and horizons. To repressed persons, exile in a metropolis like London, Paris, or New York could convey an expansion of individual autonomy, even if its sinister hidden side might turn out to be despair or death.[23] Diasporic existence, as Bhabha has so forcefully reiterated, questions fixed and static notions of cultural and communal identity. In the diaspora, identity is not conceived as a pure essence to be nostalgically preserved, but as an emancipatory project to be fashioned, in an alien territory, in a foreign language, as a polyphonic process of creative imagination. In many instances, "the restoration of a collective sense of identity and historical agency in the home country may well be mediated through the diaspora."[24]

---

[21] Frantz Fanon, *Peau Noir, Masques Blancs* (Paris: Éditions du Seuil, 1952).

[22] Graham Greene, *The Power and the Glory* (London: Penguin Books, 1990, orig. 1940), 102.

[23] This was the case for two creative Caribbean writers, marginalized and despised in their homelands, the Cuban Reinaldo Arenas and the Puerto Rican Manuel Ramos-Otero, who found in New York a wider horizon for their literary talents, a greater realm of personal freedom, and AIDS-related death. See Rubén Ríos-Avila, "Caribbean Dislocations: Arenas and Ramos Otero in New York," in Sylvia Molloy and Robert M. Irwin, eds., *Hispanisms and Homosexualities* (Durham, NC: Duke University Press, 1998), 101–122.

[24] Elazar Barkan and Marie-Denise Shelton, "Introduction," *Borders, Exiles, Diasporas*, 5.

As Walter Mignolo has so provocatively asserted,[25] diaspora, as a site of critical enunciation, compels the rethinking of the geopolitical distinction, so dear to many Third World thinkers, between center and periphery, and elicits a border thinking that challenges and changes not only the content, but also the terms of intellectual global dialogue. The émigré's cultural differences produce subaltern significations that resist the cultural cannibalism of the metropolitan melting pot. Diasporic communities are, to quote once more Bhabha, "wandering peoples who will not be contained within the *Heim* of the national culture and its unisonant discourse, but are themselves the marks of a shifting boundary that alienates the frontiers of the modern nation."[26]

Migration has become one of the main issues for theories of human rights and theological creativity done in solidarity with the pains and sorrows of displaced communities. Diasporic displacement is an essential and historical consequence of imperial domination. "There are 65 million displaced persons around the globe [...]. And the mass drowning of migrants has become so routine that it scarcely qualifies as news."[27] Many, too many, Haitian men, women, and children have, during the last couple of years, died deep in the waters of the dangerous Caribbean ocean. Their journey to freedom became a cruise to tragic death.

In the borderlands, a new poetic of political and decolonizing resistance is developed, as the late Gloria Anzaldúa so hauntingly perceived:

> In the Borderlands
> you are the battleground
> where enemies are kin to each other;
> you are at home, a stranger [...]
> To survive in the Borderlands
> you must live *sin fronteras*
> be a crossroads.[28]

---

[25] Walter D. Mignolo, Local Histories/Global Designs: Coloniality, Subaltern Knowledges, and Border Thinking (Princeton: Princeton University Press, 2000).

[26] Bhabha, The Location of Culture, 164.

[27] Jason DeParle, "The Sea Swallows People," *The New York Review of Books*, Vol. LXIV, No. 3, February 23, 2017, 31.

[28] Gloria Anzaldúa, *Borderlands/La Frontera: The New Mestiza* (San Francisco: Aunt Lute, 1999), 216–217.

We have seen, during these last decades, a tragic outcome in many Western and Northern nations: extreme xenophobia. But it also conveys urgent challenges to the ethical sensitivity of religious people and persons of good will.[29] The first step we need to take is to perceive this issue from the perspective of the migrants, to pay cordial attention to their stories of suffering, hope, courage, resistance, ingenuity, and, as so frequently happens in the wildernesses of the American Southwest or deep in the Mediterranean waters, tragic death.[30] Many of the unauthorized migrants have become *nobodies*, in the apt title of John Bowe's book, *disposable people*, in Kevin Bales' poignant phrase, or, as Zygmunt Bauman heartbreakingly reminds us, *wasted lives*.[31] They are the Empire's new μέτοικοι, *douloi*, modern servants. Their dire existential situation cannot be grasped without taking into consideration the upsurge in global inequalities in these times of unregulated international financial imperial hegemony.[32] For many human beings, the excruciating alternative is between misery in their third world homeland or marginalization in the rich West/North, both fateful destinies intimately linked together.[33]

The existential dislocation of diaspora, its cultural hybridity, recreates the complex intertwined ethnic and racial sources of many migrant communities. Asked to whom does she owe allegiance, Clare, the Jamaican protagonist of Michelle Cliff's novel *No Telephone to Heaven*, replies: "I have African, English, Carib in me."[34] She is a mestiza moving between Kingston, New York, and London, searching for a place to call home, torn

---

[29] Luis N. Rivera-Pagán, "Xenophilia or Xenophobia: Towards a Theology of Migration," *The Ecumenical Review* (World Council of Churches), Vol. 64, No. 4, December 2012, 575–589.

[30] See the poignant article by Jeremy Harding, "The Deaths Map," *London Review of Books*, Vol. 33, No. 20, 20 October 2011, 7–13.

[31] John Bowe, Nobodies: Modern American Slave Labor and the Dark Side of the New Global Economy (New York: Random House, 2007); Kevin Bales, Disposable People: New Slavery in the Global Economy (Berkeley, CA: University of California Press, 2004); Zygmunt Bauman, Wasted Lives: Modernity and Its Outcasts (Cambridge: Polity, 2004).

[32] Slavoj Žižek, *Refugees, Terror and other Troubles with the Neighbors* (Brooklyn, NY: Melville House, 2016).

[33] Branko Milanovic, "Global Inequality and the Global Inequality Extraction Ratio: The Story of the Past Two Centuries" (The World Bank, Development Research Group, Poverty and Inequality Group, September 2009); Peter Stalker, *Workers Without Frontiers: The Impact of Globalization on International Migration* (Geneva: International Labor Organization, 2000).

[34] Michelle Cliff, *No Telephone to Heaven* (New York: Plume Books, 1996, orig. 1987), 189.

between the quest for solidarity in the forging of a common identity and the lure of solitude in a strange land. To be part of a pilgrim diaspora is a difficult and complex challenge, which, to avoid utopian illusions, must be faced having in mind the superb irony of that master of twentieth-century skepticism, himself a displaced wanderer, James Joyce: "We were always loyal to lost causes [...]. Success is for us the death of the intellect and of the imagination."[35]

From the margins of empires and metropolitan centers of powers, the crossroads of borders and frontiers, in the proximity of so many different and frequently conflictive cultural worlds, in the maelstroms of the global mega cities and the virtual imagined communities of the internet, arise constantly new challenges to the international structures of power and control.[36] There colonial discourses meet their nemesis: postcolonial defiance. In the ecumenicity of diaspora, to quote again Bhabha, "we must not change merely the narratives of our histories, but transform our sense of what it means to live, to be, in other times and different places, both human and historical."[37] And certainly, decolonization is not a simple process; it requires strong resistance, as Amílcar Cabral, a resilient African anti-colonialist, asserted and wrote, before his tragic assassination.[38]

It is usually there, in the counter invasion of the "others," the "colonized barbarians," deep into the realms of the lords of the world, that the silenced peoples find the sonority of their voices and reconfigure their historical sagas into meaningful human stories. The quasi-beastly shadows of Joseph Conrad's *Heart of Darkness* (1899) dare to disrupt the imperial monologue. They hybridize the language of the colonizers to reshape and narrate their own histories. As Chinua Achebe, engaged in a critical dialogue with the specter of Conrad, so eloquently has written in a text significantly titled *Home and Exile*, "My hope for the twenty-first [century] is that it will see the first fruits [...] of the process of 're-storying' peoples who had been knocked silent by the trauma of all kinds of dispossession."[39]

Puerto Ricans constitute an essential part of the US Latino/Hispanic population, that sector of the American society whose growth, in the view of many, enriches multicultural diversity, but also led Samuel P. Huntington

[35] James Joyce, *Ulysses* (New York: Random House, 1946, orig. 1914), 131–132.
[36] Michael Hardt and Antonio Negri, *Multitude: War and Democracy in the Age of Empire* (New York: The Penguin Press, 2004).
[37] Bhabha, The Location of Culture, 256.
[38] Amílcar Cabral, *Resistance and Decolonization* (London: Rowman and Littlefield, 2016).
[39] Chinua Achebe, *Home and Exile* (New York: Anchor Books, 2000), 79.

to warn that it constitutes a "major potential threat to the cultural and possibly political integrity of the United States."[40] How interesting that the former prophet of the "clash of civilizations," beyond the frontiers of the American colossus, became the apostle of the "clash of cultures," within its borders. According to Huntington, an eminent Harvard professor, the main problem of Latinos/Hispanics is not the illegality in which many of them incur to reside in the United States, but the threat they represent to the American national identity and its allegedly traditional "Anglo-Protestant" culture.

In that clash of cultures, Puerto Ricans are distinguished warriors. They excel in the "double consciousness," the transculturation, and the border thinking that Walter Mignolo has so suggestively rescued from the African American W. E. B. Du Bois, the Cuban Fernando Ortiz, and the Chicana Gloria Anzaldúa. In Puerto Rico, people take delight in our Spanish language, in the mainland they share the linguistic fate of the diaspora, and experience "the pain and perverse pleasure of writing in a second language," in the words of that exceptional Haitian scholar Michel-Rolph Trouillot.[41] The experience of *heteroglossia*, of thinking, speaking, and writing in a different language, opens unexpected spaces for a heterodox understanding of the hybridizing encounters of peoples and cultures. For, as Mikhail Bakhtin so adeptly has written, "the word lives, as it were, on the boundary between its own context and another, alien, context."[42] Many Third World natives, including millions of Puerto Ricans, have learned to live and survive in the margins of the so-called First World.[43]

The colonial situation, encompassing its political and juridical subjugation, its ensuing cultural symbiosis, and the persisting socioeconomics inequities, constitutes the historical matrix of many modern diasporas and, thus, a crucial source of the multicultural collisions in the imperial metropolitan centers. In the words of William Schweiker, University of Chicago professor of theological ethics,

---

[40] Samuel P. Huntington, *Who Are We? The Challenges to America's National Identity* (New York: Simon & Schuster, 2004), 243.

[41] Michel-Rolph Trouillot, *Silencing the Past: Power and the Production of History* (Boston: Beacon Press, 1995), xv.

[42] Mikhail Bakhtin, *The Dialogic Imagination: Four Essays* (Austin, TX: University of Texas Press, 2006), 284.

[43] Luis N. Rivera-Pagán, *Essays from the Margins* (Eugene, Oregon: Cascade Books, 2014).

International cities are a 'place' in which people's identities, sense of self, others, and the wider world, as well as values and desires, are locally situated but altered by global dynamics [...]. The compression of the world found in massive cities is thus a boon for the formation of new self-understandings, especially for dislocated peoples [...]. This is especially pointed when those 'others' are implicated in histories of suffering. The compression of the world confronts us with the problem of how to live amid others, even enemies.[44]

Theology and Postcolonial Studies: A Critical Observation

It is not surprising that Bible scholars such as Fernando Segovia, R. S. Sugistharajah, Stephen D. Moore, Musa Dube, Roland Boer, Tat-Siong Benny Liew, Richard Horsley, and Leo G. Perdue, among others, have been first and foremost among the theological disciplines to pay close attention to postcolonial and decolonizing theories.[45] After all, it is impossible to evade the pervasive ubiquity of empires, imperial conquests, and anti-colonial resistances in the Jewish-Christian sacred Scriptures.

The geopolitical expansions or contractions of the Egyptian, Assyrian, Babylonian, Persian, Macedonian (Ptolemaic and Seleucid), and Roman empires constitute the main historical substratum of the entire biblical corpus. And let there be no doubt, imperial conquest constitutes a grave violation of human integrity. "There is no system of domination that does

---

[44] William Schweiker, *Theological Ethics and Global Dynamics In the Time of Many Worlds* (Malden, MA and Oxford: Blackwell, 2004), 6–7.

[45] Stephen D. Moore and Fernando Segovia, *Postcolonial Biblical Criticism: Interdisciplinary Intersections* (London/New York: T & T Clark, 2005); R. S. Sugirtharajah, ed., *The Postcolonial Bible* (Sheffield, England: Sheffield Academic Press, 1998); R. S. Sugirtharajah, *Postcolonial Criticism and Biblical Interpretation* (Oxford: Oxford University Press, 2002); R. S. Sugirtharajah, ed., *The Postcolonial Biblical Reader* (Malden, MA and Oxford: Blackwell, 2006); Musa W. Dube, *Postcolonial Feminist Interpretation of the Bible* (St. Louis, MO: Chalice Press, 2000); Richard A. Horsley, *Jesus and Empire: the Kingdom of God and the New World Disorder* (Minneapolis: Fortress Press, 2003); Richard A. Horsley, *Paul and Empire: Religion and Power in Roman Imperial Society* (Harrisburg, PA: Trinity Press International, 1997); Richard A. Horsley, *Paul and the Roman Imperial Order* (Harrisburg, PA: Trinity Press International, 2004); Leo G. Perdue and Warren Carter, edited by Coleman A Baker, *Israel and Empire: A Postcolonial History of Israel and Early Judaism* (London: Bloomsbury, 2015).

not produce its own routine harvest of insults and injury to human dignity [...]."[46]

From the Exodus saga to the anti-Roman apocalyptic visions of *Revelation*,[47] only a fruitless strategy of hermeneutical evasion would be able to suppress the importance of imperial hegemony in the configuration of human existence and religious faith in the Bible.[48] The dolorous cry of the conquered people was constant,

> Here we are, slaves to this day—slaves in the land that you gave to our ancestors to enjoy its fruit and its good gifts. Its rich yield goes to the kings [the Persian monarchy] whom you have set over us because of our sins; they have power also over our bodies and over our livestock at their pleasure, and we are in great distress. (Nehemiah 9:36-37)

Even a comprehensive study of gender and sex in the Bible has to take into consideration the different ways in which Esther and Judith use their female sexuality in critical historical instances in which the fate of the children of Abraham is at the stake of a powerful empire. How to forget that Jesus was executed by the Roman authorities as a political subversive? He was exposed to the horrendous rituals of moral denigration and physical assaults that traditionally constitute the tragic fate of colonized subjects who dare to defy imperial arrogance and dominion. Any theory of atonement that elides the intense political drama of the last days of Jesus transforms it in an abstract unhistorical dogma, or in a display of tasteless masochism à la Mel Gibson's *The Passion of the Christ* (2004).

Thus, it was to be expected that biblical scholars would be the first in the academic fields of religious studies to incorporate the emphases on geopolitical hegemony and resistance provided by postcolonial theories to the array of other contemporary hermeneutical perspectives. The question raised by R. S. Sugirtharajah, however, is poignant indeed:

---

[46] Scott, Domination and the Arts of Resistance, 37.

[47] João B. Libânio e Maria Clara L. Bingemer, *Escatologia Cristã: O Novo Céu e a Nova Terra* (Petrópolis, Brasil: Vozes, 1985); Pablo Richard, *Apocalipsis: reconstrucción de la esperanza* (San José: DEI, 1994) and Brian K. Blount, *Can I Get a Witness?: Reading Revelation Through African American Culture* (Louisville, KY: Westminster John Knox Press, 2005).

[48] Giorgio Agamben, The Kingdom and the Glory: For a Theological Genealogy of Economy and Government (Stanford, CA: Stanford University Press, 2011).

One of the weighty contributions of postcolonial criticism has been to put issues relating to colonialism and imperialism at the center of critical and intellectual inquiry [...]. What is striking about systematic theology is the reluctance of its practitioners to address the relation between European colonialism and the field. There has been a marked hesitancy to critically evaluate the impact of the empire among systematic theologians.[49]

To be fair, some theologians are beginning to awake from their disciplinary slumber to take into serious consideration the crucial issues of geopolitical power. Creative theologians, like Catherine Keller, Mark Lewis Taylor, Kwok Pui-lan, Wonhee Anne Joh, Mayra Rivera, Joerg Rieger, and others, have begun to face with intellectual rigor and rhetorical elegance the challenges raised by postcolonial studies and dialogues.[50] For those studies and dialogues, the Caribbean, just where I happen to live and work, might be a fine place to start.

Let me explain this last statement that many of you might find rather perplexing. Fernando Segovia has written a precise and concise exposition of the convergence between biblical scholarship and postcolonial studies.[51] Never an uncritical reader, Segovia raises several poignant critiques to the latter. Two of them are particularly relevant to the argument I want to develop: First, the lack of attention, by most postcolonial intellectuals, to the Latin American and Caribbean Iberian imperial formations as they developed between the end of the fifteenth century and the first decades of the seventeenth.[52] Second, the scarcity of analysis of religion as a crucial dimension of the imperial-colonial ideological frameworks. To quote Segovia on this second issue:

---

[49] R. S. Sugirtharajah, "Complacencies and Cul-de-sacs: Christian Theologies and Colonialism," in Catherine Keller, Michael Nausner, and Mayra Rivera, *Postcolonial Theologies: Divinity and Empire* (St. Louis, MO: Chalice Press, 2004), 22.

[50] Catherine Keller, *God and Power: Counter-Apocalyptic Journeys* (Minneapolis: Fortress Press, 2005); Mark Lewis Taylor, *Religion, Politics, and the Christian Right: Post-9/11 Powers and American Empire* (Minneapolis: Fortress Press, 2005); Kwok Pui-lan, *Postcolonial Imagination and Feminist Theology* (Louisville, KY: Westminster John Knox Press, 2005); Wonhee Anne Joh, *Heart of the Cross: a Postcolonial Christology* (Louisville, KY: Westminster John Knox Press, 2006); Joerg Rieger, *Christ & Empire: From Paul to Postcolonial Times* (Minneapolis: Fortress Press, 2007); Keller, Nausner, and Rivera, *Postcolonial Theologies: Divinity and Empire* (2004).

[51] Fernando Segovia, "Mapping the Postcolonial Optic in Biblical Criticism: Meaning and Scope," in Moore and Segovia, *Postcolonial Biblical Criticism*, 23–78.

[52] Ibid., 73.

> It is almost as if religious texts and expressions did not form part of the cultural production and as if religious institutions and practices did not belong to the social matrix of imperial-colonial frameworks. I would argue [...] that religion is to be acknowledged and theorized as a constitutive component of such frameworks, and a most important one [...].[53]

The existential relevance of both issues for Segovia, a Cuban-born person who describes himself as "a student of religion in general and of the Christian faith in particular," seems obvious. As another Caribbean-born student of religion and theological ideas, I share both concerns.

It is hard to deny that Segovia is *partially* right, for he is referring to postcolonial cultural studies as they emerged from the twilight of the European empires that developed in the wake of the Enlightenment. What has been named by some British historians the classic age of Empire is the basic matrix whence the critical texts of Said, Bhabha, and Spivak emerge. Even a very useful introductory text in the field, *Post-Colonial Studies: The Key Concepts*, edited by Ashcroft, Griffiths, and Tiffin, proceeds as if the sixteenth-century Iberian empires never existed or as if religious discourses have never been used as motivation for conquest and colonization.[54] The end result of those analytical occlusions is the homogenization of imperial experiences and, therefore, of colonial defiance.[55]

---

[53] Ibid., 74–75.

[54] Bill Ashcroft, Gareth Griffiths and Helen Tiffin, *Post-Colonial Studies: The Key Concepts* (London and New York: Routledge, 1998). Sometimes, their disregard for the sixteenth-century imperial formations leads them into egregious mistakes, like asserting that "in 1503, Bishop Las Casas [...] proposed [...] systematic importation of blacks" as "an alternative to indigenous labor" (ibid. 212). In 1503, Bartolomé de Las Casas was not yet a bishop, and he did not propose to bring Black slaves to the new Spanish territories till the middle of the second decade of that century. Cf. Luis N. Rivera-Pagán, *A Violent Evangelism: The Political and Religious Conquest of the Americas* (Louisville, Kentucky: Westminster – John Knox Press, 1992), 180–195. See also Luis N. Rivera-Pagán, "Freedom and Servitude: indigenous Slavery in the Spanish Conquest of the Caribbean," *General History of the Caribbean. Volume I: Autochthonous Societies*, edited by Jalil Sued-Badillo (London: UNESCO Publishing and Macmillan Publishers, 2003), 316–362. Several of their statements regarding Latin America are not to be trusted ("the slave system [...] persisted in the Caribbean and some South American areas until the 1830s" [ibid. 214]—whereas slavery was not abolished in Puerto Rico until 1873, in Cuba until 1886 and in Brazil until 1888), which only shows the lack of attention of some postcolonial scholars to the colonial history of Latin America and the Spanish Caribbean.

[55] Curiously, Chinua Achebe is mentioned once in Ashcroft, Griffiths, and Tiffin's textbook, but his 1958 classic novel, *Things Fall Apart*, one of the foremost literary assessments of the convergence between European colonization of African and Christian missions, is not even alluded to.

In many postcolonial texts, we learn a lot about the multifarious resonances of the notorious 1835 Macaulay's Minute on Indian Education, but almost nothing about the intense theological controversies, juridical disputes, and philosophical debates (Francisco de Vitoria, Bartolomé de las Casas, Juan Ginés de Sepúlveda, José de Acosta) during the sixteenth-century Spanish conquest of the Americas, despite the fact that they anticipate most of the latter colonial and anti-colonial discourses.[56] The discussion by Vitoria about the justice of the wars against the Native Americans foreshadows all posterior arguments on the legitimacy of imperial wars.[57] The dispute between Las Casas and Sepúlveda about the rationality of the Native Americans and the adequacy of conversion by conquest inaugurates a long series of similar latter debates.[58] The lengthy treatise of Acosta on the Christianization and civilization of the American "barbarians" is paragon of subsequent analogous imperial justifications.[59]

Segovia is therefore right in his critique of the mainstream postcolonial studies. Yet, his critique reiterates that same mistake. He also excludes from the rather porous and vague boundaries of postcolonial studies' authors that do in fact pay serious attention to both the Iberian sixteenth-century imperial formations and, as an unavoidable consequence, the role of religious discourses in those geopolitical structures of control and dominion. The initial shaping of European global imperial expansion in Latin America and the Caribbean during the sixteenth century, in conjunction with the emergence of early modernity, capitalist accumulation, transatlantic slave trade, the proclamation of the Christian gospel as imperial ideology, and the othering of non-European peoples, have been topics of rigorous academic research and publications by two Argentinean émigrés, Walter Mignolo and Enrique Dussel.[60] Lewis Hanke and Anthony

---

[56] Enrique Dussel, *Política de la liberación. Historia mundial y crítica* (Madrid: Editorial Trotta, 2007), 186–210.

[57] Francisco de Vitoria, "On the American Indians" (*De indis*, I), *Political Writings*, trans. Jeremy Lawrance (Cambridge: Cambridge University Press, 1992), 231–292.

[58] Bartolomé de las Casas, *In Defense of the Indians*, trans. Stafford Poole (DeKalb, IL: Northern Illinois University Press, 1992).

[59] José de Acosta, *De procuranda indorum salute* (2 vols.), translated and edited by G. Stewart McIntosh (Tayport: Scotland, UK: Mac Research, 1996).

[60] Walter D. Mignolo, The Darker Side of the Renaissance and Local Histories/Global Designs; Enrique Dussel, Invention of the Americas: Eclipse of "the Other" & the Myth of Modernity (New York: Continuum Publishing Co., 1995).

Pagden[61] have also dealt extensively with that complex configuration of themes, engaging frequently in a comparative critical analysis with more recent empires. I myself have scholarly engaged the theological debates that accompanied the emergence of the transatlantic Iberian empire in the sixteenth century.[62]

Decoloniality, as Catherine Walsh has asserted, requires "understanding and accepting the precepts and praxis of interculturality as a decolonial project."[63] The postmodern and postcolonial mega cities compress times and spaces into borderlands of cultures, religiosities, traditions, and values. There it is impossible to evade the gaze of the Other and the primordial biblical question—"am I my brother's keeper?"[64]—acquires new connotations and urgency. A new sensitivity has to be forged to the rendering ambivalences, the sorrows and joys, of diasporic existence of the peoples who live day and night with the uncanny feeling of existing as Gentile aliens within the gates of holy Jerusalem. Puerto Ricans need to always remember that they are fellows of a colonized and subordinated nation and therefore are called to creatively imagine and forge a critical decolonial theology.[65]

---

[61] Lewis U. Hanke, The Spanish Struggle for Justice in the Conquest of America (Philadelphia: University of Pennsylvania Press, 1949); Lewis U. Hanke, Aristotle and the American Indians: A Study in Race Prejudice in the Modern World (Chicago: Henry Regnery Co., 1959); Lewis U. Hanke, All Mankind is One; A Study of the Disputation Between Bartolomé de Las Casas and Juan Ginés de Sepúlveda in 1550 on the Intellectual and Religious Capacity of the American Indians (DeKalb, IL: Northern Illinois University Press, 1974). Anthony Pagden, The Fall of Natural Man: The American Indian and the Origins of Comparative Ethnology (Cambridge: Cambridge University Press, 1982); Anthony Pagden, Spanish Imperialism and the Political Imagination (New Haven and London: Yale University Press, 1990); Anthony Pagden, Lords of all the World: Ideologies of Empire in Spain, Britain and France, c.1500–c.1800 (New Haven and London: Yale University Press, 1995).

[62] See Luis N. Rivera-Pagán, *A Violent Evangelism*, op. cit.; and *Entre el oro y la fe: El dilema de América* (San Juan: Editorial de la Universidad de Puerto Rico, 1995). Among theologians, Joerg Rieger is a distinguished exception. He devotes a chapter of one of his books to the critical analysis of Bartolomé de las Casas's Christology in the context of the sixteenth-century imperial expansion. *Christ & Empire*, 159–196.

[63] Walter D. Mignolo & Catherine E. Walsh, *On Decoloniality: Concepts, Analytics, Praxis* (Durham and London: Duke University Press, 2018), 72.

[64] Genesis 4:9.

[65] Teresa Delgado, *A Puerto Rican Decolonial Theology: Prophesy Freedom* (New York, NY: Palgrave Macmillan, 2017); Luis N. Rivera-Pagán (editor), *Fe Cristiana y descolonización de Puerto Rico* (San Juan, PR: Mesa de Diálogo Martin Luther King, Jr., 2013).

And in that process of forging a critical decolonial theology, they must never forget the extraordinary statement of Dietrich Bonhoeffer, in prison, soon to be assassinated by the Nazi regime, when he wrote to his close friend Eberhard Bethge the following:

> We have for once learnt to see the great events of world history from below, from the perspective of the outcast, the suspects, the maltreated, the powerless, the oppressed, the reviled—in short, from the perspective of those who suffer [...][66]

---

[66] Dietrich Bonhoeffer, *Letters and Papers from Prison* (London, England: Folio Society, 2000), 16.

CHAPTER 3

Immigration, Immunity, Community, and the Church: Roberto Esposito's Biopolitical Immunitary Paradigm

Craig A. Phillips

In his 1977–1978 lecture at the Collège de France, "Security, Territory, Population," Michel Foucault employed the term "biopolitical" to describe ways that emerging European nation-states exercised political sovereignty not only over the life and death of the populations under their control, but also to ensure the health, safety, and well-being of their citizens.[1] His lecture identified the role of governmental systems in regulating populations and the spaces they inhabit. While Foucault's lecture did not focus explicitly on immigration and the status of refugees, it did make clear the links between populations and their respective territories and the security apparatuses regulating the flow of people within and across the

---

[1] Michel Foucault and Paul Rabinow, *The Foucault Reader*, 1st ed. (New York: Pantheon Books, 1984). See also, Michel Foucault and Robert Hurley, *The History of Sexuality. Volume 1, An Introduction*, Vintage Books Edition ed. (New York: Vintage Books, 1990), 140–45.

C. A. Phillips (✉)
Saint Anselm College, Manchester, NH, USA

© The Author(s), under exclusive license to Springer Nature Switzerland AG 2023
R. C. Barreto, V. Latinovic (eds.), *Decolonial Horizons*, Pathways for Ecumenical and Interreligious Dialogue,
https://doi.org/10.1007/978-3-031-44839-3_3

established borders of territories. Security apparatuses seek to protect populations both from internal threats within the borders of the modern nation-state and from external threats, real and imagined, posed by populations outside its borders.

At the time of his death in 1984, Foucault had not completed his study of biopower. He had proposed that biopower first arose to ensure the health, safety, and well-being of citizens. If that were the case, how is it then that biopower can also exhibit such a negative and controversial force in modern life? This question is central to the work of three contemporary Italian political theorists, Giorgio Agamben, Roberto Esposito, and Antonio Negri.

Contemporary Italian political theory is uniquely equipped to address the challenges of refugees, asylum seekers, and migrants within the context of modern biopolitics, because, as Esposito maintains, "it is grounded in concrete action on current issues while at the same time it investigates more ancient *dispositifs*," that is, configurations and mechanisms of power that serve to maintain and reinforce the exercise of power within the social body.[2] Where Agamben espouses a persistently negative stance toward modern biopolitics, seeing in it an excessive use of governmental force (or sovereignty), and Negri maintains a generally more positive view of its benefits, Esposito is best located in the intersection of these two positions, seeing both the positive and negative effects of the exercise of modern biopolitics.[3] He advances the concept of immunity as a way of understanding the internal and external actions of modern biopolitics toward those within the state (citizens), and those outside it (noncitizens). Esposito situates modern "biopolitics" in the tension between living in community

---

[2] Roberto Esposito and Zakiya Hanafi, *Living Thought: The Origins and Actuality of Italian Philosophy*, Cultural memory in the present (Stanford, California: Stanford University Press, 2012), 4.

[3] This is evident in the respective views of how different nations have addressed the COVID pandemic. Where Agamben sees science as the new religion and vaccine legislation as a sign of the repressive use of sovereignty under the "state of emergency," Esposito holds a more dialectical view of the cost/benefits of such laws and restrictions. See Giorgio Agamben, *Where are we Now?: The Epidemic as Politics*, ed. Valeria Dani (Lanham, Maryland: Rowman & Littlefield, 2021). See also, Roberto Esposito. Interview by Tim Christiaens, "The Biopolitics of Immunity in Times of COVID-19: An Interview with Roberto Esposito," *Antipode Online* (June 16 2020), https://antipodeonline.org/2020/06/16/interview-with-roberto-esposito/. *Antipode Online* (June 16, 2020).

and immunizing it from internal or external threats to its health and well-being. His work, therefore, with its focus on community, immunity, life, and biopolitics, offers a cogent lens through which to interpret crises surrounding immigration in both Europe and North America.

This chapter employs Esposito's concept of *immunitas* to reflect theologically on immigration and the status of refugees and asylum seekers in contemporary political discourse in the United States. It identifies implicit theological themes found in current debates on immigration in the United States as they relate to the processes of immunity (*immunitas*), the formation of community (*communitas*), and sanctuary, which is itself a form of immunity.[4] While Esposito is not a postcolonial theorist, his biopolitics can be read profitably alongside the work of contemporary decolonizing theorists who investigate the colonialist invention and subsequent construction of *race* as way to categorize, differentiate, divide, and rule people of non-European descent. The constructed category of race continues to be employed to exclude migrants, immigrants, and asylum seekers from legal immigration and to divide these persons into categories of desirable vs. undesirable, productive vs. unproductive, and welcome vs. unwelcome persons solely based on designated race or national origin. The concluding section suggests practical ways the church might confront the racism implicit in current immigration practices and set an example of radical hospitality and welcome to those seeking refuge and protection.

Refugee and Refugee Studies

The field of refugee studies developed in the aftermath of World War II.[5] "The distinction between displaced persons (assumed to have, somewhere, a home to go to) and refugees (who were classified as homeless)," as Tony Judt notes, "was just one of many nuances that were introduced" in the

---

[4] Mayra Rivera, "Theological Metaphors in Anti-immigration Discourse," *American Journal of Theology & Philosophy* 40, no. 2 (2019).

[5] In her influential anthropological study, Liisa Malkki asserts that refugees do not constitute "a naturally self-delimiting domain of anthropological knowledge." "The term refugee has analytical usefulness not as a label for a special, generalizable 'kind' or 'type' of person or situation, but only as a broad legal or descriptive rubric that includes within it a world of different socioeconomic statuses, personal histories, and psychological or spiritual situations." Liisa H. Malkki, "Refugees and Exile: From 'Refugee Studies' to the National Order of Things," *Annual Review of Anthropology* 24 (1995): 496.

years following the war.[6] In an effort to understand displacement and the state of being in exile, emerging refugee studies crossed "discursive and institutional domains within which the refugee and/or being 'in exile' have been constituted," including, but not limited to, international law, the work of the United Nations in the formulation of documents to accommodate and protect displaced persons, and the formation of refugee agencies.[7]

In the aftermath of the massive refugee crisis caused by World War II, Hannah Arendt noted that when people displaced from their homes arrived at national borders seeking entrance, they found that if they were not citizens, they had no rights at all. She argued that these individuals would have received better treatment as criminals than they received as stateless persons, because even criminals would have been afforded some rights and protections under the law.[8]

Refugees simultaneously represent a political life that is threatened and in need of saving and a threat to the body politic, perceived as fragile and vulnerable to the alien other of the refugee. In short, the migrant/refugee is both a threatened life and a threat to life. When perceived as a threat, border politics exposes refugees and migrants to dehumanizing and, at times, lethal security measures.[9] A key humanitarian and theological question is how to deal humanely with refugees and migrants while at the same time protecting the social body from the real and perceived threats posed by them.[10]

---

[6] Tony Judt, *Postwar: A History of Europe Since 1945* (New York: Penguin Press, 2005), 29.

[7] Malkki, "Refugees and Exile: From 'Refugee Studies' to the National Order of Things," 497.

[8] Hannah Arendt, *The Origins of Totalitarianism*, New ed., A Harvest book, (New York: Harcourt Brace Jovanovich, 1973), 286. See, Craig A. Phillips, "The Refugee as 'Limit-Concept' in the Modern Nation-State," in *The Church, Migration, and Global (In)Difference*, ed. Jaroslav Z. Skira Darren J. Dias, Michael S. Attridge, and Gerard Mannion (Springer International Publishing, 2021), 185–99.

[9] Nick Vaughan-Williams, "Europe's Border Crisis as an Autoimmune Disorder," Online Journal, *Green European Journal* (April 20, 2016 2016), https://www.greeneuropeanjournal.eu/europes-border-crisis-as-an-autoimmune-disorder/

[10] See Heidrun Friese, "The Limits of Hospitality," *Paragraph* 32, no. 1 (2009): 51–68. Friese notes that "Historically, hospitality has been considered a religious and ethical duty [...]." "With the development of the modern nation-state, these ethical obligations have been inscribed into the procedures of the public political deliberation and legal institutions that determine rights, duties and the social spaces of foreigners, residents and citizens." See 51–52.

Where the dominant way of thinking about refugees, asylum seekers, and migrants blames the gap between humanitarian rhetoric and the management of security measures at the border of the nation state, Esposito's examination of the mechanisms of modern biopolitics allows us to see the entanglement between the protection and negation of life, and the complex relationships between inclusion and exclusion, hospitality and securitization, in current refugee crises around the world.

THE IMMUNITY PARADIGM

Central to Esposito's account of *immunitas* is the relationship between immunity and community. For him, "Community is affirmative where immunity is negative."[11] Both terms are derived from the Latin root *munus* (gift, office, duty, or obligation). *Immunitas* is a privative term whose meaning is derived from what it negates, namely the *munus* (gift, office, duty, or obligation). Whoever is exempt or discharged from paying tributes or duties that might be done for others is defined as immune.[12] At the same time, however, this person becomes separated from the *communitas* in which the *munus* is accepted and taken up. The *munus* is always already imbricated in community since it is defined and allocated by the larger political body or *communitas*.[13] Esposito explains that the nature and operation of the political body of the state and the practice of the law within it are best explained within the immunitary paradigm. He observes:

> The state is a great immunitary dispositif to protect life, as Hobbes said. The law is also an immunitary dispositif against conflicts that would otherwise destroy society. In modern times, there has been a very strong acceleration in the need for immunitary security and, today, immunity has become, in my opinion, the pivot around which all our entire modern symbolic universe revolves. However, immunity is something ambivalent: it generates its own risks and dangers as well.[14]

---

[11] Roberto Esposito, *Terms of the Political: Community, Immunity, Biopolitics*, ed. Rhiannon Noel Welch, 1st ed. (New York: Fordham University Press, 2013), 58–59.

[12] Roberto Esposito, *Immunitas: The Protection and Negation of Life* (Cambridge, UK; Malden, MA: Polity, 2011), 5.

[13] Esposito, *Terms of the Political: Community, Immunity, Biopolitics*, 58.

[14] Christiaens, "The Biopolitics of Immunity in Times of COVID-19."

"Hostipitality"

The Latin roots *hostis* (guest) and *hospes* (stranger, foreigner, or alien), corresponding to the Greek ξένος, capture the tension at the heart of current debates and practices on refugees and migrants and their inclusion in, or exclusion from, the communities in which they seek refuge. In English, moreover, the Latin word, *hostis*, is the root of both "host" and "hostile"—one welcomes guests, the other excludes them. Derrida's neologism "hostipitality" (*hostipitalité*) highlights the tension between host and guest and the implicit violence of the encounter in which they each seek to appropriate a space for themselves.[15]

Esposito's immunitary paradigm highlights the tensions between hospitality and hostility, inclusion and exclusion, and welcome and securitization, within modern biopolitics. Within these tensions, the two-sided nature of the biopolitical calculus that is applied irregularly, often irrationally, according to the exigencies of the current political environment, is made evident. At the same time, as Luca Mavelli observes, the "dynamics of inclusion/exclusion of refugees have been informed by a biopolitical racism that redraws the boundary between 'valuable' (to be included) and 'not valuable' (to be excluded) lives according to the refugees' capacity to enhance the biological and emotional well-being of host populations."[16] Underpinning that, moreover, is the historical legacy of European colonial powers, that, as Sylvia Wynter argues, did more than divide the world into regions and nations. Their denial of the full being of non-European peoples was always already inscribed by the category of race.[17]

---

[15] "On Hostipitality," in Jacques Derrida, *Acts of Religion*, ed. Gil Anidjar (New York: Routledge, 2002), 358–420. See 419. See also the editor's notes, 356–7. See also, Jacques Derrida, *Of Hospitality*, ed. Anne Dufourmantelle (Stanford, Calif.: Stanford University Press, 2000).

[16] Luca Mavelli, "Governing Populations through the Humanitarian Government of Refugees: Biopolitical Care and Racism in the European Refugee Crisis," *Review of International Studies* 43, no. 5 (2017): 809–32. See 809.

[17] Sylvia Wynter, "Unsettling the Coloniality of Being/Power/Truth/Freedom: Towards the Human, After Man, Its Overrepresentation – An Argument," *The New Centennial Review* 3, no. 3 (2003): 257–337. See 300–303.

Coloniality and Race

Esposito does not include a biopolitical account of race, or what Mavelli calls "biopolitical racism," as it is operative in the contemporary global order.[18] The work of the Peruvian sociologist and postcolonial theorist, Anibal Quijano, offers a helpful supplement to Esposito's immunitary paradigm, particularly as it relates to exclusion of immigrants, migrants, and asylum seekers based on their race.

"The model of power that is globally hegemonic today," Quijano asserts, "presupposes an element of coloniality, that is, that modernity and colonialism are so inextricably connected that they are two sides of the same coin."[19] The process of globalization, Quijano argues, "began with the constitution of Americas and colonial/ modern Eurocentered capitalism as the new global power." Central to the European colonial project is the category of race. The colonial project began with "the codification of the differences between conquerors and conquered in the idea of 'race,' a supposedly different biological structure that place some in the natural situation of inferiority to others."[20] Quijano writes:

> The idea of race is certainly the most effective instrument of social domination invented in the last 500 years. Produced at the very beginning of the formation of America and capitalism, in the transition from the fifteenth to the sixteenth century, in the following centuries it was imposed on the entire population of the planet as part of the colonial domination of Europe.[21]

[18] See, John McMahon, The "Enigma of Biopolitics": Antiblackness, Modernity, and Roberto Esposito's Biopolitics," *Political Theory* 46, no. 5 (2018), 750–771. McMahon observes that the lack of an account of race, racism, racialization, and other related terms in Esposito's work "circumscribes the possible analytical power of his account: while in my assessment the questions and paradoxes he poses are crucial, his limited purview means that his responses will always be insufficient […]." By comparison, for a description of how racism is configured within Michel Foucault's biopolitics, see Kim Su Rasmussen, "Foucault's Genealogy of Racism," *Theory, Culture &Ssociety* 28, no. 5 (2011), 34–51. Rasmussen observes that Foucault's account of racism "is rather incomplete, lacking for example any substantiual discussion of European colonialism of the history of the idea of race." See Rasmussemn, 35. See also, Michel Foucault, *"Society Must Be Defended": Lectures at the Collège de France 1975–1976*, trans. D. Macey (New York: Picador Books, 1997).

[19] Anibal Quijano and Michael Ennis, "Coloniality of Power, Eurocentrism, and Latin America," *Nepantla* 1, no. 3 (2000), 533–580.

[20] Quijano, Coloniality of Power, 533.

[21] Quijano, Aníbal. "Que tal Raza!" *Revista del CESLA: International Latin American Studies Review.* No. 1 (2000). (Author's translation.) Quijano writes, "La idea de raza es, con toda seguridad, el más eficaz instrumento de dominación social inventado en los últimos 500 años. Producida en el mero comienzo de la formación de América y del capitalismo, en el tránsito del siglo XV al XVI, en las centurias siguientes fue impuesta sobre toda la población del planeta como parte de la dominación colonial de Europa.

While "the racial axis has a colonial origin and character," Quijano asserts, "[…] it has proven to be more durable and stable than the colonialism in whose matrix it was established."

Within the logic of the coloniality of power, there is an implicit connection between racial capitalism and migration/immigration. Encarnacíon Gutierrez Rodríguez writes:

> Migration within the emergence of the modern nation-state in the nineteenth century in former European colonies illustrates the divide created between the insider and outsider of the nation. This divide evokes the logic of coloniality, as it creates a racial difference between the insiders, considered members of the nation, and the outsiders, considered "migrants." Thus the dichotomy between citizens and migrants is embedded in a racializing logic produced within social relations shaped by the enduring effects of colonial epistemic power.[22]

Migration policies, operating within this racializing logic of coloniality, are evident in Europe and North American "border and migration control technologies" and in the "organization of labor recruitment." Rodriguez concludes that within the "current asylum-migration nexus, the 'refugee' has been reduced to a potential worker," who may or may not be welcomed across the border depending on their perceived value to the host nation.[23]

Recognizing the need for an account of the racializing logic operative in contemporary biopolitics and its absence in Esposito's biopolitics, his immunitary paradigm, nonetheless, offers a helpful explanatory model that highlights what is at issue in debates concerning inclusion/exclusion of refugees and migrants and the security apparatuses that have been created to protect the social body from the real and perceived threats posed by them. Esposito writes:

---

[22] Encarnacíon Gutierrez Rodríguez, "The Coloniality of Migration and the 'Refugee Crisis': On the Asylum-Migration Nexus, the Transatlantic White European Settler Colonialism-Migration and Racial Capitalism," *Refuge (Toronto. English edition)* 34, no. 1 (2018), 16–28. See, 25.

[23] Rodríguez, The Coloniality of Migration and the Refugee Crisis, 25.

The fact that the growing flows of immigrants are thought (entirely erroneously) to be one of the worst dangers for our societies suggests how central the immunitary question is becoming. Everywhere we look, new walls, new blockades, and new dividing lines are erected against something that threatens, or at least seems to, our biological, social, and environmental identity.[24]

When migrants and asylum seekers are used within the identity politics of nationalist political rhetoric to heighten tensions between the "us" within the borders of "our" nation and the dangerous otherness of "them" outside the border of that state, an increased emphasis is placed on the security apparatuses needed to exclude the alien other. This leads to a dangerous predicament for people seeking refugee from political and economic oppression at the border: even appearing at the border constitutes a criminal act, for which they can be imprisoned and deprived of the same rights that would have been proffered to them as citizens. When the irregular migrant is identified as a form of chaos in need of control or elimination, the unleashing of the power of the state to control that chaos is presented as the only reasonable option. This takes its form in the shape of fences and walls and an increased securitization at the borders of the nation.

It might appear that the answer to existing inhumane conditions for refugees and migrants is to embrace a completely affirmative biopolitics that would lessen security measures and open the border of the state to all seeking entry. A mass influx of population would lead to a xenophobic autoimmune response that would make conditions worse for both refugees and citizens already living within the state. Too little of a border, however, is as problematic as too much of one.

In his 2016 analysis of "Europe's Border Crisis as Auto-Immune Disorder," Gareth Vaughan-Williams observes, "Borders are not only sites of closure and excessive militarised defence; they are also sites of encounter with the other and an opening onto the common."[25] He suggests several "moves" that might make the border a safer, less militarized, and more hospitable place, for those appearing at the border seeking refuge, including "subjecting border security practices to greater democratic oversight," creating "legal channels for labour migration," and recalibrating "present conditions to allow for potentially transformative encounters between self and other[…]." These changes "could turn the present crisis

---

[24] Esposito, *Terms of the Political: Community, Immunity, Biopolitics*, 59.
[25] Vaughan-Williams, "Europe's Border Crisis as an Autoimmune Disorder."

into an opportunity to shatter the mirror in which Europe is reflected without seeing anything but itself."[26]

Vaughan-Williams' suggestions to mitigate the European border crisis are directly applicable to the border crisis in the United States. Unfortunately, as is often the case in Europe, the borders of the United States do not have sufficient democratic oversight and the US Congress has not been able to produce bipartisan solutions to address an influx of legal asylum seekers.

The asylum process in the United States is broken due to an inability of the US Congress to enact meaningful provisions for those seeking legal asylum. In theory, asylum seekers should be able to work with the US Embassy in their home countries and then with permission travel to the United States for asylum. In fact, this often is not available to them due to the politicization and the demonization of persons seeking asylum. Immigration and forced migration scholar Kathleen Arnold notes that "one of the most interesting aspects of current discourse on immigration is the widespread use of the term 'illegal' when discussing waves of immigrants arriving at the southern border" of the United States. "Although these immigrants would most likely be designated "refugees" if they were screened properly," she observes, "their treatment and confinement seems to be evidence of their 'guilt 'and 'illegality.'"[27] If bipartisan solutions for legal immigration and a more humane screening of refugees and asylum seekers were put in place at the border, this would open new spaces for hospitality and welcome, while at the same time it could assure security at the nation's borders. This is exactly the sort of thing Esposito is suggesting with his immunitary paradigm; it allows for inclusion and exclusion, and for the protection of life, even as it, in its exclusionary practices, can be seen as a negation of life.

---

[26] Vaughan-Williams, "Europe's Border Crisis as an Autoimmune Disorder."
[27] Kathleen R. Arnold, *Arendt, Agamben and the Issue of Hyper-legality in between the Prisoner-Stateless Nexus* (2018), 2.

Katechon and Immunity

The Pauline figure of the *katechon* (τὸ κατέχον) is central to the logic of Esposito's immunitary paradigm.[28] The *katechon* is the "restraining" or "withholding" power that restrains the unleashing of the forces of lawlessness. The exact identity of this power is not explicitly identified in 2 Thessalonians; Paul only says that he had told the Thessalonians about it when he was with them. Paul writes, "And you know what is now restraining him, so that he may be revealed when his time comes. For the mystery of lawlessness is already at work, but only until the one who now restrains it is removed" (2 Th. 2:6–7 NRSV).

Within the field of "political theology," with its application of an assemblage of secularized theological concepts, the analysis of power of the *katechon*, or more generally *katechonic* forces, is central to critiques of empire, the political sovereignty of the State, as well as the Church. Immunity in its exclusionary form, endeavoring to hold the forces of chaos within the community at bay, is that of *katechonic* power. The *katechon*, for Esposito, "is located precisely at the point of intersection between politics and religion: in the horizon defined as political theology."[29]

According to the logic of Romans 7, Esposito argues, "the law is that which simultaneously produces sin and its remedy; that which, by fighting it, reinforces it."

Interpreted within Esposito's immunitary paradigm, therefore, "the law injects within itself the death that sin brings to life, and thus brings life to death and death to life."[30] The *katechon*, similarly, "restrains evil by containing it, by keeping it, by holding it within itself. [...]. It confronts evil [...] but does not eradicate it, because if it did, it would eradicate itself."[31] By the same token, Esposito argues that "Christianity is the religion *of* secularization," and because creation and redemption are always already rooted in history, it is a "religion that dialectically separates from

---

[28] Esposito, *Immunitas: The Protection and Negation of Life*, 62–3. See also Roberto Esposito, *Two: The Machine of Political Theology and the Place of Thought*, First edition. ed. (Fordham University Press, 2015), 76–82. Analysis of the *katechon* is also central to the Italian political theologies of Massimo Cacciari and Giorgio Agamben. See Massimo Cacciari, *The Withholding Power: An Essay on Political Theology*, ed. Edi Pucci and Howard Caygill (London: Bloomsbury Academic, 2018). See also, Giorgio Agamben, *Stasis: Civil War as a Political Paradigm* (Stanford, Calif.: Stanford University Press, 2015).

[29] Esposito, *Immunitas: The Protection and Negation of Life*, 66.

[30] Esposito, *Immunitas: The Protection and Negation of Life*, 62.

[31] Esposito, *Immunitas: The Protection and Negation of Life*, 63.

itself to preserve itself as such." Esposito writes: "To immunize the community—as indeed all religions do—Christianity must immunize itself primarily through the assumption of its secular opposite."[32] He tends to see the primary task of religion as protective, that is, as an immunizing force that protects the social body (community); in other words, he stresses the katechonic or immunizing forces of religion over those that build community by welcoming and incorporating new members within it. Esposito's immunitary understanding of religion does not offer a complementary account of how religions, including Christianity, can offer a vision of wholeness that can be implemented, even if imperfectly, in concrete religious communities for their own benefit and for the benefit of the wider communities in which they are located. A fuller description of ways that katechonic forces of religion might build community would account for religious communities that seek to care for refugees and migrants who do not share the same ethnic, national origin or religious tradition. How then might Christian communities offer this sort of care and protection for those outside of their own community? How might they cross the boundary between internal protection of their own and the protection of vulnerable people, such as refugees, migrants, and asylum seekers of different national, ethnic, and religious communities?

THE CHURCH AND IMMIGRATION

Mayra Rivera, a Puerto Rican scholar of religion, employs Esposito's immunitary paradigm to examine the theological metaphors operative in the immigration and border politics of the Trump administration (2017–2021). She describes "a vision of the United States as a sacred enclosure, creating a people bounded to a territory yet threatened by contact with foreign bodies."[33] "Anti-immigration discourses," she observes, "are concretized in walls, fences, and other partitions. Their effects materialize in human bodies."[34] In the face of this reality, how might churches respond to current debates on immigration and set an example of hospitality and welcome to those seeking refuge and protection? To address this question, it is helpful to differentiate between the church as an institution and the church as a local parish or congregation. As an institution, the

---

[32] Esposito, *Immunitas: The Protection and Negation of Life*, 71–2. See also 60.
[33] Rivera, "Theological Metaphors in Anti-immigration Discourse," 70.
[34] Rivera, "Theological Metaphors in Anti-immigration Discourse," 70.

church and its leaders can lobby for changes to legal immigration and the welcoming of refugees and migrants. The church can also reject the legal fiction that denies personhood to certain individuals and assert the fundamental dignity of every human being, no matter their race or national origin.

The oldest immunitary practice of the church is that of providing sanctuary. This ecclesiastical practice was rooted in a suspicion of the punishments meted out by civil authorities. The Sanctuary Movement in the United States arose in the 1980s to provide refuge to Central American refugees fleeing civil conflict. In response to deportations during the Trump administration, a new "Sanctuary Movement" formed. It is self-described as "a growing movement of immigrants and over 1100 faith communities doing what Congress and the Administration refuse to do to protect and stand with immigrants facing deportation."[35]

By way of example, in 2016, the Episcopal Diocese of Los Angeles declared itself a "sanctuary diocese." The diocese resolved to make its congregations and diocesan institutions serve "as places of welcome, refuge, healing, and other forms of material and pastoral support for those targeted by hate due to immigration status or some perceived status of difference" and to "work alongside our friends, families, and neighbors to ensure the dignity and human rights of all people [...]."[36]

Similarly in 2019, the Evangelical Lutheran Church in America Churchwide Assembly declared itself to be a "sanctuary denomination."[37] The "Talking Points" issued by the Evangelical Lutheran Church in America to explain its actions asserted that "becoming a sanctuary denomination means that the ELCA is publicly declaring that walking alongside immigrants and refugees is a matter of faith." The same "Talking Points" stressed "that being a sanctuary denomination does not call any person, congregation, or synod to engage in any illegal actions."[38]

---

[35] "Sanctuary Movement," https://www.sanctuarynotdeportation.org. Accessed December 8, 2022.

[36] "Episcopal Diocese of Los Angeles Becomes 'Sanctuary Diocese,'" Monday, December 5, 2016, https://www.pasadenanow.com/main/episcopal-diocese-becomes-sanctuary-diocese. Accessed May 24, 2022.

[37] "ELCA: Sanctuary Denomination," https://elca.org/sanctuarychurch. Accessed December 8, 2022.

[38] Sanctuary Denomination Talking Points, https://download.elca.org/ELCA%20Resource%20Repository/ELCA_SanctuaryDenomination_TalkingPoints.pdf?_ga=2.99330525.2103513490.1670537333-521380656.1670537333. Accessed December 8, 2022.

Some congregations are willing to go further than that and are willing to shelter those who are threatened with deportation because of their immigration status, thus risking subsequent legal encounters with immigration officials. Kathleen Arnold argues that church-based sanctuary as a form of resistance is "potentially revolutionary because it interrupts and challenges sovereign power." It is the most logical path in the current situation, she argues, because "sovereign power formations increase at local and federal levels, leaving no other remedy except through grass-roots action." "If sanctuary is broadened to include any individual seeking protection and not just foreigners," Arnold continues, "this method of resistance could be used as a broad tool to interrupt and reconfigure sovereign power affecting citizens and foreigners alike."

While the institutional church can bear witness to the way Christians can offer hospitality to the stranger, refugee, and migrant by theological statements and pronouncements and by reference to the biblical stories of welcome in Holy Scripture in sermons and other teaching opportunities, authentic hospitality can only be offered in person within the context of local parishes and congregations. When a parish community, for example, helps a refugee family settle into the community in which it is located, their hospitality allows for the interpersonal encounter that breaks down the hostile barriers between the refugee and members of their adopted community. In some cases, parish families might offer their own homes as sites of hospitality and housing for refugees and migrants. The ELCA suggests other ways that church members can assist in the welcome of immigrants, refugees, and asylum seekers: hosting English as a second language (ESL) classes, marching in protest of the detention of children and families, providing housing for persons facing deportation, and even engaging in "thoughtful conversations about what our faith says about immigration."

Mayra Rivera identifies additional practices of churches and secular organizations that offer hope and hospitality to migrants in the face of a hostile xenophobic nationalism that stigmatize and threaten them: "strangers looking for lost children and arranging for their care until they are reunited with their families, flying with immigrants to make sure they reach a family member in a different state, [and] leaving bottles of water in the desert[…]."[39]

---

[39] Rivera, "Theological Metaphors in Anti-immigration Discourse," 72.

In September 2022, Ron DeSantis, the governor of Florida, gathered a group of Venezuelan asylum seekers in Texas, who had crossed the border from Mexico, and put them on a chartered flight unannounced to Martha's Vineyard, Massachusetts. He apparently hoped that the unannounced arrival of the asylum seekers would demonstrate the hypocrisy of "liberals" who have declared themselves to be site of sanctuary but when actually confronted with the reality of the presence of asylum seekers in their midst would vociferously protest their arrival. From a cynical perspective, the governor's actions seem to assume that no one legitimately could be concerned for such persons and that those from afar who seem to care would not if they had to deal with the real, physical human needs of these persons.

On the one hand, DeSantis' actions exhibited a callous disregard for the dignity of human life, while at the same time it visibly demonstrated the truth behind Arendt's assertion that once noncitizens cross the border, they essentially have no rights. On the other hand, the arrival of persons seeking asylum in Martha's Vineyard, and the hastily organized welcome they received, manifested the contours of a generous hospitality. The people of numerous congregations on the island quickly joined together to assist the newly arrived migrants. They gathered food, found temporary lodging, and garnered legal support for them. Their hospitality highlighted the fragile network of religious and nonprofit organizations who work tirelessly behind the scenes to treat migrants and asylum seekers with dignity and respect.

In the face of the "biopolitical racism" that discriminates between valuable and invaluable refugees, migrants, and asylum seekers, the various Christian acts of hospitality and welcome identified above directly confront the legacy of colonialism that underlies that racism, and as such are decolonizing practices that can be implemented within Christian congregations.[40]

Decolonization in its broadest sense is predicated on the understanding that the current structures of economic exploitation are connected to an overdetermined web of racialized power that is the legacy of European colonialism. Because contemporary racism is integrally connected to the legacy of colonialism, when people within a parish or congregation of European descent welcome an individual migrant, refugee, or asylum seeker or a family of a different racial background, this constitutes a

---

[40] Mavelli, "Governing Populations through the Humanitarian Government of Refugees: Biopolitical Care and Racism in the European Refugee Crisis," 809.

decolonizing practice. It might seem to be a small step forward in the process of decolonization, but from small steps like this often come larger, more important ones. When members of Christian congregations of European descent welcome and form genuine, interracial and interpersonal friendships with immigrants and immigrant families within the context of a Christian community that affirms their fundamental human dignity, they counter the racism that is inherent in current immigration practices that distinguishes between valuable and invaluable persons and excludes persons because of their race or national background. Members of the congregation learn firsthand that all people have something to offer the wider community into which the congregation is helping to integrate them.

When a congregation in Hallowell, Maine, decided to close its doors due to financial constraints, the Episcopal Diocese of Maine transferred the ownership of the property to the Capital Area New Mainers Project, a nonprofit dedicated to "meeting immigrant needs," cultivating interpersonal between immigrants and local community members and educating the broader public about diverse cultures and immigration issues. Their building now hosts two families and serves as a multicultural center in which immigrants share their lives with the people of the broader community. In a report from the Episcopal News Service, Chris Myers Asch, cofounder and executive director of the project, explained that with the arrival of numerous refugees in 2017 from Iraq to Augusta, "Many of us…felt like we needed to do more as a community to be welcoming, to help these folks get their feet on the ground and thrive here." He explained further, "We're helping people understand that we benefit a lot from what immigrants bring, and they're not, like, taking our jobs or taking things from the community. They're actually bringing rich traditions … and ideas that can help infuse this area with some much-needed energy."[41]

Esposito's immunitary paradigm highlights the tensions between hospitality and hostility, inclusion and exclusion, and welcome and securitization, within modern biopolitics. The paradigm operates within the space of the larger concept of community. At the time of the origin of modern biopolitics, the state took on the role of providing for the health and

[41] Egan Millard, "Closed Maine Church becomes Housing, Community Center for Immigrants." Episcopal News Service, Feb 2, 2023. https://www.episcopalnewsservice.org/2023/02/02/closed-maine-church-becomes-housing-community-center-for-immigrants. Accessed February 15, 2023.

well-being of people within its purview in much the same way the church had done with its concept of the body of Christ, of which each Christian was a part. For the state to provide for the safety and security of its citizens, it seeks to exclude what it perceives will threaten them. When fear, hatred, and hostility toward the migrant and refugee are incited, the space and conditions for hospitality become rare or impossible. If the church is to be faithful to its ministry of reconciliation (2 Cor. 5:18), then it and its people must seek to establish common spaces in which hospitality and welcome for those seeking refuge can flourish. The task for the church amid an immigration crisis is to help members of the wider society move from hatred and hostility to welcome and hospitality. This move can best be accomplished by example and concrete practice within the local community.

CHAPTER 4

Decolonizing Among Filipin@ Migrant-Settlers

Cristina Lledo Gomez

Parque Retiro, or Retiro Park, is Madrid's most famous and largest park and made a UNESCO World Heritage site in July 2021.[1] This park was also the site of a human zoo, named *Exposición de las Islas Filipinas,* or the "Exhibition of the Islands of the Philippines", opened in 1887 by Queen María Cristina.[2] Madrid journalist, Leah Pattem, describes the purpose of the exhibition:

---

[1] "Unesco adds Madrid's Paseo del Prado and Retiro Park to heritage list", *BBC News*, 25 July 2021, https://www.bbc.com/news/world-europe-57955966; UNESCO World Heritage Convention, *Paseo del Prado and Buen Retiro, a landscape of Arts and Sciences,* https://whc.unesco.org/en/list/1618/
[2] "La Exposición de las Islas Filipinas (1887): UN Encuentro con Hispanoasia", *Madrid Historico,* Jan 14, 2021, at https://www.revistamadridhistorico.es/2021/01/la-exposicion-de-las-islas-filipinas-1887-un-encuentro-con-hispanoasia/

C. Lledo Gomez (✉)
BBI-The Australian Institute of Theological Education and Research, Sydney, NSW, Australia

© The Author(s), under exclusive license to Springer Nature Switzerland AG 2023
R. C. Barreto, V. Latinovic (eds.), *Decolonial Horizons,* Pathways for Ecumenical and Interreligious Dialogue, https://doi.org/10.1007/978-3-031-44839-3_4

Over the course of six months, tens of thousands of Spaniards would have the chance to visit one of the farthest corners of the Spanish Empire – and even meet some of its people – without ever having to leave the country.[3] [...] The grand inauguration of this exhibition took place in the *Palacio de Cristal* (Crystal Palace) – a beautiful, giant greenhouse built to house tropical plants brought over from the Philippines. Textiles were also added, as museum curators laid out paths using rugs woven by Filipino women. It was not just these items on display: the people who crafted them were too. Spanish colonisers brought 43 Igorot women and men from the mountainous island of Luzon in the Philippines, instructing them to act out their daily lives in front of spectators. A small village was built for them next to the palace, complete with streets, raised thatched huts and places of worship. A pond was dug in front of the palace and filled with water and fish for the Igorot people to catch. Traditional canoes made of hollowed-out tree trunks sat at the water's edge. Small farms were laid out and cattle were brought in to plough the land, all for the amusement of curious onlookers.[4]

This human zoo is indicative of how often the indigenous were seen by their colonizers as exotic, subhuman, uncivilized creatures to be ruled over, according to the whims of their invaders. A pamphlet created by the Spanish Ministry of Culture for a 2017 exhibition of the 1887 *Exposicion de las Islas Filipinas* similarly admits how Filipin@s were viewed at the time through the eyes of Spanish photographers who recorded two types of images: the first, in their own clothing, portraying them as "folkloric" or "exotic"; the second, in 'modern' European clothes, suggesting a vision of a possible future for the Philippines. The pamphlet explained these two visions, which worked hand in hand to justify the colonization of the Philippines by the Spaniards:

> The duality of backwardness/savagery and modernity were two sides of the same coin. The existence of the former justified – in the eyes of many people at the time – the need for intervention by the Spanish authorities (civil and religious) to bring Christian and Western 'civilisation' to these peoples.[5]

---

[3] Leah Pattem, "UNESCO's new world heritage site in Madrid was once a human zoo", August 2021, https://gal-dem.com/madrid-unesco-retiro-park-human-zoo-history/; cf. also https://madridnofrills.com/unescos-new-world-heritage-site-in-madrid-was-once-a-human-zoo/, accessed June 19, 2022.

[4] Ibid.

[5] *Imágenes De Una Exposición Filipinas en el Parque de el Retiro, en 1887*, Museo Nacional de Antropología, From 30 June to 15 October, 2017, pp.1–30, at 12.

Pattem comments on how these recorded images presented racist narratives which she argues exist to this day: "These staged images involved nudity and dramatized aggression, presenting a racist narrative that goes relatively unchallenged even today, especially in Retiro Park itself".[6] It is confronting and hurtful to hear about this history. The knowledge of such a reality connects me more deeply with the suffering of my people in those early days where they were made to feel like animals, for the entertainment of another population. Considering how people treasure and love their pets these days, one might say that my people were regarded as less than animals then.

Politically Independent, Psychologically Trapped

Whilst the Philippines is politically and economically independent from Spain and America,[7] this chapter argues that a considerable number of Filipin@s are far from being independent from their colonizers in their minds. For the dominant and pervasive narrative of 'whiteness', whether it is being white-European or white-American, can intrude and invade the Philippine sense of self, communicating always to them that they are never enough. Studies by David and Okazaki including their 2006 essay on colonial mentality and the mental health of Filipin@ American show an association between internalized colonialism and the psychological well-being among Filipino Americans.[8] Whilst some postcolonial theorists argue that indigenous reclamation of stolen land is and should be the primary or even sole concern in this postcolonial era, in turn enabling other indigenous rights to be acknowledged, for Filipin@s, this chapter argues, dealing with 'whiteness' and the association between colonial mentality and mental health (such as tendency towards anxiety, depression, eating disorders and suicidality) is the higher priority.

[6] Pattem, "UNESCO's New World Heritage Site in Madrid was Once a Human Zoo".

[7] The colonial invasion of the Philippines began with the Spaniards in 1521. The islands were then ceded to the United States by Spain in 1898, lasting 48 years until the Philippines became a republic on July 4, 1946.

[8] David & Okazaki, "Colonial mentality"; E. J. R. David & S. Okazaki, "The colonial mentality scale (CMS) for Filipino Americans: Scale construction and psychological implications", *Journal of Counseling Psychology* 53.2 (2006):241–252; Della Maneze, Yenna Salamonson, Chandra Poudel, Michelle DiGiacomo, Bronwyn Everett, Patricia M. Davidson, "Health-Seeking Behaviors of Filipino Migrants in Australia: The Influence of Persisting Acculturative Stress and Depression", *Journal of Immigrant and Minority Health* 18 (2016): 779–786.

Agenda

This chapter proceeds as follows: First, it locates the Philippines geographically and sociologically as part of the Austronesian language group to show their connection with their Pasifika brothers and sisters, and not just with the southeast Asian group, briefly presenting the spread of Filipin@ migrants around the world and also define how Filipin@ migrants can be called 'migrant-settlers'.

Second, it explores colonial mentality as it presents for a number of Filipin@s in diaspora. Note that there are differences in experience according to location and between 1.0, 1.5 or 2.0 generation migrants. As well, they can be dealing with multiple traumas. Thus, in addition to colonial trauma, they have the usual added burden of migrants such as experiences of dislocation, cultural amnesia and living in two worlds on the land of one's own colonizers, or on lands that have been colonized by 'white persons'. Due to the constraints of space, it will not be possible to explore the differences in experience among generations and the combined difficulties of colonial trauma and migrating, but they are simply noted.

Finally, this chapter presents a decolonial view emerging among the Philippine diaspora. This chapter's intention is to suggest how churches might begin to think about and take up decolonial practices in their interactions with this population.

Locating Filipin@s

The Philippines is considered part of the Austronesian-speaking family which includes the countries of the Pacific region: Micronesia, Melanesia and Polynesia. The Austronesian-speaking family is said to have originated in Taiwan and is considered "the second most diverse linguistic group in the world with nearly 1200 languages".[9] The family is said to have originated in Taiwan, expanding through sea migration somewhere between 3000 and 1500 BCE. As Pasifika peoples saw themselves as boat or water people, Filipin@s could self-identify in similar ways, given the amount of water that connects the diverse language groups of the Philippines. Today,

---

[9] C. Padilla-Iglesias, E Gjesfjeld, L Vinicius (2020), "Geographical and social isolation drive the evolution of Austronesian languages", *PLoS ONE* 15 (12): 1–16, at 3.

the Philippines remains the largest supplier of seafarers and officers at sea in the world.[10]

The experience of Christian colonization and its enduring effects in the Austronesian-speaking region aligns with the experience of colonization and its effects upon the Pacific region, as described by Tongan pastor and biblical scholar Jione Havea. According to him,

> We owe a big part of the troubling of Pasifika waters to our 'discovery' by European explorers, the most celebrated of whom are Abel Tasman of the Dutch East India Company (1640s) and James Cook of the British Royal Navy (1760's and 1770s). Their expeditions came in the spirit of Pope Alexander VI's 1493 papal bull *Inter Caetera* (cradle of the Doctrine of Discovery), which sanctioned Catholic empires to *colonize, convert, and enslave* non-Christian (is)lands and peoples [...]. They registered the islands for their respective crowns, infected native bodies with diseases that had no local remedies, and they colonized the minds of generations to come.[11]

Another consideration is the significant presence of Filipin@s in the diaspora. According to the Commission on Filipinos Overseas, 10.2 million Filipin@s live overseas:[12] 4.8 million are permanent migrants, 4.2 million are temporary migrants and 1.2 million are irregular migrants, living in more than 200 destinations countries and territories, the majority moving to the United States, followed by Canada, Japan and Australia. An indication of the numbers that migrated to these countries can be seen in the Commission on Filipinos Overseas' data on registered Filipino Emigrants by Major Country of Destination, from 1981 to 2020. The Commission records the following totals for this period: United States 1,513,314 or 60.15%; Canada 512,638 or 20.38%; Japan 156,120 or 6.21%; and Australia 146,953 or 5.84%.

Whilst being a migrant often refers to permanently settling on new land, as an Australian Filipina migrant, this author acknowledges her context as also being a settler on Aboriginal Australian land. Moreover, she

---

[10] "The Philippines Continues to be the Leading provider of Seafarers and Officers", *Marine Insight,* 24 November 2021, https://www.marineinsight.com/shipping-news/philippines-continues-to-be-the-leading-provider-of-seafarers-and-officers/

[11] Jione Havea, "Sea of Theologies", in Jione Havea (ed.), *Theologies from the Pacific, Postcolonialism and Religions Series,* Joseph Duggan and J Jayakiran Sebastian (series eds.) (Cham, Switzerland: Springer, 2021) pp.1–12, at 6.

[12] "Philippine Migration at a Glance", *Office of the President of the Philippines, Commission on Filipinos Overseas,* https://cfo.gov.ph/statistics-2/

acknowledges that Australian Aboriginal sovereignty remains unrecognized in the Australian constitution. The non-recognition of the first nations peoples of Australia has consequent ongoing detrimental effects for them. Here, the Australian historian Lorenzo Veracini's distinction between 'migrant' and 'settler' can help illuminate the importance of identifying as a migrant-settler. Veracini says 'settlers' are "beneficiaries", whereas 'migrants' are "targeted by assimilatory processes".[13] This points to the hybrid existence of migrants who whilst experiencing issues of oppression and disadvantage as they settle on new lands as migrants (including subtle or underhanded racism and classism), they also reap the benefits of the colonial takeover of indigenous land, as settlers to the land. In Australia, the land was considered *terra nulius*—nobody's land or land without a master, justifying its takeover. Thus, in any discussions on issues of race and colonialism, it is important to remember the realities and voices of the indigenous who are often left out of the picture in these investigations.

Returning to the statistics on Filipin@ migrants in diaspora, with a majority of this population in the United States, it is important to consider the research undertaken by Filipino-Americans among Filipino-Americans such as professors E. J. R. David and Kevin Nadal. As psychologists, David and Nadal, continually encountered colonial mentality (CM) in their clinics, eventually leading them to co-publish the 2013 article "The Colonial Context of Filipino American Immigrants' Psychological Experiences".[14] They concluded that:

(a) Filipino American immigrants experienced ethnic and cultural denigration in the Philippines prior to their U.S. arrival,
(b) ethnic and cultural denigration in the Philippines and in the United States may lead to the development of colonial mentality (CM), and
(c) that CM may have negative mental health consequences among Filipino American immigrants.[15]

---

[13] Lorenzo Veracini, "Settlers are not Migrants" pp.32–48, *The Settler Colonial Present* (London: Palgrave Macmillan, 2015), 32.

[14] E.J.R David and Kevin L. Nadal, "The colonial context of Filipino American Immigrants' psychological experiences", *Cultural Diversity and Ethnic Minority Psychology* 19 (2013): 298–30.

[15] Ibid., 298.

Colonial Mentality

What is colonial mentality?[16] According to David and Okazaki, when observing Filipino-Americans, colonial mentality is "a product of colonialism [...] a broad multidimensional construct that refers to personal feelings or beliefs of ethnic or cultural inferiority".[17] It can manifest in the following ways:

(1) degradation of the self,
(2) degradation of the culture or body,
(3) discriminating against less Americanized in-group members and
(4) tolerating historical and contemporary oppression.[18]

It is believed that the effects of this form of internalized oppression "range from admiration of the colonial legacy and culture to feelings of shame and embarrassment about the indigenous culture".[19] Therefore, colonial mentality is often "associated with bullying, acculturative stress and maladaptive behaviors".[20] Internalized colonialism weakens not only individual self-identity, but also collective self-esteem. David and Okazaki write that for the Filipin@s, Colonial Mentality appears as:

(a) degradation of the Filipino self (that is, feelings of inferiority, shame, embarrassment, resentment, or self-hate about being Filipino).

---

[16] I have written on colonial mentality among Filipin@s in other publications and have used the same definitions on colonial mentality as is used in this chapter. Those publications are: Cristina Lledo Gomez, "Noli me Tangere: A Church for the Oppressed – Putting the Abused & Vulnerable at the Forefront of Ecclesial Change" pp.67–76, in Mark Chapman and Vladimir Latinovic (eds.) *Changing the Church: Transformations of Christian Belief, Practice & Life. Pathways for Ecumenical and Interreligious Dialogue* (London: Palgrave Macmillan, 2020); Cristina Lledo Gomez, "Deleted and Reclaimed Borders: Embracing my Native Self" pp.119–138, in *Bordered Bodies, Bothered Voices: Native and Migrant Theologies*, edited by Jione Havea (Eugene, Oregon: Wipf and Stock, 2022).

[17] E. J. R. David and S. Okazaki, "The Colonial Mentality Scale (CMS) for Filipino Americans: Scale construction and psychological implications," *Journal of Counseling Psychology* 53, (2006): 241–252; Shawn O. Utsey, Jasmine A. Abrams, Annabella Opare-Henaku, Mark A. Bolden, Otis Williams, "Assessing the Psychological Consequences of Internalized Colonialism on the Psychological Well-Being of Young Adults in Ghana", *Journal of Black Psychology* 41 (2015): 195–220, at 198.

[18] Utsey et al., 198.

[19] Ibid., 199.

[20] Ibid., 198.

(b) degradation of the Filipino culture or body (that is, the perception that anything Filipino is inferior to anything White, European, or American, including culture, language, physical characteristics, material products, and government).
(c) discriminating against less-Americanized Filipinos (that is, distancing oneself from characteristics related to being Filipino and becoming as American as possible); and
(d) tolerating historical and contemporary oppression of Filipinos and Filipino Americans (that is, the acceptance of oppression as an appropriate cost of civilization, believing maltreatment is well intentioned).[21]

The power of colonial mentality is such that even if the colonization by Spaniards and Americans occurred in a by-gone era, and through migration Filipinos left the physical space which reminded them of this destructive part of their past, a number of Filipin@s continue to carry colonial mentality as part of their diaspora experience.[22] While the likes of David, Nadal and Okazaki have published on this phenomenon among Filipin@ Americans, in Australia, a 2010–2011 joint study between scholars from the University of Technology Sydney and the University of Western Sydney has shown similar acculturative stress and depressive results among Filipin@ Australians.[23]

In "Deleted and Reclaimed Borders", this author shares her experience of internalized inferiority due to the brownness of my skin, attributing this

---

[21] David and Okazaki, "The Colonial Mentality Scale (CMS) for Filipino Americans"; Cf. also Victor E. Tuazon, Edith Gonzalez, Daniel Gutierrez, and Lotes Nelson, "Colonial Mentality and Mental Health Help-Seeking of Filipino Americans", *Journal of Counselling and Development* 97 (October 2019): 352–363; E.J.R. David and Dinghy Kristine B. Sharma, "Losing Kapwa: Colonial Legacies and the Filipino American Family", *Asian American Journal of Psychology* 8 (2017): 43–55; and Elizabeth Protacio Marcelino, "Towards Understanding the Psychology of the Filipino", *Women & Therapy* 9 (Oct 2008): 105–128.

[22] E.J.R. David & S. Okazaki, "Colonial mentality: A review and recommendation for Filipino American Psychology", *Cultural Diversity and Ethnic Minority Psychology* 12.1 (2006):1–16; E.J.R. David, "A colonial mentality model of depression for Filipino Americans", *Cultural Diversity and Ethnic Minority Psychology* 14.2 (2008): 118–127; E.J.R. David, "Testing the validity of the colonial mentality implicit association test and the interactive effects of covert and overt colonial mentality on filipino american mental health", *Asian American Journal of Psychology* 1.1 (2010):31–45.

[23] David and Nadal, "The colonial context of Filipino American Immigrants' psychological experiences"; David & Okazaki, "Colonial mentality"; David & Okazaki, "The Colonial Mentality Scale (CMS) for Filipino Americans"; Maneze et al., "Health-Seeking Behaviors of Filipino Migrants in Australia".

internalization to my socialization in the Philippine culture.[24] In *"Narrativas y experiencias de racializacion de las mujeres de Oceania"*, Carroll and Lledo Gomez explain that a common socialization practice among mothers in the Austronesia-Oceania region is the daily massaging of their daughters' noses "in the hopes of shaping them into pointy European noses".[25] Such practice was not seen as an act of denigration of their daughters but rather care for and protection of them given the value of 'whiteness' (i.e. having 'whiter' or lighter skin and European facial features) in their cultures. This is without surprise given the prevalence of discrimination and abuse against women and girls in the region, based on shadeism or colourism, whether subtle or overt. Often "racism has been masked under the dominant narrative of gender-based violence which has its roots in colonialism".[26]

There are scholars who are reluctant to use the phrase 'colonial mentality'. For Elaine Marie Carbonell Laforteza, for example, while the idea of 'colonial mentality' might seek to bring awareness to the superstructure that supports and perpetuates this form of oppression, it is limited as a descriptive term. For Laforteza, the descriptive expression "the somatechnics of whiteness and race" better explains the superstructure that supports and perpetuates internalized oppression from the perpetuation of colonial mentality, as she explains:

> [...] somatechnics is revealed as the means through which everyday belonging to the world becomes constituted. It reveals the ways in which technologies of power/knowledge become consolidated through embodied practice. Consequently, the concept of somatechnics considers the ways in which *soma* [body] and *techne* [technologies] intersect to inform interpersonal/intercorporeal relations. This focus on embodied practice and its enmeshment with technologies of power is relatively absent from the concept of colonial mentality which depends on a Cartesian logic and a subject/object split.[27]

---

[24] Cristina Lledo Gomez, "Deleted and Reclaimed Borders: Embracing My Native Self", in Jione Havea (ed.) *Bordered Bodies, Bothered Voices: Native and Migrant Theologies*. Intersectionality and Theology Series. Series Editor: Jione Havea (Eugene, Oregon: Pickwick, 2022), 119–138.

[25] Cristina Lledo Gomez y Seforosa Carroll, *"Narrativas y experiencias de racializacion de las mujeres de Oceania"*, en Sharon A Bong, Bernadeth Caero Bustillos y Susan Abraham (eds.) *Concilium. Racismo: Perspectivas Interculturales de las Mujeres*, Vol. 399 (Febrero 2023): 75–90, de 81.

[26] Lledo Gomez y Carroll, *"Narrativas y experiencias de racializacion de las mujeres de Oceania"*, 86.

[27] Ibid., 6.

As an ecclesiologist, this idea of the somatechnics of whiteness and race can lead one to question the role of Christian churches. One needs to ask how church members, particularly the migrant Filipin@ communities find their belonging and how many ever consider race and gender in the embodied practices (the *soma*) of worship, combined with the "technologies" (the knowledge and leadership) in the liturgy, in turn forming them into interpersonal relations that either perpetuate or resist white Western normativity. Filipin@ decolonizing elders, Marian Pastor Roces and Felipe de Leon Jr, themselves point to the power of reclaiming and relearning Filipino arts and crafts as embodied practices to reclaim Philippine native heritage.[28] They are essentially inviting Filipin@s to the practice of somatechnics. For this would involve becoming more in touch with our bodies (the *soma*) by checking how we feel, locating those bodies in a particular place, allowing those bodies to be what connects us—not just to each other but also with land, spirit ancestors and God or divinity. Philippine arts and crafts as practiced by our ancestors were not simply about making clothing, homewares or just art. They were spiritual practices engaged with spirits including ancestor spirits in the room. The craft connected, one to the land, to the universe, to the living and the dead, to one's God and to oneself. Thus, a possible decolonizing practice for the Filipin@ would involve not just learning Philippine history and constructing family trees (the *techne*) but also reclaiming lost arts and crafts (the *soma*). Together, these can replace the rituals and thinking imbedded in Filipin@s that 'whiteness' and anything 'Euro-American' is superior, whilst their own brown bodies and connection with spirits and land are deemed inferior, to be dismissed and rejected.

Clarifying White Western Normativity

This chapter has repeatedly referred to 'whiteness' and 'white' normativity. Let me clarify the meanings of these words. In their 2014 classic text *Ethnoautobiography*, Kremer and Jackson-Paton cite the work of Henrich,

---

[28] Felipe M. De Leon, Jr., "Defining the Filipino through the Arts: From Specialistic Innocence to Participatory Consciousness", *Philippine Humanities Review* Vol 13.1 (2011):3–41; Felipe De Leon Jr., "On Philippine Indigenous Arts" *Project Virkurso Lecture Series YouTube*, accessed Feb 16, 2023, at https://fb.watch/iJp-xff8cP/; Felipe De Leon Jr. and Marian Pastor Roces, "Reclaiming Our Narratives: Inclusivity & Decolonization", *Post Pandemic Futures Video Series YouTube*, accessed Feb 16, 2023, at https://www.youtube.com/watch?v=IjTqdQlztiU

Heine and Norenzayan who reviewed research on human psychology and behaviour, searching for generalizations.[29] Henrich et al. interestingly found that "members of Western, educated, industrialized, rich, and democratic" cultures are actually the "exceptional" rather than the normative. Yet, they were seen as the normative in the past as they often constituted most of the sample populations in surveys and tests. They further concluded that the more you fit into these five categories: Western, educated, industrialized, rich and democratic, "the more you see a world full of separate objects, rather than relationships".[30] Henrich and his colleagues compared Western, educated, industrialized, rich and democratic persons to East Asians, stating that the former tended towards individualism whilst the latter towards roles and relationships. Moreover, the norm for the former was to have individuals split themselves from the priority of group goals, place, myth, ritual, ancestry, spirits, gods and goddesses. Meanwhile, the latter complete "I am ..." sentences with families, communities or religious groups. Their relationships to others and the feelings, thoughts and behaviours of others have greater significance and consequently impact upon one's own actions.[31]

Kremer and Jackson-Paton add a third group to these two, which is Indigenous peoples and their cultures. For Kremer and Jackson-Paton, "Indigenous traditions are consciously based on locally, ecologically, and seasonally contextualized truths that are narratively anchored—their stories are embedded—in natural communities".[32] Their worldview, ways of being and doing are non-dualistic, where spirits are not removed from their human relations but rather participate in an ongoing conversation; stories and ceremonies facilitate internal and external harmony which includes harmony with plants, animals, ancestors, stars, humans, rocks, mountains and other beings. The goals of conversation with all of creation are balance, being present in a particular time and location, and attending to "the obligations arising from one's being" in that time and location. It can be described as *beingknowing* which participates with its surroundings.[33]

---

[29] Joseph Henrich, Steven J. Heine, & Ara Norenzayan, *The Weirdest People in the World?* (New York, USA: Cambridge University Press, 2010) cited by Jürgen Werner Kremer and R Jackson-Paton, *Ethnoautobiography: Stories and Practices for Unlearning Whiteness, Decolonization, Uncovering Ethnicities* (Sebastopol, California, 2014).
[30] Ibid., 45.
[31] Ibid., 46.
[32] Ibid., 48.
[33] Ibid., 49.

Kremer and Jackson-Paton's definition for WEIRD cultures (Western, educated, industrialized, rich and democratic) implicitly points to what whiteness studies, such as that by Jessica Terruhn, have explicitly named. That is, "whiteness as an invisible norm, a structural location of privilege, and a set of cultural practices and discourses that serve to reinforce white supremacy".[34] As Terruhn explores white settler narratives from her location Aotearoa/New Zealand, she importantly points to whiteness as "a contemporary phenomenon which persists at a time when most white people insist that racism is a thing of the past [...]".[35] What informs her analysis are "theories and research that examine how majorities respond and adapt to 'dilemmas about how to maintain their own identity and the national identity they largely shaped, when their hitherto privileged situation is increasingly under threat'".[36] Quoting Andrea Smith, Terruhn proposes that "whiteness operates in three distinct but sometimes concurrent or overlapping ways: [...] a 'logic of slavery', a 'logic of genocide', and / or a 'logic of orientalism'".[37] In other words, dominating, erasing and othering.

Decolonizing Filipin@s: Being Babaylan-Inspired

Once one knows how whiteness operates and how it can pervade Filipin@s identity, the following question emerges: how might they decolonize? According to the Centre for Babaylan Studies (CfBS), decolonizing involves recovering ancestry, learning about indigenous spirituality and becoming inspired by indigenous figures, which for Filipin@s are the Babaylans. These figures had certain powers and freedoms until European colonizers invaded their lands (and introduced misogyny, patriarchy, racism and colonialism). As the CfBS explains:

> A central part of this ancestral work is learning about indigenous spirituality as embodied in the tradition called by various names among our indigenous peoples: babaylan, balian, baylan, mumbaki, patutunong, mandadawak, and others...[38]

---

[34] Jessica Terruhn, *Being Pākehā: White Settler Narratives of Politics, Identity, and Belonging in Aotearoa/New Zealand*, PhD Thesis, University of Auckland, 2015, 46.
[35] Ibid.
[36] Ibid.
[37] Ibid., 46–47.
[38] "What is a Babaylan?", *Centre for Babaylan Studies*, https://www.centerforbabaylanstudies.org/history.

The CfBS lists several core principles and values for engaging in decolonizing/ancestral work. Two examples are shown below:

- We seek to be guided by and rooted in the Ancestral Knowledge from both our Motherland and the Diasporic lands we occupy.
- We relate to kin and to all experiences with a Decolonizing lens, working with all our relations to transform dynamics that have been shaped by systems and legacies of domination (including those influenced by capitalism, racism and patriarchy) and replace them with *Kapwa* relationships of mutuality, respect, humility and reciprocity.[39]

The organizers of the CfBS, including co-founder Leny Strobel, encourage decolonizing Filipin@s to become 'Babaylan-inspired' rather than claiming a 'Babaylan' identity for themselves, out of respect for living land-based Babaylans. Strobel names the former (those inspired by Babaylans) as Secondary Babaylans, whilst the latter (living Babaylans) as Primary Babaylans. To decolonize as a Filipin@ thus involves becoming a 'Secondary Babaylan', turning to the Babaylan Tradition for inspiration. The CfBS explains how the Wisdom and Power of Babaylan tradition is already in the Filipin@, waiting only to be recognized:

> You may carry the traditions of the Babaylan within you because you have answered a calling of leadership in one or more of the following: advocacy, activism, teaching, increasing awareness, healing, spirituality and vision, struggling and working for justice—actions and motivation deeply connected to the context of being Filipino.[40]

Who were the Babaylans? Filipina Catholic theologian, Agnes Brazal, explains:

> The early history of evangelization in the [Philippine] islands is characterized by a clash on the one hand, between the indigenous religions led by the shamans called Babaylan or Catalonan who are mostly older women with a few transgender female, and on the other hand, Christianity headed by an

---

[39] "Roots of Our Sacred Work", *Center for Babaylan Studies*, https://www.centerforbabaylanstudies.org/roots-of-our-sacred-work.
"*Kapwa*" is a foundational value for all other values of the Filipin@s. This value will be explained later in the chapter.
[40] Ibid.

all-male priesthood. At the start of the 17th century, it's estimated that over half the population of the Philippines had heard the Gospel and one third had been baptized, but Christianity had not really taken deep roots. The people continued to go to the priestesses for all their problems. The conversion of the native shamans was important to ensure the evangelization of the islands. The Spanish priests condemned the shamans as priestess[es] of the devil. In accordance with the Instructions to Commissary of the Inquisition in the Philippines, young boys were removed from their families to live in a convent where they received catechism and baptism, and then employed to catechize the older generation, or if not, report their clandestine animist practices. The babaylan tradition however was not completely eradicated. Indigenous religions and beliefs will merge with Christian beliefs to galvanize resistance against colonizers.[41]

For the decolonizing Filipin@s, the Babaylan becomes one of the Philippine nation's anticolonial and feminist figures of empowerment, representing what is possible for disempowered Filipin@s all over the world, as they decolonize. Whilst Christian colonizers sought to dismantle the indigenous systems of the Babaylans, just as the Babaylans resisted total erasure, so is inspiration found in the Babaylans' way of resisting erasure as Filipin@s, breaking in turn the cycles of intergenerational colonialism and colonial trauma among the diaspora.[42]

---

[41] Agnes Brazal, "Rethinking the Encounters", *500 years of Christianity and the Global Filipin@* webinar, hosted by the Berkley Centre for Religion, Peace, and World Affairs, 8 February 2022, at https://berkleycenter.georgetown.edu/events/500-years-of-christianity-and-the-global-filipin. See also Agnes M. Brazal, Cristina Lledo Gomez, and Marilou S. Ibita, "Christianity in the Philippines: 500 Years of Resistance and Accommodation", in Cristina Lledo Gomez, Agnes M. Brazal, and Marilou S. Ibita (eds.), *500 Years of Christianity and the Global Filipino/a: Postcolonial Perspectives* (Cham: Palgrave, 2024).

[42] Whilst this method of decolonizing has and continues to help numerous Filipin@s in diaspora, connected particularly to the CfBS, Grace Nono, author of *Babaylan Sing Back (2021)*, makes sharp critiques regarding this method. I discuss those critiques in another publication and propose rather that for Christian Filipin@s, Jesus is a more appropriate figure of empowerment and anti-colonialism. I agree with Nono that the danger of this method is turning the Babaylan into symbol and in turn their living voice and agency, leading then to further oppression. By using Jesus instead, he becomes both a symbol of empowerment but also a symbol for the oppressed, giving voice to both disempowered Filipin@s in diaspora as well as living land-based Babaylans experiencing ongoing oppression as the indigenous. For more on this, see Cristina Lledo Gomez, "Bangon Na, Pinays Rise Up: Reclaiming Pinay Power Dismantled by a Christian Colonial Past and Present", in Lledo Gomez, Brazal and Ibita, 500 Years of Christianity and the Global Filipino/a.

Decolonizing: The Methods and Traps

How might this decolonizing look like in practice? Here, I speak from my own observations as someone who has been engaged with decolonizing groups in Australia, Canada and the United States in the last six months. First, whilst there is an element of individual work necessary in embracing the whole self, the difficult work of decolonizing is ultimately only sustainable within a community of others who are also decolonizing. It would in fact be antithetical to the work of integrating the whole self, in connection with land, divinity and others, to do otherwise.

Second, elders who themselves have undertaken the decolonial journey are important guides for the journey of their children. They know all too well about the feelings of discouragement, self-doubt, shame, anger, hopelessness and helplessness as one awakens to internalized oppression carried without question for decades. They also know how tempting it is to be judgmental of those at earlier stages of the decolonizing process or to deny the need for the process at all. It is important to understand too that decolonizing will look differently for different generations of migrants. For first-generation migrants, they will have some memories of living in the Philippines, whilst the third generation not only will have no memory of that, but will also be encouraged to disregard this identity even if they show a deep desire to connect with their native heritage.

Third, decolonizing is about embracing ethnoautobiography. Discovering one's own elders, building the family tree and grappling with the history of your people are all ways of beginning to redress the feelings of being erased, lost, dismissed, ignored and rejected as brown-skinned. Thus, for example, learning about the grandmother who was the *abularyo* or healer of her community is empowering and encourages the Filipin@s to become healers themselves of their own communities. Note how ethnoautobiography is about memory—recovering and rewriting over other 'memories' which are really internalized narratives of oppression.

Fourth, there is the temptation to imagine that one can recover a pure Philippine identity but in truth we cannot erase our experiences, location and hybrid identities. This is the temptation to think dualistically: imagining that the past before colonization was pure whilst after colonization everything became a mess for Filipin@s. Similarly, the indigenous, Babaylan tradition was only good for the Filipin@ people whilst Christianity and other religions entering the Philippines such as the Muslim and Jewish religions have been bad for Filipin@s; they haven't been helpful at all. We know this to be untrue because it was the Christian sense of social justice that led to the People Power revolution, overturning the dictator, president Marcos, and freeing the people from the oppression of martial law. I thus understand the goal of decolonizing for the oppressed as about embracing native identity which has been demonized and shamed. It is about understanding we cannot live in a golden age of Babaylan tradition. Rather, for the Filipin@s in diaspora, it is about living a matrix identity which includes both native and urban identities and living with 'white' and 'non-white' systems in continual need of critique and reform.

Fifth, it is important to be aware that people who come together to decolonize, who carry colonial trauma or in the least carry a sense of inferiority and/or loss of identity because of their skin colour and/or racial identity and heritage are possibly bringing with themselves other experiences of rejection, abuse and/or trauma. For it is often the abused who find themselves in other abusive and re-traumatizing situations. With such vulnerabilities, in addition to differences in personality and backgrounds, there can be clashes within the group that were unexpected. This can lead to the dismantling of relationships and the group itself. In other words, just because a group of individuals come together to decolonize, it cannot be assumed that the group dynamics will be smooth and there will simply be a common understanding of "ground rules of interaction". Thus, some expectations and ground rules for interaction must never be assumed but communicated if there is to be mutual understanding on what is appropriate and not appropriate behaviour towards another within a group. While in the Filipino culture, *pakikiramdam*, or feeling your way around the other person, is the usual way of interacting with other persons, in a group setting that already carries vulnerabilities and trauma, to establish safety for all within the group, it helps to establish ground rules of respectful communication with one another. This in turn builds trust which is important in a group that is centres around the sharing of deep hurts because of the suppression and/or rejection of being Filipin@.

Sixth, because of Christianity's role in dismantling some indigenous systems in the Philippines, in abuse of its people and the denigration of their culture and senses of self as indigenous and brown, some Filipin@s consider rejection of Christianity as an important part of decolonizing. Thus, if one chooses to decolonize but remain a Christian, that person must be prepared to conflict with the person decolonizing from Christianity and vice versa. This is where the ground rules for respectful communication become highly significant. If both types learn to understand that each of them have as much right to exist in the group, that each have equal dignity and worth, that the group can have diversity in beliefs, that people can agree to disagree and that they are trying to achieve something positive together, by agreeing on such principles from the beginning of their interactions, then this sets the tone for their consequent communications with each other, even when they have fundamentally different values.

Last, overall, it is important to check the assumptions we hold about decolonizing. First, we are not all on the same page about decolonizing. Second, just because one is committed to 'decolonizing', it does not mean that they are self-aware of their own colonial practices or of their support of colonizing practices. Further, talking about decolonizing does not lead to its automatic practice.[43]

The Church That Decolonizes

When one looks to the key elements that make up good practices for decolonizing among the oppressed, one can as an ecclesiologist identify these same elements in what makes good churches: a community committed to each other, the divine/the spiritual life and a vision of what is possible for themselves and each other; elders of the community who carry the memories; embracing past, present and future through the concept of memory; and living with complex hybrid identities. On community, churches cannot build God's kingdom except as community. The very existence of the trinitarian God is as a communion of persons; God cannot exist except as a community. Building this kingdom includes critiquing colonial elements in the community and decolonizing from it. For colonialism is so antithetical to the Good News of Jesus.

Second, just as decolonizers need elders to guide and walk with them so the church also has elders/leaders—but these leaders need to have undergone the hard work of decolonizing themselves. I think of St.

---

[43] For more on decolonizing especially as a Filipin@, see Leny Mendoza Strobel, *Babaylan: Filipinos and the Call of the Indigenous* (Davao, Philippines: Ateneo de Davao University, 2010); Leny Mendoza Strobel, *Coming Full Circle: The Process of Decolonization Among Post-1965 Filipino Americans* 2nd edition (Los Angeles: Center for Babaylan Studies, 2015); Susannah Lily L. Mendoza and Leny Mendoza Strobel (eds.), *Back from the Crocodile's Belly: Philippine Babaylan Studies and the Struggle for Indigenous Memories* (CreateSpace Independent Publishing Platform, 2013). Jurgen Werner Kremer, R. Jackson-Paton, *Ethnoautobiography: Stories and Practices for Unlearning Whiteness, Decolonization, Uncovering Ethnicities* (Sebastopol, California: ReVision Publishing, 2014).

Augustine here who once said to his congregation, you were once spiritual infants, now you are called to grow up and mother others.[44] Thus, the work of decolonizing is not to be left with the hierarchy but a call for the entire people of God to become decolonizing elders themselves.

Third, just as ethnoautobiography is about reclaiming the past while attending to the present, and rewriting memories to affirm the Tagalog, Visayan, Cebuano or (insert language group)... self, so does the Eucharist recollect memory, rewrite memory and attend more fully to the present. The Eucharist rewrites the narratives of tendencies towards violence, revenge and abuse of power. Thus, the work of the Eucharist in decolonization is to recall our dignity in God, made in the image of God ourselves, in goodness, for goodness, and to rewrite those tendencies to either self-denigrate (because of one's own skin colour and race or nationality) or to denigrate what is different or unfamiliar to ourselves (in overt or subtle ways). It must be remembered too that the Eucharist and the Bible were central tools for colonizing the so-called uncivilized non-European or non-American persons in so-called newly discovered lands.

Finally, just as decolonizing involves living hybridity, similarly the Church is meant to live its beliefs in unity in diversity. I think in this case hybridity needs to include not only embracing the various denominations of Christianity and other faiths and religions, but especially indigenous spiritualities, religious lenses and religious practices.

These thoughts challenge us to consider the Liturgy of the Church. The liturgy is often referred to as *Theologia Prima*, the first theology, as it is the primary expression of the beliefs of the Church. I am led to ask how indigenous practice can be incorporated not just at the superficial level but at the level which equally values them in revealing God's Good News. As Vatican II's *Nostrae Aetate* (n. 2) states: "The Catholic Church rejects nothing which is true and holy in these religions", but rather looks "with sincere respect upon those ways of conduct and of life, those rules and teachings, which, though differing in many particulars from what she holds and sets forth, nevertheless often reflect a ray of that Truth which enlightens all people".[45] The Babaylan Tradition thus, in its way of engag-

---

[44] Augustine, "Sermon 72A," ch.8 in *The Works of St. Augustine: A Translation for the 21st Century*, trans. Edmund Hill, ed. John Rotelle (New York: New City Press, 1991).

[45] Pope Paul VI, *Nostra Aetate*, Declaration on the Relation of the Church to Non-Christian Religions, 28 October 1965, https://www.vatican.va/archive/hist_councils/ii_vatican_council/documents/vat-ii_decl_19651028_nostra-aetate_en.html

ing somatechnics, body, knowledge and practice, with its potential to help decolonize both the oppressed and oppressor, can be taken seriously as revealing what is true and holy about the God of liberation and salvation. If it is true that the seeds of the logos and the Holy Spirit were present among the indigenous including the Babaylans, how do we take more seriously indigenous and native cultures? How do we recover and incorporate what has been in the past demonized by colonizers?

Dom Anscar Chupungco, a Filipino Benedictine theologian and liturgist, is known for his work on inculturation of the liturgy. His work was broadly rejected under Benedict's 2001 *Liturgiam Authenticam* with its insistence on formal equivalence but is finding new flower under the current pontificate. For Chupungco, liturgical inculturation is:

> [...] a process whereby pertinent elements of a local culture are integrated into the worship of a local Church. Integration means that culture will influence the way prayer formularies are composed and proclaimed, ritual actions are performed, and the message is expressed in art forms. Integration can also mean that local rites, symbols, and festivals, after due critique and Christian reinterpretation, will become part of the liturgical worship of a local Church.[46]

Chupungco explains a key consequence of inculturating in the liturgy:

> One significant effect of inculturation is that the liturgical texts, symbols, gestures, and feasts will evoke something from the people's history, traditions, cultural patterns, and artistic genius. We might say that the power of the liturgy to evoke local culture is a sign that inculturation has taken place.[47]

This shows the potential of inculturating both native and indigenous Tagalos, Cebuano, Visayan, Pampangan or (insert Philippine language group) spiritualities and cultures as a way forward in decolonizing—work that must be performed in collaboration with native or indigenous elders and their communities, cultural anthropologists and liturgists.[48]

---

[46] Anscar J. Chupungco, OSB, "Liturgical Inculturation: The Future that Awaits Us", *Institute of Liturgical Studies Occasional Papers* 96 (2003) https://www.valpo.edu/institute-of-liturgical-studies/files/2016/09/chupungco2.pdf, p.2.

[47] Ibid.

[48] Chupungco promotes two methods of inculturation: Creative Assimilation and Dynamic Equivalence, both of which have much relevance for decolonizing the Christian liturgy. For more on these two methods, see ibid.

Conclusion: The Ongoing Work

Let me conclude by pointing out that the work of decolonizing is ongoing. Elsewhere, I have written on the necessity of this work. I repeat my concluding remarks on creating cultures of encounter rather than cultures of colonialism as they are pertinent to this essay:

> Thinking through and executing ways in which we might no longer dominate over others, regardless of race, nation, age, sex, sexuality, or other background or grouping is a process. If done well, it will take a toll on us all emotionally, spiritually, and intellectually. It will also remain a never-ending process. Like the reign of God, it is an ideal we envision and seek to make present in this world. While we might only ever hope to experience it in its fullness when we meet our Maker, we should not be discouraged in seeking to build in this world a culture that is less about colonialism and domination and more about encounters of respect, mutuality, safety, trustworthiness, and empowerment. Maybe then, just maybe, Indigenous peoples [...] might be able to imagine the possibility that people who are used to being in the center are willing to share that center—or even better—are willing to go to the margins so that there might be more room for[...] other marginalized people, those who have never known what it means to be heard, to be considered important enough, to truly be considered fully human and of intrinsic value.[49]

Decolonizing in so many ways can be seen as challenging human empire as Jesus did during his life and ministry. Moreover, it can be seen as building a different reality, what one might traditionally call as the reign of God, where those at the periphery are centred and all are acknowledged as having worth and dignity no matter one's race, skin colour, gender, sexuality, background, filial or friendship ties and other human categorizations. In the Filipin@ cultural view, this reality is *kapwa* where I see the other as myself rather than an 'other'. In this way, we are one and the same

---

[49] Cristina Lledo Gomez (August 22, 2022), "From Cultures of Colonialism to Cultures of Encountering Others", Reflections on Rome: The Experience of Encounter, *The Culture of Encounter and the Global Agenda Project,* Berkley Centre for Religion, Peace, and World Affairs and Georgetown University. Project Director: Tom Banchoff, https://cultureofencounter.georgetown.edu/responses/from-cultures-of-colonialism-to-cultures-of-encountering-others

(*pagkakaisa*) as opposed to someone different to myself and therefore are to be treated differently (*pagkakaiba*) and even deserving to be treated less than myself. Both Filipin@s and non-Filipin@s would learn much from learning or re-learning *kapwa* as they decolonize. It is the very basis of all other values for Filipin@s and can give much insight into the current papal enthusiasm for synodality in the Church.

PART II

Decolonizing Dialogue

CHAPTER 5

"A World in Which Many Worlds Fit": Ecumenism and Pluriversal Ontologies

Raimundo C. Barreto

In his book *Decolonizing* Oikoumene, Gladson Jathanna revisits the colonial nature of the project that gave rise to what became known as the modern ecumenical movement. Connecting the origins of the modern ecumenical movement to modern missions as envisioned by individuals such as William Carey (1761–1834) and Gustav Warneck (1834–1910), he unveils two major theological motivations that informed the establishment of the modern *Oikoumene*:

> [O]ne, an attempt to draw human beings out of a "sinful" world and to absorb them into the church, just as the Roman Empire attempted to 'redeem' the 'uncivilised' non-Roman world to the oikoumene of Rome; and the other, to accentuate the need for 'social transformation' and 'redemption of history' as a demand of Christian faith and commitment,

R. C. Barreto (✉)
Princeton Theological Seminary, Princeton, NJ, USA
e-mail: raimundo.barreto@ptsem.edu

© The Author(s), under exclusive license to Springer Nature Switzerland AG 2023
R. C. Barreto, V. Latinovic (eds.), *Decolonial Horizons*, Pathways for Ecumenical and Interreligious Dialogue,
https://doi.org/10.1007/978-3-031-44839-3_5

similar to what the Roman Empire claimed as bringing 'social transformation' and 'redemption' through its colonial project Pax Romana.[1]

Dale Irvin, by his turn, situates the origin of the modern ecumenical movement as taking place toward the end of the period that Eric Hobsbawm aptly called "the age of empire" (1875–1914). According to him, modern ecumenism was shaped under the influence of powerful "lingering memories of Christendom East and West" still haunted by the specter of Constantine.[2] Accordingly, the incipient Ecumenical Movement at the beginning of the twentieth century reflected the image of the Protestant communions that mostly comprised it. While disestablished in the United States, they nevertheless aligned themselves primarily with the dominant culture and its political and social life.[3]

By contrast, Irvin also argues that a new ecumenism is emerging. This new ecumenism, according to him, "resembles the fluid assemblages and cross-border flows of globalization and exile."[4] This chapter aims to contribute to this analysis by interrogating the worldview emerging from those cross-border flows of globalization and exile and their own contributions to the notion of 'the ecumenical,' reinterpreting this concept through decolonial lenses. The chapter draws, in particular, from Latin American experiences and recent theoretical developments in decolonial studies. Concurring with both Jathanna and Irvin about both the signs of an incipient new ecumenism, this chapter argues that the decolonizing of the ecumenical movement is an ongoing process. The lingering colonial memories that both Jathama and Irvin connect with the origins of modern ecumenism persist informing ecclesiastical and ecumenical structures

---

[1] Carey was a key pioneer of modern missions and Warneck the founder of the field of missiology as an academic discipline. See Gladson Jathanna, *Decolonizing Oikoumene* (London: ISPK and Council for World Mission, 2020), 27. The Greek word *Oikoumene* is at the roots of the word "ecumenical" and in its origins, in the context of the Roman empire, meant "the whole inhabited world" or "a house that includes the whole inhabited world." (p. 21) As Jathanna underscores, this Greek word is the overarching slogan in the logo of the World Council of Churches. His book examines the ambiguity implied in the use of *Oikoumene* in the modern ecumenical movement and seeks to shift its understanding through the use of a postcolonial lens.

[2] Dale Irvin, "Specters of a New Ecumenism: In Search of a Church 'Out of Joint,'" in *Religion, Authority, and the State: From Constantine to the Contemporary World*, ed. Leo D. Lefebure (New York: Palgrave Macmillan, 2016), 3–32 (17).

[3] Ibid., 20.

[4] Ibid., 24–25.

nowadays, affecting contemporary understandings of church and society. As Anibal Quijano has convincingly shown, the settler colonialism started by European colonizers at the turn of the sixteenth century gave birth over the centuries to a colonial matrix of power, which colonized not only bodies (coloniality of power) but also minds (coloniality of knowledge), and ways of existing in the world (coloniality of being).[5] While these three forms of coloniality are interwoven, this chapter pays special attention to the coloniality of knowledge, under the premise that at this historical juncture, the captivity of the mind has been key to the control of the body and of human institutions.

Considering the epistemic and ontological dimensions of the colonial matrix of power, thinkers like Walter Mignolo have indicated that a process of delinking is necessary for epistemic decolonization.[6] For the sake of the argument this chapter advances, the emphasis on delinking implies that the process of decolonizing ecumenism cannot be restricted to a reflection on new ecumenical dynamics, challenges, and possibilities but also on the need to unlearn and relearn what ecumenism means; i.e., to change the terms of the conversation. Among other things, delinking implies "cognitive decolonization,"[7] the unlearning of colonial conceptions of the ecumenical, and the reinvention of the ecumenical through the engagement of what Boaventura de Sousa Santos calls "the epistemologies of the South," i.e., "the production and validation of knowledges anchored in the experiences of resistance of all those social groups that have systematically suffered injustice, oppression, and destruction caused by capitalism, colonialism, and patriarchy."[8] To achieve that, this chapter looks into the terms that have shaped particular conceptions of the universal and the particular, the one and the many, in communities whose

---

[5] Anibal Quijano uses the term coloniality to refer to the persistence of colonialism through structures of power formed during the modern/colonial period, forming a global hegemonic matrix (the colonial matrix of power). See, for instance, Anibal Quijano, "Coloniality of Power, Eurocentrism, and Latin America," in *Nepantla: Views from South* 1/3 (2000): 533–580. For the distinction between coloniality of power, coloniality of knowledge, and coloniality of being, see Nelson Maldonado-Torres, "On the Coloniality of Being: Contributions to the Development of a Concept," *Cultural Studies* 21/2–3 (2007): 240–270.

[6] Walter Mignolo, "Delinking: The Rhetoric of Modernity, the Logic of Coloniality and the Grammar of Decoloniality," *Cultural Studies* 21/2–3 (2007): 449–514 (453).

[7] A term used by *Boaventura de Sousa Santos* in *The End of the Cognitive Empire: The Coming of Epistemologies of the South* (Durham & London: Duke University Press, 2018), 107.

[8] Ibid., 1.

experiences of resistance to colonialism, capitalism, and patriarchy challenge colonial ecumenical discourses, thus contributing to liberate contemporary ecumenism from its lingering colonial legacies.[9] While modern ecumenism has focused on Christian unity in terms that often do not take certain cultural ways of being and knowing into consideration, the ecumenical possibilities emerging from "the underside of modernity"[10] point to the possibility of a pluriversal ecumenicity; i.e., the existence of a world in which many worlds can fit.[11]

The view of unity expressed in a number of indigenous struggles in Latin America, for instance, is inclusive of a plurality of worlds. Speaking on behalf of the Indigenous Clandestine Revolutionary Committee, the General Command of the Zapatista Army of National Liberation, in January of 1996, insurgent *subcomandante* (subcommander) Marcos published the "Fourth Declaration of the Lacandona Jungle," which states:

> Many words walk in the world. Many worlds are made for us. Many worlds make us. There are words and worlds which are lies and injustices. There are words and worlds that are truth and truthful. [...] In the world of the powerful there is no space except for anyone but themselves and their servants. The Nation which we construct is one where all communities and languages fit, where all steps may walk, where all may have laughter, where all may live the dawn.[12]

---

[9] Jathanna, op. cit., 15.

[10] Enrique Dussel, *The Underside of Modernity: Apel, Ricoeur, Rorty, Taylor, and the Philosophy of Liberation* (Highland, New Jersey: Humanities Press, 1996).

[11] Arturo Escobar, *Designs for the Pluriverse* (Durham and London: Duke University Press,2018), xvi. While the Zapatistas developed this view of the world independently and prior to S. N. Eisenstadt's concept of multiple modernities, there is some resemblance among the two ideas. See, for instance, Eisenstadt's "Multiple Modernities," *Daedalus* 129/1 (2000): 1–29.

[12] Subcomandante Insurgente Marcos, Indigenous Clandestine Revolutionary Committee General Command of the Zapatista Army of National Liberation Mexico, January of 1996, "Fourth Declaration of the Lacandona Jungle." https://schoolsforchiapas.org/library/fourth-declaration-lacandona-jungle/. As cited in *A World of Many Worlds*, edited by Marisol de la Cadena and Mario Blaser (2018). Citation also found in Subcomandante Marcos, *Our Word is Our Weapon*. Edited by Juana Ponce de León (New York, NY: Seven Stories Press. Kindle Edition), 88.

While the modern ecumenical movement was originally formed under "a one-world world,"[13] a universalistic perspective that does not consider the possibility of other ways of being in the world, decolonial ecumenism creates a home where many worlds can coexist.

The Origins of the Ecumenical Movement

The modern ecumenical movement results from the evangelistic impetus of its architects. The World Missionary Conference in Edinburgh (1910), which is widely considered the bedrock of the contemporary ecumenical movement, focused on the least Christianized lands, aiming to extend Christendom once and for all throughout the world. Brian Stanley describes this evangelistic impetus driving that conference in the following terms:

> Edinburgh 1910 was conceived as a great deliberative council of the Church Protestant that would prepare its missionary armies to launch a concerted and final onslaught on the dark forces of heathendom that still ruled supreme beyond the frontiers of western Christendom.[14]

The third World Missionary conference in Edinburgh materialized the hopes expressed by William Carey a little more than a century earlier, when he unwittingly exposed the connection between British imperialism and mission as he stated,

> The Cape of Good Hope is now in the hands of the English; should it continue so, would it not be possible to have a general association of all denominations of Christians, from the four quarters of the world, held there once in about ten years. I earnestly recommend this plan, let the first meeting be in the year 1810, or 1812 at furthest.[15]

---

[13] John Law, "What's Wrong with a One-World World," *Heterogeneities*, http://www.heterogeneities.net/publications/Law2011WhatsWrongWithAOneWorldWorld.pdf.

[14] Brian Stanley. *The World Missionary Conference, Edinburgh 1910*. Studies in the History of Christian Missions (SHCM). (Grand Rapids, MI: Wm. B. Eerdmans, 2009), 4.

[15] "William Carey's Proposal for a World Missionary Conference (1806)," in Klaus Koschorke; Frieder Ludwig; Marian Delgado; Roland Spliesgart (eds.). *A History of Christianity in Asia, Africa, and Latin America, 1450–1990: A Documentary Sourcebook* (Grand Rapids, MI: Wm. B. Eerdmans, 2007), 61.

Twenty-two years earlier, the first World Missionary Conference in 1888, in London, had celebrated the centenary of modern Protestant missions.[16] After another twelve years, the second World Missionary Conference gathered in New York to continue that task in a new century. In contrast with its predecessor, that second conference added the qualifier 'Ecumenical' to its title, "not as claiming to be representative of all portions of the Christian Church, but because it represented mission work in all parts of the 'inhabited world.'"[17] These two initial conferences were organized by the British, Continental European, American, and Canadian Foreign Mission Societies.

The third World Missionary Conference, which gathered in Edinburgh in 1910, while dropping the word 'ecumenical' from its title, was meant to move that ecumenical missionary fervor forward. Edinburgh 1910 was distinct from the previous two conferences, though, because of its articulation of the creation of an institutional embodiment of the conference goals, which would take the form of a permanent body for international cooperation. One of the most consequential decisions made in the Edinburgh Conference was the formation of a Continuation Committee composed of 35 members "to carry forward the spirit of co-operation in the work of mission."[18]

While that Committee was largely dominated by representatives from the Western Missionary Societies and the churches that formed them, China, India, and Japan had each one representative in it. In the decade that followed, the Edinburgh Continuation Committee inspired the formation of similar continuation committees on the national level in a number of countries, including China, Japan, and Korea. Some of those continuation committees evolved later into national councils of churches. By going beyond its predecessors, Edinburgh 1910 offered a concrete path for the realization of the ecumenical ideal. Christian unity was perceived as fundamental for the fulfillment of the church's mission. Such a mission at the time was primarily conceived as planting "self-governing, self-supporting, and self-propagating Churches" all over the world.[19] Such an ideal, paradoxically, opened the doors for the rise of the so-called

---

[16] See World Missionary Conference, 1910. *The History and Records of the Conference Together with Addresses Delivered at the Evening Meetings* (Edinburgh and London: Oliphant, Anderson & Ferrier/Fleming H. Hevel Company, 1910), 4.

[17] Ibid., 5.

[18] Stanley, op. cit., 110.

[19] Kenneth Scott Latourette, "Ecumenical Bearings of the Missionary Movement and the International Missionary Council," in *A History of the Ecumenical Movement 1517–1948*, edited by Ruth Rouse and Stephen Charles Neil, 4ed (Geneva: World Council of Churches, 1993), 353–402 (358). Ideally, these churches would be undivided (359).

younger churches in Asia, Africa, and Latin America. Christians from those regions would later raise questions about the nature of Christian collaboration and the need to acknowledge the colonial wounds still impacting relations between colonizers and the colonized. Some of those younger churches began to develop their own ideas about overcoming the denominational divisions imported from the West, challenging the European churches to rethink them.[20]

The event of World War I (1914–1918), on the one hand, put a hold on the work of the Edinburgh Continuation Committee. On the other hand, it led to the rise of an Emergency Committee whose work culminated with the formation of the International Missionary Council (IMC) in 1921. The IMC would be "the forerunner and the first comprehensive embodiment of the Ecumenical Movement" until the formation of the World Council of Churches in 1948.[21] Its founding participants were still overwhelmingly from the North Atlantic churches. Only seven of them represented the so-called "younger churches." Two African-American participants were included among those seven. In many ways, though, the IMC would function as an incubator of world Christian leaders.

The Incubation of a World Christian Ecumenism

The formation of the IMC was part of a concerted ecumenical response to a time of crisis and uncertainty, when the rise of a world Christian worldview was shattered by increasing fears of fragmentation, divisions, and conflicts. John R. Mott, one of the masterminds of the IMC, argued that Christians were "demanded to counteract the growth of divisive forces in the world."[22] According to him, missionary agencies were world leaders and as such were urged to show an alternative moral way "[a]midst all the discord and strife in international affairs."[23] Missionary leaders were those in Christian circles who dealt "with the world as a whole" and held "world horizons." The "world," according to such a perspective, was divided into

---

[20] An extended version of this argument can be found in my forthcoming book *Base Ecumenism: Latin American Contributions to Ecumenical Praxis and Theology* (Minneapolis, MN: Fortress Press).

[21] International Missionary Council, *The International Missionary Council: What It Is, What It Does* (New York, NY: International Missionary Council, 1951), 2.

[22] John R. Mott, "International Missionary Co-operation," *International Review of Missions* 11/1 (1922): 43–72 (44).

[23] Ibid.

two halves: the Christian nations and the non-Christian world. The task of the Christian nations was to evangelize the rest of the world. The increasing presence of Asian and African Christians in the gatherings of the IMC among other ecumenical gatherings starting in the 1920s, though, began to put questions to that simplistic view of the world. In the first enlarged meeting of the IMC, in Jerusalem, 1928, non-Western participants began to raise questions about the complex nature of "the impact of the so-called Christian nations upon the non-Christian world."[24]

One-fourth of the participants of Jerusalem 1928 came from churches, which Mott described as resulting "from missionary labour in the preceding century in Latin America, Africa, Asia, and the Islands of the Seas."[25] It was the following meeting of the IMC in the village of Tambaram, near Madras, India, though, that brought greater attention to the increasing participation of non-Western voices on ecumenical conversations. Four hundred seventy-one representatives from sixty-nine countries were in attendance at Tambaram 1938. This was the first time when the majority of the representatives in any ecumenical meeting so far had come from "the younger churches."[26] The largest delegations in Tambaram were the ones from India and China. Dr. Wu Yi-fang, who led the Chinese delegation, was one of the seventy-seven women present in Tambaram. In the 1930s, initial preparations for the creation of the World Council of Churches were being put in place. Those non-Western churches received particular attention in that process. Among other things, the IMC recommended William Paton to the WCC Provisional Committee "as one of the general secretaries of the World Council of Churches [still in formation], in an honorary capacity, with special concern for the relation of the

---

[24] John R. Mott, "Foreword," in *Roads to the City of God: A World Outlook from Jerusalem*, by Basil Mathews (Garden City, NY: Doubleday, Doran & Company, 1928), vii–ix (vii–viii).

[25] William R. Hogg, *Ecumenical Foundations: A History of the International Missionary Council and Its Nineteenth-Century Background* (New York, NY: Harper, 1952), 253.

[26] L. S. Albright, *The International Missionary Council: Its History, Functions and Relationships* (New York, NY: The International Missionary Council, 1946), 16. Tambaram also counted with the presence of members of existing and emerging ecumenical bodies, including the World Conferences on Life and Work and on Faith and Order, and Provisional Committee of the World Council of Churches (an outgrowth of the Oxford and Edinburgh conferences of 1937), creating the opportunity for consideration about the IMC and the future WCC. (17).

Younger Churches to the World Council."[27] Not by coincidence, the conference in Tambaram devoted a great deal of attention to "the growing development of the Younger Churches."[28] In reference to Tambaram, American historian Kenneth Scott Latourette noticed, "The Church was becoming world-wide."[29]

Tambaram also made the increasing tensions in the relationship between representatives of "older" and "younger" churches more evident. Dutch missionary and historian of religions Hendrik Kraemer was asked to write a book to serve as a resource for the conference, furthering the discussion initiated in Jerusalem 1928 about the Christian message to the non-Christian world.[30] The book, according to Kraemer, should state "the fundamental position of the Christian Church [...] towards other faiths, dealing in detail with the evangelistic approach to the great non-Christian faiths."[31] The two main theses advanced in his book were: (1) "[T]he Christian revelation is absolutely 'sui generis'"; and (2) "the relation between Christian revelation and other religions 'is not one of continuity, but discontinuity.'"[32] While not relegating the teachings of other religions necessarily as errors, Kraemer explicitly affirmed the superiority and uniqueness of the Christian revelation, concluding that "if one were to decide to follow Christ, he or she should make a clean break with their religious past."[33]

A group of Indian theologians, though, challenged that emphasis on discontinuity. As Joshua Kalapati notices,

---

[27] Albright, op. cit., 18. It is worth noting that Asian and African delegates at Tambaram opposed the IMC having full membership in the WCC because they rightly feared they would remain a minority in that new structure. It was not until the Asian and African churches had formed their own regional bodies that the IMC was merged into the WCC, by vote in 1958 and as a WCC Commission with a new name in 1961 [Special thanks to Dale Irvin for bringing my attention to this].

[28] Ibid., 17.

[29] Latourette, op. cit., 369.

[30] Hendrik Kraemer, *The Christian Message in a Non-Christian World* (New York, NY: Harper & Brothers, 1938).

[31] Ibid., v.

[32] Joshua Kalapati, "Tambaram International Missionary Council Conference, 1938," in *The Oxford Encyclopedia of South Asian Christianity*, edited by Roger E. Hedlund, Jesudas M. Athyal, Joshua Kalapati, and Jessica Richard (Oxford University Press, 2011), available at: https://www.oxfordreference.com/view/10.1093/acref/9780198073857.001.0001/acref-9780198073857-e-0961?print. Accessed on March 28, 2022.

[33] Ibid.

This Rethinking Christianity Group broadly argued that Indian philosophy, culture, and tradition could not be ignored by those engaged in Christian mission on Indian soil, and secondly, that the 'Kingdom of God' rather than 'church' would provide a better platform for defining and doing mission in the pluralist context of India.[34]

The discussions of Kraemer's proposed theses led to two significant outcomes. On the one hand, it forced the conference to "rethink every theological presupposition upon which it acted."[35] On the other, that conversation pointed to an emerging change in the relationship between Western missionary agencies and the increasingly self-governing non-Western churches whose representatives were no longer afraid of expressing their views on such important matters. For the Asian theologians, what was at stake in those conversations was more than theology. As M. M. Thomas pointed out,

> Tambaram 1938 took place at a time when the churches of Asia were awakening to the need of a selfhood oriented to witnessing to Jesus Christ among Asian peoples who were themselves struggling for self-identity and for the renaissance of their nations in the world of nations.[36]

The "march towards authentic Asian selfhood" was crucial for the future of the Asian churches. Most Asian churches represented in Tambaram were discerning their Christian identity in contexts where growing nationalist sentiments informed the ongoing transition from a colonial past to a process of nation-building that required their participation in "dialogue with religions and secular faiths within that context."[37] Despite is focus on the church, Tambaram 1938 had to stay tuned to the broader transformations taking place in the world, which provided a unique opportunity for self-critique on the part of the Christian missionary agencies at the origins of the twentieth-century ecumenical instruments. As William Hogg underscored, the Madras meeting "saw the church standing under God's

---

[34] Ibid.
[35] Ibid.
[36] M. M. Thomas, "An Assessment of Tambaram," *International Review of Mission*, 77/307 (1988): 390–397 (390).
[37] Ibid., 397.

judgement. Madras concentrated on the church but did not absolutize it."[38]

Those difficult conversations in Tambaram can be seen as a direct consequence of the widening of the church's ecumenicity, which increasingly included a larger number of non-Western Christians. In particular, Tambaram created the conditions for the rise of an understanding of ecumenism that moved beyond an ecclesiocentric perspective. The social, economic, political, and cultural demands that many of the so-called younger churches were facing forced them to reconsider questions of identity and belonging in religiously plural contexts. Their participation in the IMC and other organisms of the incipient global ecumenical movement brought their concerns closer to the center stage of ecumenical conversations. One could come to similar conclusions by looking at the 1937 Universal Christian Council for Life and Work Conference in Oxford, England. However, Tambaram was unique for its location in the east and the larger non-Western representation it gathered. Tambaram 1938 offered a first significant contribution to changes in the discourse of modern mission, which would be intensified in the second half of the twentieth century. With the formation of the World Council of Churches (WCC) in 1948, the distinction between older and younger churches began to fade; mission began to be increasingly understood as the task of a worldwide church.

Tambaram sparked a debate that would contribute later to expand the understanding of unity within diversity within the ecumenical movement. Ecumenism could not be only concerned with church unity. As the WCC Vancouver Assembly would state in 1983, "the unity and the renewal of the Church and the healing and destiny of the human community" are interrelated. The late Uruguayan theologian Julio de Santa Ana described such a change in the path of ecumenism as a spiritual liberation helping us move beyond "an idolatrous attachment to outdated values and patterns of life which are passing away."[39]

Upon the IMC merging into the WCC in 1961, the ecumenical emphasis on mission shifted significantly toward the need for Christian witness to be rooted in indigenous cultural and social patterns, especially in

---

[38] Hogg, op. cit., 298.
[39] Julio de Santa Ana, *Beyond Idealism: A Way Ahead for Ecumenical Social Ethics*. Edited by Robin Gurney et al. (Grand Rapids, MI: William B. Eerdmans Publishing Group Company, 2006), 50.

theological training. The growing conviction at the time was that "If the Gospel is to become fully incarnate in the training of the ministry, it must take on indigenous flesh and expression."[40] This process coincided with the period when a number of countries in Africa and Asia were undergoing a process of decolonization. Both the turn to the indigeneity of Christianity everywhere and the decolonizing processes are at the root of the rise of the field of world Christianity.

World Christianity's Turn to Indigeneity and the Rise of Decolonial Ecumenism

The resilience of indigenous cultures in the global south despite centuries of colonization offered an alternative utopia, challenging Christendom's pretension to universality. The counter-colonial/decolonial initiatives that emerged in the 1950s challenged colonial and neocolonial hegemonic projects, including the idea of Christendom at the root of the ecumenical movement. Whereas Christendom presented an ecumenical vision that promoted a misguided approach to universalization, the turn to the indigenous in world Christianity offered another possible ecumenical path, carved through an intercultural hermeneutics that decenters colonial Christianity, relocates the Christian loci of enunciation, and critically multiple cultures, traditions, and religions, allowing them in that interaction to manifest their own pretension to truth. This is why the inversion of Christendom's inversions, to borrow Enrique Dussel's language,[41] is important, as it manifests the resilience and resistance of those who continue to be crucified and whose aspirations to universality continue to be repeatedly negated.

The tension between unity and indigeneity is a problem only when confined to a fallacious binary rationality. There is a widespread fear that the turn to the indigenous in world Christianity risks a loss of Christianity's catholicity. In my opinion and in the opinion of many others, such a fear is unwarranted. The rise of indigenous consciousness that resulted from the process of decolonization has not let to isolation. An example of this is the formation of the Third World Movement at the peak of the wave of

---

[40] Ibid., 23.
[41] Enrique Dussel, "Epistemological Decolonization of Theology," in *Decolonial Christianities: Latinx and Latin American Perspectives*. Edited by Raimundo Barreto and Roberto Sirvent (Cham, Switzerland: Palgrave Macmillan, 2019), 25–42.

decolonization in the 1950s. The rise of the Third World Movement was meant to unite the struggles for autonomy and liberation in Africa, Asia, and Latin America.

Post-World War II geopolitics was polarized between the Western capitalist empire and Eastern communism. The nations struggling for autonomy in Asia, Africa, and Latin America were expected to fall in line, siding with one of the two major blocks. While that ideological divide impacted them, a growing need for new spaces to coordinate their agency and interests gave birth to conferences and networks meant at articulating common ideals. Those articulations formed an incipient idea of the Third World. While the expression Third World has often been used in a depreciative manner to refer to impoverished countries and peoples, the term was embraced by political and religious leaders of what is now known as the global south to refer to formerly colonized and nonaligned nations who organized as a movement. As Vijay Prashad underscores, in the context of this conversation, "The Third World was not a place. It was a project."[42] What united this group of nations was the anticolonial struggle. Together, they created a number of organizations through which they articulated common hopes and demands. In the process, they organized important conferences. Be it in Bandung or in Havana, the political leaders of this moment "crafted an ideology and a set of institutions to bear the hopes of their populations. The 'Third World' comprised these hopes and the institutions produced to carry them forward."[43]

The Bandung Conference (1955) and two gatherings that followed, one in Cairo (1961) and other in Havana (1966), were the landmarks of the movement, but not its exclusive manifestation.[44] The Third World project combined many initiatives addressing economic, political, and cultural concerns. On top of the demands for political autonomy on the state level and "political equality on the world level," Third World leaders

---

[42] Vijay Prashad, *The Darker Nations: A People's History of the Third World* (New Press People's History) (New York, NY: The New Press, 2007), xiv.

[43] Ibid., xv.

[44] Other anti-imperialist gatherings took place during that decade, some of which led not by politicians and heads of state but by popular movements such as the Peace Movement in the Cold War years. That was the case, for instance, of the Conference of Asian Countries on the Relaxation of International Tension (CRIT), convened in Delhi eleven days prior to the Bandung Conference. For more on that people's conference, also known as the Asian Solidarity Conference, see Carolien Stolte, "'The People's Bandung': Local Anti-imperialists on an Afro-Asian Stage," *Journal of World History* 30/1–2 (2019): 125–156.

lobbied for the creation of specific international platforms to address their demands, focusing particularly on the United Nations.[45] Moving beyond concern for political autonomy, they advocated for "the redistribution of the world's resources, a more dignified rate of return for the labor power of their people, and a shared acknowledgment of the heritage of science, technology, and culture."[46]

As Prashad rightly points out, the Third World project was at the end of the day a battle for the future, the dream of a new world order. In their incessant struggle against colonialism, "the peoples of Africa, Asia [...] longed for dignity above all else, but also the basic necessities of life (land, peace, and freedom)."[47] While this collective struggle for autonomy, freedom, and liberation was not able to deliver the new world order they dreamed about, it became pervasively inspirational for the struggles for liberation that followed around the world.

This Third World spirit influenced a number of global south Christian leaders from the 1950s onward, leading some of them to dream of "a Christian Bandung."[48] Such aspirations were particularly on display in ecumenical and Catholic international gatherings, which provided opportunities for them to articulate common dreams of global solidarity with the poor and form south–south networks. In the following decades, the articulation of those liberating hopes coming from the global south impacted the ecumenical movement on at least two fundamental levels: (1) its agenda and priorities; and (2) its self-understanding and structures. While one can see the impact of the "Third World" spirit upon the ecumenical agenda and priorities in a variety of ways, including its impact on theology *per se*, the remaining of this chapter focuses on how it impacted some critical international Christian movements that followed.[49]

---

[45] Prashad, op. cit., xvi.
[46] Ibid., xvii.
[47] Ibid., xv.
[48] This was explicitly expressed, for instance, by Brazilian Catholic Archbishop D. Helder Camara as he reached out to bishops from Africa, Asia, and Latin America during the Vatican II, dreaming of forming a Christian network inspired by Bundang. Luiz Carlos Luz Marques, "As Circulares Conciliares de Dom Helder," in *Dom Helder Camara: Circulares Conciliares*, vol. 1, ed. Luiz Carlos Luz Marques and Roberto de Araujo Farias (Recife, Brazil: Companhia Editora de Pernambuco, 2008), 52–70 (68).
[49] The rise of what became known as contextual theology is an expression of how pervasive the Third World influence became within Christian circles worldwide. Stephen Bevans' words are expressive of this movement as he declared the end of a universally valid theology: "There is no such thing as 'theology'; there is only contextual theology: feminist theology, black theology, liberation theology, Filipino theology, Asian-American theology, African theology, and so forth." See Stephen B. Bevans, *Models of Contextual Theology* (Maryknoll, NY: Orbis, 2002), 3.

One of the first international gatherings where the aspiration for a Christian Bandung emerged was the Vatican II, a truly worldwide gathering with six hundred delegates only from Latin America. In the decade preceding the Council, the Latin American Catholic Church strived to understand its role and identity in the context of the dire circumstances in which most Latin Americans lived. The formation of the National Conference of Bishops of Brazil (CNBB) in 1952 and the Episcopal Conference of Latin America (CELAM) in 1955 were important benchmarks in the journey to understand the Church's mission in light of the "social question."[50] At Vatican II, many delegates from the global South were particularly concerned with the Church's solidarity with the impoverished masses around the world. They aspired for a coalition of Christians to stand in solidarity with the poor and oppressed of the world in the mold of the Third World movement.

Among other initiatives, a group of bishops inspired by Pope John XXIII's use of the phrase "the Church of the Poor" in a speech prior to the Council gathered during the council to form the "Church of the Poor" group, which envisioned the incarnation of a serving and poor Church.[51] Likewise, on November 16, 1965, forty-nine bishops, many of whom from Latin America, celebrated the Eucharist in the Catacombs of Saint Domitilla. In that symbolic location, they signed the *Pact of the Catacombs*, a life-long commitment to nurture a special sensibility to the poverty of the Church and the evangelization of the poor.[52] By championing the cause of the poor, those bishops sowed the seeds of the Medellin Conference in 1968, which became the birthplace of the liberation turn in Latin American theology.[53]

The liberationist movement that stemmed from such developments gave birth, among other things, to initiatives such as *ação ecumênica*

---

[50] José Miguez Bonino, "The Reception of Vatican II in Latin America," *Ecumenical Review* 37/3: (1985): 266–74 (267).

[51] See John XXIII, "*Nuntius Radiophonicus*," September 11, 1962, in *Discorsi-Messaggi-Colloqui del Santo Padre Giovanni XXIII*, vol. 4, ed. Domenico Bertetto (Vatican: Tipografia Poliglotta Vaticana, 1962), 520–28.

José Oscar Beozzo, *O Pacto das Catacumbas: Por uma Igreja Servidora e Pobre* (São Paulo: Paulinas, 2015), 11–12.

[52] José Oscar Beozzo, *O Pacto das Catacumbas: Por uma Igreja Servidora e Pobre* (São Paulo: Paulinas, 2015), 11–12.

[53] Rohan Curnow, "Stirrings of the Preferential Option for the Poor at Vatican II: The Work of the 'Group of the Church of the Poor,'" *Australasian Catholic Report* 89, no. 4 (2012): 420–32.

popular (popular ecumenical action) in Latin America and the movement known as *Leitura Popular da Bíblia*.[54] These grassroots initiatives have informed the Latin American ecumenical movement's praxis of "solidarity in the search for the reign of God and in the service to the poor."[55] Popular ecumenical action became a critical feature in national and international ecumenical networks of resistance to the military dictatorships that plagued Latin America between the mid-1960s and the late 1980s. In response to numerous cases of imprisonment, torture, and disappearance of individuals who dared to resist the violence of Latin American authoritarian regimes, creative ecumenical efforts of resistance emerged mostly at the margins of the Church. The ecumenical networks of resistance that emerged during this tenebrous moment in the history of Latin America can all be traced to the ideal of the "Christian Bandung" that began to emerge in the 1960s and which inspired numerous national and international liberationist movements in basically every continent ever since.

Another expression of a Christian Bandung is found in the Ecumenical Association of Third World Theologians (EATWOT). EATWOT was founded during a meeting in Dar-Es-Salam, Tanzania, in 1976 by "a group of theologians committed to a common concern for doing theology in a way that would be relevant to so called Third World contexts."[56] This Association was formed with the goal of overcoming "the gap between the rich and the poor among the nations, producing a theology that could overcome social injustice and the dependence of Third World theologies on models inherited from the affluent West." To achieve that goal, EATWOT has sought to create a sense of solidarity among Third World theologians "in spite of their cultural, religious, economic and political situations for the purpose of strengthening the struggles for liberation."[57]

The use of 'Third World' in the name of this association is not a coincidence. Inspired by the movement that emerged in the 1950s, EATWOT uses "Third World" to refer to "the poor and the oppressed in the continents of Africa, Asia and Latin America, the regions of the Caribbean and the Pacific, the peoples of the diaspora from Africa, Asia, and Latin

---

[54] Julio de Santa Ana, *Ecumenismo e Libertação* (São Paulo, Brazil: Vozes, 1991), 303. See also Gerhard Tiel, *Ecumenismo e Reino de Deus* (São Leopoldo, Brazil: Sinodal, 1998).
[55] Ibid.
[56] Luiza E. Tomita, "Presentation," *EATWOT News Letter*, May 2017. Manuscript received by email on the occasion of the celebration of the 40th anniversary of EATWOT.
[57] Ibid.

America, and all marginalized peoples in other parts of the world" as theological subjects and social and cultural agents.[58] Its assemblies in the course of forty years of existence have focused on numerous matters of significance to those contexts, including gender issues (1996), interreligious praxis (2001), the renewal of theological language for the sake of a new humanity and creation (2006), and ecological vision and planetary survival (2011). A particular topic informing the theological task of EATWOT since its inception is the idea initially conceived by Gustavo Gutierrez of "the participation of Christians in the process of liberation" as "simply an expression of a far-reaching historical event: the irruption of the poor."[59] While some—often white—theologians from the global north tend to ironically dismiss global south theological networks such as EATWOT as elitist,[60] they miss the point of the existence of these networks by focusing only on the professional theologians that are part of them and the books they write. When EATWOT refers to the "irruption of the poor" in history, it is not merely an abstract reference invented by an intellectual elite, but the recognition of popular experiences which are informing theological developments in among 'the poor and oppressed.' In Latin America only, EATWOT (through its members and sponsorship) has facilitated forums of women, black, and indigenous peoples formulating their own theological discourses.

For instance, the Third Latin American Ecumenical Encounter of *Teología India* (Indigenous Theology) in Cochabamba, Bolivia, on August 24–30, 1997, counted with the participation of EATWOT members from Africa, Asia, and the United States. Eleazar López Hernández, one of the Indigenous coordinators of that encounter, welcomed their participation with the following words:

> You are indigenous like us. You live realities of pain like us. In their hearts there are forces of life and hope as in us. Their presence is an expression of the alternative globalization that we can build with all the poor, who are children of Mother Earth, to face the globalization of death that comes

---

[58] Ibid.

[59] Gustavo Gutiérrez. *A Theology of Liberation: History, Politics, and Salvation*. 15th Anniversary Edition (Maryknoll, NY: Orbis Books, Kindle Edition, 2019 [1971]), Location 246.

[60] See, for instance, Henning Wrogemann's reference to EATWOT as elitist in his article "Intercultural Theology as In-Between Theology," *Religions* 12: 1014. https://doi.org/10.3390/rel12111014.

from neoliberalism. Although the problem of spoken language prevented direct communication, the language of life and spiritual attunement made us feel deeply identified. The rituals, the celebrations, the dance, the singing and the coexistence united us deeply. In the end we experience that we speak the same language of life, pain and hope. With your presence we are laying clearer foundations to consolidate the indigenous EATWOT. And with the proposal that you bring about an intercontinental meeting on Indigenous Theology, we will open the way to a theological perspective that will surely be a serious contribution to the search for and understanding of God in our current history. The methodology that we follow in our Third Meeting of Indian Theology will be our contribution to the realization of the intercontinental meeting, where we hope to meet theological and spiritual processes that work with methodologies like ours. We would not want to find ourselves with people who only speak of God from books.[61]

As the words from Father Hernández make clear, EATWOT is not simply an association of professional theologians. It is instead an organic network, whose capillarity is difficult to measure, since most of its numerous members are deeply embedded in diverse communities throughout the world. The various networks it forms regionally and globally are not institutionally connected with one another, rather being organically related, acknowledging their common participation in a sort of ecumenism from below, an *ecumenismo de base* (grassroots ecumenism), which expands the horizons of the ecumenical movement not only by enlarging its circles and giving voice to new participants, especially those at the margins of both church and society, but also by allowing their contributions to add to the toolkit of ecumenical discourse, as implied in the citation above.

In Lieu of a Conclusion: The Irruption of the Poor as a Decolonial Act

The liberationist turn to the poor as historical subjects in Latin America and in other parts of the world has provoked an intellectual revolution, opening a range of new epistemic possibilities, which directly contribute to decolonial thinking. In a liberation key, the poor are not only the object

---

[61] Eleazar López Hernández, "III Encuentro Ecumenico Latinoamericano de Teologia India," Vinto, Cochabamba, Bolivia 31 de agosto de 1997. https://usuaris.tinet.cat/fqi_sp02/docs/eatwot.doc. Last accessed by the author on April 17, 2023. Translation from Spanish is mine.

of solidarity but also the subject of rights and the owners of their own destiny. It is not a coincidence, therefore, that Gutiérrez speaks of the irruption of the poor as also being the irruption of the Third World. As historical beings, subjects of rights, and agents of their own liberation, the poor (those made subaltern in history) can now speak in their own theological voices, giving rise to black, indigenous, feminist, and queer liberation theologies, among others. In other words, the poor are not only economic subjects, but also subjects of knowledge.

The decolonial project that has emerged among Latin American and Latinx scholars in the past two decades emphasizes not only colonialism, but also coloniality, "a concept originally developed by Peruvian scholar Anibal Quijano, and later expanded by Walter Mignolo, which refers to the systemic legacy of colonialism."[62] With its focus on coloniality, decolonial thought addresses the various configurations of power—the "gradual propagation of capitalism, racism, the modern/gender system, and the naturalization of the death ethics of war"—that outlived the imperial conquest. In order to resist and overcome "the coloniality of power, the coloniality of knowledge, and the coloniality of being," we are challenged to engage "in epistemic disobedience and delinking from the colonial matrix," promoting "a vision of life and society that requires decolonial subjects, decolonial knowledges, and decolonial institutions."[63] As Nelson Maldonado-Torres notices, the decolonial turn is not only about making visible those who have been made invisible but also "about analyzing the mechanisms that produce such invisibility or distorted visibility in light of a large stock of ideas that must necessarily include the critical reflections of the 'invisible' people themselves." In other words, it recognizes the "intellectual production" of those who have been subjugated, as proper knowledge, "not only as culture or ideology."[64]

As Walter Mignolo and Catherine Walsh put it, by acknowledging how the lived experience of coloniality "traverses practically all aspects of life, including the realms of subjectivity, knowledge, being, sexuality, spirituality (including soul-body, spirit-mind, and ancestor-relation), and nature (understood interrelationally as Pachamama)," decoloniality promotes "a

---

[62] Walter D. Mignolo. *The Darker Side of Western Modernity: Global Futures, Decolonial Options* (Durham and London: Duke University Press, 2011), 2.
[63] Raimundo Barreto & Roberto Sirvent, "Introduction," in *Decolonial Christianities*, 5.
[64] Ibid.

perspective and analytic that challenges [sic] many of the presuppositions of Western knowledge and thought."[65]

As the examples above show, while decoloniality has the important task of unmasking the colonial matrix of power and dismantling it, it is not simply about undoing or deconstructing. A great amount of the work of decoloniality is creative and constructive, as it advances the possibility of thinking, doing, and being otherwise. Decolonial thought thus is not binary. Speaking in the World Forum of Theology and Liberation in Salvador, Bahia, on March 14, 2018, Union Theological Seminary professor Cláudio Carvalhaes equated the task of resisting oppression to the ideas of transforming and creating another possible world based on the experience of those for whom colonialism and coloniality have not yet ended—in particular, he was referring to the experiences of Indigenous and Black Brazilians. Playing with the closeness of the phonetics of the Portuguese words "existir" (to exist) and "resistir" (to resist), he came up with the proposal of "resistir como re-existir," resisting as re-existing, existing all over again.[66] For those who have survived colonialism and coloniality for more than five centuries, the act of resistance is a creative act. There is no time to lose by limiting oneself to adversarial tactics. Even when that is necessary, it is only the means for a new creation.

What does a decolonial perspective bring to the ecumenical table, then? As Chicana cultural theorist Gloria Anzaldúa highlights, the fractured, traversed existence of the colonized, which she describes through the lenses of the borderlands, turns what was an open wound into an existential space where people impacted by the colonial matrix of power live in the *entremedios* (in-between) cultural, political, epistemological, and ontological edges, constantly experiencing dislocation and disorientation, "not quite at home here but also not quite at home over there."[67] Colonial subjects living in these existential *entremedios*, these in-between spaces reject essentializing identities and binary logics. The borderlands, originally a place of violence and separation, become a site of creativity and renewed consciousness. Anzauldua's borderlands enable us to speak of "intersectional conditions of language, gender, religion, sexuality, class,

---

[65] Walter D. Mignolo & Catherine E. Walsh, *On Decoloniality: Concepts, Analytics, Practices* (Durham and London: Duke University Press, 2018), 90.

[66] Cláudio Carvalhaes, "Resistir é Criar, Resistir é Transformar," Fórum Mundial de Teologia e Libertação Salvador, Brazil, March 14, 2018. Author's files.

[67] Gloria Anzaldúa, *Light in the Dark: Rewriting Identity, Spirituality, Reality*. Edited by Analouise Keating (Durham and London: Duke University Press, 2015), 81.

culture, and space,"[68] and "to re/create spaces in which the multiple worlds we inhabit and the various identities we have developed mesh and blend with/out conforming to no/one in particular."[69]

The new consciousness emerging from these in-between spaces creates new challenges for our understanding of 'the ecumenical.' Ecumenism is no longer about universalizing understandings of unity. In fact, the same universalistic modern design at the origins of the modern ecumenical movement has created the crisis of being, knowing, and doing we face today, limiting our possibilities of existing. In response to that multifaceted crisis, inspired, among other things, by the Zapatista quote at the beginning of this chapter, Arturo Escobar calls for a new design, a new world-making which moves us beyond "the dualist ontology of separation, control and appropriation" prevalent in "patriarchal capitalist modernity" to explore models of being that emphasize profound "relationality and connectedness."[70] These models are not new. They can be found both in nature and in many Indigenous cultures around the world. They are, however, increasingly necessary as ecumenical Christians seek to respond to the crises of this century. Redesigning ecumenical structures on the basis of deeply engaging the ways of knowing and being in the world are resurfacing through the irruption of the poor as new historical and epistemic subjects.

Decolonizing ecumenism may require to be uneasy about it. It may demand a move beyond the modern-colonial limits of rationality, which still inform ecumenical and interfaith dialogues, toward "Nondualist and relational forms of life,"[71] which may help us to reconnect in new ways with "the endless and ceaseless changing weave of life on which all life depends."[72]

---

[68] Margaret Cantú-Sánchez et al., "Introduction," in *Teaching Gloria E. Anzaldúa: Pedagogy and Practice for Our Classrooms and Communities*. Edited by Margaret Cantú-Sánchez et al. (Tucson, AR: University of Arizona Press, 2020), 3.

[69] Margaret Cantú-Sánchez, "Breaking the Mold: Redesigning Curricula for the 'Planetary Citizen, in *Teaching Gloria E. Anzaldúa*, 16.

[70] Escobar, op. cit., 19–20.

[71] Ibid., x.

[72] Ibid., xi

CHAPTER 6

Colonization, Proselytism and Conversion: Can Interfaith Dialogue Be the Answer? Pope Francis' Contribution

Roberto Catalano

INTRODUCTION

For centuries, colonialism carried out by Western Christian countries—especially Spain, Portugal, England, Netherlands, France and, to a lesser degree, Germany and Belgium—has often contributed to forced or, at least, induced forms of evangelization characterized by proselytism and conversion. The original motivation could appear somehow justifiable from the Western Christian viewpoint in that the understanding of the times, based on the quasi-dogma *extra Ecclesiam nulla salus*,[1] resulted in the strong and unshakable conviction that all those who were not baptized

---

[1] For the emergence and evolution of this principle, see Francis A. Sullivan, *Salvation outside the Church? Tracing the History of the Catholic Response*, (London: Chapman, 1992).

R. Catalano (✉)
Sophia University Institute, Loppiano-Firenze, Italy

© The Author(s), under exclusive license to Springer Nature Switzerland AG 2023
R. C. Barreto, V. Latinovic (eds.), *Decolonial Horizons*, Pathways for Ecumenical and Interreligious Dialogue,
https://doi.org/10.1007/978-3-031-44839-3_6

were, without exception, condemned to eternal damnation.[2] As a consequence, *missio ad gentes* became a sort of a race against time to save as many people as possible. Although the intention at the root of the process might have been somehow understandable—at least for the comprehension of the time—the fact that it was carried out hand in hand with colonial powers progressively led to a violent imposition not only of religious beliefs and doctrines but also of cultural patterns, which were alien to the colonized worlds.

The colonizers and the missionaries in Asia, Africa and the Americas were convinced that the European cultural model was superior, and as a consequence, they sought to subjugate or even erase non-Western cultures. Western values and traditions were considered to be expressions of the only culture and religion worthy of the name. Against this ethnocentric and exclusivist background, the Good News was preached all over the world with contrasting results. On the one hand, in Meso and South America, the local cultures were erased and Christianity took over as the only religion, to the point that today that part of the world is the one with the highest concentration of Christians. Nevertheless, many Meso and South American originary peoples resisted and survived, along with their cultures and religious traditions, which have actually experienced some revitalization in the past three decades. Recently, Christianity of that side of the world showed its maturity and depth with the election of the first pope ever outside of the European continent and the Near East. On the other side, in Africa, local traditional religions survived side by side with Christianity. Finally, we note that Asia—with the exception of the Philippines and Timor and, more recently, of South Korea—remained somehow insulated, if not repellent, to the Gospel to the point that for many "it is indeed a mystery why the Savior of the world, born in Asia, has until now remained largely unknown to the people of the continent".[3] Nevertheless, while Christianity remains a tiny minority in most Asian countries, that part of the world is the home of almost 400 million

---

[2] See *Cantate Domine*, Council of Florence, 1452 in Bernard Sesboüé, *Fuori della Chiesa nessuna salvezza? Storia di una formula e problemi di interpretazione* (Cinisello Balsamo - Milan: San Paolo Ed., 2009).

[3] Pope John Paul II, *Ecclesia in Asia*, New Delhi, 06.11.1992, n.2.

Christians, and a continent where some of the most ancient forms of Christianity continue to exist despite their religious minority.[4]

COLONIALISM AND MISSIONS

Ever since the *Treaty of Tordesillas*[5] was signed on 7 June 1494, a tight collaboration was established between the colonial powers and the Catholic missions.[6] In the course of the following centuries, this strong bond met with different evolutions, characterized by times of tensions and consequent detachment, followed by epochs of strong mutual and close cooperation. The cultural and spiritual hegemony of the Western world was the element, which constantly accompanied the different phases of the history of the mutual cooperation between colonialism and mission. For centuries, the conviction of the political, economic, financial and military superiority of the West prevailed as if that part of the world were called by God's plan to dominate over the rest of the planet. This perspective was deeply engraved not only in the political and economic spheres but also within the Church. Real progress and true civilization and faith could come only through colonizers and missionaries. All this led to the conviction that the rest of the world was inferior to the West and to Christianity. Consequently, missionaries were called to hard-work for promoting their faith and civilization in order to save a great number of souls and enable peoples to progress from ignorance and primitivism to true civilization.[7] Moreover, the Christian message, which was preached, was the one that grew in the previous fourteen centuries in Europe and, partially, in the

---

[4] It is enough to think of the so-called Thomas Christians in South India, especially in the state of Kerala. There Christianity claims to have arrived as early as the first century. Today, several Churches (Syro-Orthodox, Armenian, Mar-Thomas and Catholic Syro-Malabar and Syro-Malankara) survive and maintain their own Oriental rites, which, often, represent also a conflict ground among themselves and with Catholics of Latin rite.

[5] The *Treaty of Tordesillas* divided the "New World" of the Americas between Spain and Portugal, then the true world superpowers. The partition was implemented by drawing a north-to-south line of demarcation in the Atlantic Ocean, about 555 kilometers west of the Cape Verde Islands, off the coast of northwestern Africa and then controlled by Portugal. All lands east of that line were claimed by Portugal. All lands west of that line were claimed by Spain.

[6] The same happened later for the protestant missionaries who followed Dutch and British colonizers.

[7] For more details, see the interesting text (in Italian language): Mauro Forno, *La cultura degli altri. Il mondo delle missioni e la decolonizzazione*, (Roma: Carocci Editore), 2017.

Middle East. With a few exceptions, there was no attempt to adapt the announcement of the *Good News* to the local cultures and categories. The exceptions came from specific individual missionaries or from certain missionary orders.[8]

In the second half of last century, especially with the end of the Second World War, this whole Western superiority paradigm started being strongly criticized and had begun to show signs of a decaying process which was faster than expected. The western powers which had dominated large portion of other continents started showing signs of weakness and soon it became clear that they could not continue any longer to dominate the world in the way they had done till then.[9] In fact, within three decades, almost all countries, which had been under colonial rule, obtained their independence. At the same time, the majority of the evangelizing methods of Christian missions, which developed with the backing of colonial rule, had to be rethought and reformed. In fact, the wind of change, at least initially, was more evident in Rome, at the center of Christianity, especially thanks to the Second Vatican Council. There were new consideration regarding mission and relationship of the Gospel with different cultures, provoked by some of the Council documents and by significant changes which occurred in some of the Vatican Dicasteries. On the contrary, at the peripheries, in faraway mission stations, the process was unavoidably much longer.[10] Among the many and significant steps toward a decolonization process, the one which was probably more effective was the *Day of Pardon* convened by Pope John Paul II on 12th March 2000.

> Today, the First Sunday of Lent, seemed to me the right occasion for the Church, to implore divine forgiveness for the sins of all believers. [...] *Let us forgive and ask forgiveness!* [...] we cannot fail to recognize *the infidelities to the Gospel committed by some of our brethren,* especially during the second millennium. Let us ask pardon for the divisions which have occurred among Christians, for the violence some have used in the service of the truth and for the distrustful and hostile attitudes sometimes taken towards the followers of other religions. Let us confess, even more, *our responsibilities as Christians for the evils of today.* We must ask ourselves what our responsibili-

---

[8] We refer here to the Jesuit experience of the '*adaptation*' in Japan and China and to the pioneer work of catechisms carried out by the Dominican Bartolomé de Las Casas in South America.

[9] See Mauro Forno, *La cultura degli altri*, 14–15.

[10] See Ibidem, 16.

ties are regarding atheism, religious indifference, secularism, ethical relativism, the violations of the right to life, disregard for the poor in many countries.[11]

The same concept of courageously and humbly asking for forgiveness for having imposed our own culture and religion without respecting local people, their cultures and faiths has been taken up several times by Benedict XVI[12] and Pope Francis. Bergoglio spoke about this topic in different occasions, especially during his recent trip to Canada when he met the 'first nation' people to apologize for the evil and violence perpetrated by the Catholic Church against them. Already in 2017, during one of his morning meditations at Santa Marta, he underlined the temptation of persecuting people in the name of a cultural colonization which is also ideological and destroys everything because it transforms everything in something uniform, while rejecting differences that it cannot tolerate. Pope Francis underlined that ideological and cultural colonization focus only on the present, while they deny the past and refuse to look at the future. Those who impose on others such a process of colonization commit a sin of blasphemy as they refuse to accept creation the way He had done it.[13] Pope Francis, therefore, strongly criticized such an attitude which is guilty of a conversion-oriented mission imposed on people of other faiths. The only remedy indicated by the pope is 'witness', a genuine and true witness.[14] At the same time, for some decades, local Churches have been involved in de-colonizing processes with a large spectrum of initiatives at the theological, liturgical and pastoral level.

CONVERSION: A KEY PROBLEM

In this context, the phenomenon of 'conversion', often imposed, deserves special attention. For centuries, it represented a distinguishing characteristic of Christianity—and also of Islam—in different parts of the world. Until today, it remains a controversial key point in the complex and articulated unfolding of its encounter with other cultures and religions. In fact, conversions have always been the aim of Christian missions, and yet, this

---

[11] Pope John Paul II, *Homily, Day of Pardon*, Vatican City, 12 March 2000.
[12] See Benedict XVI, *Address to the Meeting of Peace*, Assisi, 27 October 2011.
[13] See Pope Francis, *No alle colonizzazioni ideologiche*, Homily at Santa Marta, 21 November 2017.
[14] Ibidem.

practice remains largely mysterious and unacceptable to others, especially in Asia. For a large part of South, South-East and East Asia, and their respective religious traditions, the effort to convince others to change their faith is almost inconceivable. Hinduism, Buddhism, Confucianism and Taoism identify themselves with the respective cultures much more than Christianity does in Europe, especially in the last centuries. As such, conversion to another religion goes against the Asian cultural frame of mind and sensitiveness. Moreover, we cannot ignore that the theological Christian perspective has progressively modified the original meaning of the word and concept of conversion by narrowing down its interpretation to only one point: the move toward Christian faith.

For this reason, it may be interesting to return briefly to some of the original meanings of this term, respectively in the Greek and Jewish context. For Greek philosophers, 'conversion' implied a maturing process of the human being and a sort of change of his/her mental and ethical frame.[15] In Israel, instead, 'conversion' had a more articulated significance with a clear religious dimension, as it indicates a return to YHWH. In fact, for Judaism, the process of conversion means to re-establish the personal relations with God, after it has been broken: returning to YHWH with a contrite heart, after having drifted away. This is possible only through sincere repentance, which favors an existential change of direction, as the root *šûbh* suggests. The Hebrew word indicates that, if we have moved away from the initial starting point, we can always return to the origins and continue on the right path. It may be significant to note that the verb has a strong 'communitarian' connotation: In fact, it is the Jewish people, as a whole, who are called to return to God after having abandoned Him. Without underplaying the personal repentance, the stress, more often than not, is on the entire people of Israel, who together are called to re-establish the original relationship with God.[16]

The New Testament also follows the same line by insisting on a return back to God, but with a novelty: This turning back is mediated through Jesus Christ, our Savior. With respect to Greek, there are two verbs which express 'conversion' in the Gospels: *metanoéin* and *epistréphein*. The first one implies repentance, displeasure and change of mind in order to ensure

---

[15] See Ugo Sartorio, *Conversione. Un concetto controverso, una sfida per la missione cristiana*, Biblioteca di Teologica Contemporanea n. 207, (Brescia: Queriniana, 2021), 41.

[16] See William Lee Holladay, *The Roots šûbh in the Old Testament: With Particular Reference to its Usages in Convenetal Contexts*, (Leiden: Brill, 1958), 53.

renouncing sin and going back closer to God and to Jesus, while the second verb expresses the move of turning to Him to attain salvation. The two verbs express both dimensions of the conversion process in accordance with the Gospel's new sensitivity: the detachment from idolatry and sin and the effort to address one's own way of thinking and acting toward the God of Jesus Christ, while placing one's own existence at His service. In the frame of the New Testament, God's intervention and human man's and woman's action have to enter into a synergic relation. Only this activates the true process of conversion.[17] It is crucial to underline the sense of 'process', which is attached to the idea of conversion as it requires a long transformation period.

In hindsight, a further point has to be taken into account. In the course of the past two millennia, 'conversion' has constantly maintained a self-referential meaning for the Christian world, which, for its part, has proposed different models of conversion, often highlighting and drawing inspiration from exceptional protagonists.[18] These proposed models suggest a sudden and dramatic change of life style due to the discovery of God, through Christ. Today, we find ourselves in a different epoch where to convert does not necessarily mean moving toward Christianity. We all witness 'conversions'—in the sense of change of religions—also toward other faiths and traditions. At times, the concept has even lost its specific meaning, only to be replaced by what is commonly known as a double or a multiple belonging: to follow two or more religious traditions, at the same time, without denying any of them. There are also cases of 'de-conversion' with people going back to the original faith they used to follow.[19] Nevertheless, conversion has become an object to be studied, and this can be undertaken from the religious, psychological, social, relational and even spiritual perspectives.[20]

---

[17] See Sartorio, *Conversione*, 42–43.

[18] It is enough to think of Paul and Augustine, but also Ignatius of Loyola, J. H. Newman, T. Merton, D. Day or, closer to us, C. De Foucauld etc.

[19] Consider the *ghar wapsi* (returning home) phenomenon suggested by some fundamentalist currents of *Sanatana Dharma* traditions in the Indian sub-continent. For this highly controversial topic, we suggest to see Yashasvini Rajeshwar and Roy C. Amore, "Coming Home (Ghar Wapsi) and Going Away: Politics and the Mass Conversion Controversy in India", Religions 10 no.5 (2019), 313; doi: 10.3390/rel10050313.

[20] See Pierre Yves Brandt - Claude-Alexandre Fournier, *La conversion religieuse. Analyses psychologiques, anthropologiques et sociologiques*, (Genève, Labor et Fides, 2009) and William James, *The Varieties of Religious Experience. A Study on Human Nature*, Longmans, Green And Co., (London and Bombay, 1902) in Sartorio, *Conversione*, 19–20.

In present societies, things are far more complex. We often witness a contrasting panorama. In the western world, characterized by a strongly progressive process of secularization, religion is more and more detached from culture and social life, while globalization has also contributed to a de-culturalization of all religions, which are no longer identified with a certain territory and culture. They have become—or are still in the process of becoming—more and more global. This dimension, however, shows new characteristics. Religions are often chosen, or made use of, without considering their cultural origins and even less the cultural provenience of the individual who follows them. Their spirit and insights often appear somehow watered down.[21] Nevertheless, after a sort of exile, which has lasted for quite some time, especially, during last century, religions are on the come back to the public sphere of life[22] and are acquiring a new social visibility in the public domain,[23] although, at times, they may appear to be blurred and without a sharp identity. The fact that they appear de-culturalized makes them, so to say, more 'universal' and acceptable, but, at the same time, more culturally homologated.[24] As a consequence, in the Western world, whose roots are Judaic and Christian, a change of religion is no longer considered as a dramatic event. There is a prevailing perception that the truth we are leaving behind and the one we are likely to find are provisional Truths without any claim to objective certainties. From this perspective, religions can be compared to the latest fashion trend which changes regularly.[25] This might be considered a real novelty in the Western world, but for the Hindu culture in India, it remains still highly unacceptable. On the other side of this scenario, one may be confronted with 'fundamentalism', which nowadays, at least in the understanding of the general public, is more often than not, mainly associated with Islam.

Against this complex and often contrasting panorama, two questions arise from many corners: what is the sense of a Christian mission today? What are its implications and impact?

---

[21] Olivier Roy, *Holy Ignorance: When Religion and Culture Part Ways*, (New York: Oxford University Press), 2014.

[22] See Sartorio, *Conversione.*, 48 and Giuseppe Angelini, "Il fattore religioso e il destino dell'Occidente. Verso una santa ignoranza? La Rivista del Clero Italiano 100 no. 4 (2019), 303–313, here 308.

[23] See Ibidem, 49.

[24] See Ibidem, 48 and Angelini, *Il fattore religioso*, 307.

[25] See Ibidem, 51.

Pope Francis: Mission and Relations, Attraction by Witnessing

Notwithstanding the evidence that large portions of humanity are becoming progressively indifferent to any faith,[26] there remains the fact that many people change their faith, while others adhere to two or more religions. This in itself offers clear evidence that religions still have an important role to play in our societies. The phenomenon, therefore, should not be approached superficially and surely deserves further scrutiny. In this complex panorama, also globalization is playing an important role, and religions, often, appear as any other good in a globalized market. It is enough to think of the rampant growth of Pentecostalism, which is often defined as the 'religion of globalization'.[27] All this had a powerful impact on all religions, which are experiencing deep inner evolutions that were simply unthinkable a few decades ago. For instance, today for the Catholic Church, truth and salvation seem to be no longer the crucial points, as it used to be in the past. For centuries, in fact, these two paradigms were used to more-or-less justify a dogmatic application of the *extra Ecclesiam nulla salus*. In contrast, Pope Francis from the time of his election has indicated that in our present world the better reference point should be 'relationships'. This emphasis is not a novelty. It was true also at the origins of the Christian experience when what we could define as *agapic* relationships characterized the internal dynamics of the early communities of the new religion, including care and concern for the weaker members sections of society around them. These were (and I think still are) the striking elements capable of attracting people toward the new faith. Drawing inspiration from the model of those early communities, today more than ever, the Church if it is to be still credible should not be primarily preoccupied with its own growth but, rather, genuinely concerned for women and men living in our times and the quality and strength of its

---

[26] See Peter L. Berger, *The Many Alters of Modernity: Toward a Paradigm of Religion in a Pluralist Age*, (Boston/Berlin: Walter de Gruyter, Inc., 2014); Joseph Ratzinger/Benedetto XVI, *Il problema di Dio nel mondo contemporaneo. Un'antologia*. (Umberto Casale ed. by) (Torino: Lindau, 2011); Olivier Roy, *L'Europe est-elle Chrétienne?* (Paris: Seuil, 2019).

[27] See Joel Robbins, "The Globalization of Pentecostal and Charismatic Christianity", Annual Review of Anthropology, 33 (2004), <RefSource/>117–143; Matthias Deininger, Global Pentecostalism: An Inquiry into the Cultural Dimensions of Globalization, (Hamburg: Bedey Media GmbH, 2013), https://www.anchor-publishing.com/document/287372.

relationship with them. It is a matter of leaving behind centuries old habits and consolidated certainties in order to move fearlessly toward others—people who believe differently from Christians and those who claim to have no religious affiliation—with the 'fragrance of the Gospel',[28] centering the practice of faith in daily life through concrete expressions of love, joy, mercy and sharing in the others' suffering. In so doing, Christians may evoke questions such as *'why do they live like this?'*, *'what pushes them?'*[29] in people around them, some of whom will show an interest in the Church. Indeed, because of this unconditional selflessness, others may feel drawn to closer contact with Christianity and may even become part of their community,[30] especially if the believers' concern for them is genuine and contagious.

Proclamation does not consist only in announcing some concepts and truths but, rather, in being committed to draw people's attention to a lifestyle, which is attractive. It was through their 'witness' (a key category) and not proselytism that early Christian communities grew. In fact, during his speech at the opening of the CELAM General Assembly held at Aparecida (Brazil) in 2007, Pope Benedict XVI clearly underlined this: "The Church does not engage in proselytism. Instead, she grows *'by attraction'*".[31] Pope Francis, on his part, offers a further and significant contribution to this point that has become a key paradigm of his teaching. He proposes it with courage and determination, through his preaching, traveling and personal witness. By keeping safe distance from proselytism that he has unambiguously defined as "a solemn idiocy and non-sense",[32] he makes clear the real nature of the Church mission. Nevertheless, the present pope still perceives proselytism as a great resurgent problem for Christianity: "There is a danger that crops up again — it seemed to have been overcome but it reappears, confusing evangelization with proselytism".[33] In Rabat in 2019, he stated that "the paths of mission are not those of proselytism, which leads always to a cul-de-sac". The mission

---

[28] See Papa Francesco, *La gioia della missione*, (Cinisello Balsamo-Milano: San Paolo Ed. 2019), 14.

[29] Ibidem, 75.

[30] See Christoph Theobald, *Urgenze pastorali. Per una pedagogia della riforma*, (Bologna: EDB, 2019), 114 in Sartorio, *Conversione*, 104.

[31] Benedict XVI, *Holy at Mass for the opening of V General Assembly of CELAM*, Aparecida, Brazil, May 13, 2007.

[32] See Pope Francis, "Interview" by Luigi Scalfari in La Repubblica, October 1, 2013.

[33] Pope Francis, *Address to Pontifical Mission Society of Milan (PIME)*, May 20, 2022.

proposal he advances is rather one focused on finding "our way of being with Jesus and with others".[34] In fact, already at the beginning of his pontificate, he underlined that "the Church missionary spirit is not about proselytizing, but the testimony of a life that illuminates the path, which brings hope and love".[35] To evangelize and to announce the Gospel is, therefore, first of all, a commitment in building relationships, which are not to be used in order to proclaim the message of Christ as a sort of an 'assault' on people's 'freedom'.[36] To proclaim Christ and His good news should be a respectful Christian practice and not an imposition. It requires that we be courageous and joyful witnesses who not only respect others as persons but also their culture, faith and freedom. From this attitude and approach, the great relevance of 'witness', as a key element for proclamation, emerges even more clearly as the true priority of mission. Already in the thirteenth century, Francis of Assisi represented a clear example of this attitude.

> As for the brothers who go, they can live spiritually among [the Saracens and nonbelievers] in two ways. One way is not to engage in arguments or disputes, but to be subject to every human creature for God's sake (1 Pet 2:13) and to acknowledge that they are Christians. Another way is to proclaim the word of God when they see that it pleases the Lord [...].[37]

The saint from Assisi had the intuition that witnessing has to precede announcing. In fact, practicing the words of the Scripture makes the announcement more credible and convincing. He invited his friars "to go and announce the Gospel, [and] if necessary, even [use] words".[38] The adverb 'even' carries a crucial importance and calls for another necessary clarification. Christians are called to announce the Gospel not in order to become more numerous than others but rather to be like leaven in the dough. "For Jesus did not choose us and send us forth to become more numerous! He called us to a mission. He put us in the midst of society like a handful of yeast: the yeast of the Beatitudes and the fraternal love by

---

[34] Pope Francis, *Address to Priests, Religious, Consecrated Persons and the Ecumenical Council of Churches*, Rabat (Morocco), March 31, 2019.
[35] See Pope Francis, *Message for the World Mission Day 2013*, Vatican City, May 19, 2013.
[36] See Ibidem.
[37] Francis of Assisi, *Regula non Bullata*, Cap. XVI. Available online at https://friarmusings.com/tag/regula-non-bullata/. Accessed 15.05.2022.
[38] Ibidem.

which, as Christians, we can all join in making present his kingdom".[39] Moving from the paradigm of proselytism to offering a witness opens us to the possibility of discovering the true nature of the Church, which should not be that of an imposing fortress, isolated under lock and key, and opening its doors only to impose its own beliefs. The model for the Church should be the one of Abraham's tent: open on all sides in order to allow everyone to enter.[40] Everyone is welcome to enter, never forced in. And through those same doors Christians are called to go forth to meet others, to encounter their brothers and sisters. We are called to go toward other people, to meet them and stay with them, taking care of them. Pope Francis reminds us of how crucial the relationship with people coming from outside, the so-called *Gentiles*, had been even for the first Christian community.

> [... D]*oors open* to whom? To the *Gentiles,* because the Apostles were preaching to the Jews, but the Gentiles came to knock at the Church's doors; and this novelty of doors open to the Gentiles triggers a very lively controversy. Several Jews affirm the need to become Jewish through circumcision in order to be saved [...] first the Jewish rite and then Baptism [...] and to resolve the issue, Paul and Barnabas seek the advice of the Apostles and of the elders of Jerusalem, and what takes place is what is held to be the First Council in the history of the Church, the Council or Assembly of Jerusalem. [...] A very delicate theological, spiritual and disciplinary issue is addressed, that is, *the relationship between faith in Christ and observance of the Law of Moses*. During the Assembly [...] Peter and James [...] exhort not imposing circumcision on the Gentiles but, instead, asking them only to reject idolatry and all its expressions.[41]

Today, in order to be credible, Christianity needs communities of believers that are truly mature, which celebrate their faith with joy, through liturgy and proclamation of the word but also by living charity with people around them with a special care for those living at the '*peripheries*' who often do not know Christ yet.[42] Personal and community relations are fundamental in creating always new and effective processes of faith transmission.

---

[39] Pope Francis, *Address to Priests*.
[40] See Pope Francis, *General Audience*, St. Peter's Square, October 23, 2019.
[41] Ibidem.
[42] See Pope Francis, *Message for the World Mission Day 2013*, Vatican City, May 19, 2013.

Missionary spirit is not only about geographical territories, but about peoples, cultures and individuals, because the "boundaries" of faith do not only cross places and human traditions, but the heart of each man and each woman.[43]

Interfaith Dialogue: A Privileged Way to Evangelize

The power of witness offered to people who believe differently, or even to those who claim to have no faith, opens the way to dialogue. Dialogue, in the present understanding, and more specifically for our interest here 'interfaith dialogue', made its appearance on the ecclesial and missiological scene a few decades ago. After initial uncertainty and understandable suspicion, the dialogical approach toward followers of other religions has contributed to reduce—though not yet fully overcome—the image of a proselytizing Church aiming at converting 'others'. In 1965, *Nostra Aetate* exhorted Catholics to commit to dialogue and collaboration with the followers of other religions, recommending that this should be "carried out with prudence and love and in witness to the Christian faith and life".[44] The following decades have shown how the Church is greatly enriched and encouraged by the experience of Christians who engage in dialogue with faithful of other traditions. Broadly speaking, the dialogical approach, which emerged from the Vatican Council, represents a great challenge for the Catholic Church, both at the universal level and in the local communities. Primarily, it is a method of discerning and listening to God's word within our hearts.[45] This commitment to listening allows us, on the one side, to be attentive and to welcome God's word and, on the other, to be attentive and welcoming of God's people to whom we offer it. Subsequently, the Christian community announces Jesus' good news in dialoguing with other cultures and religions.[46]

Through this new attitude, which is more dialogical than apologetic, the Catholic Church has engaged in the attempt to place and offer the patrimony of Christian faith in a positive relationship with other great religious traditions of the world.[47] The richness of Christian faith, which

---

[43] Ibidem.
[44] *Nostra Aetate*, (Vatican City, 28 October 1965.), n.2.
[45] See Papa Francesco, *La gioia*, 57.
[46] See Ibidem, 55–56.
[47] See Bertram Stubenrauch, *Pluralismo anziché cattolicità? Dio il cristianesimo e le religioni*, (Brescia: Queriniana, 2019). 22. (Original title: *Pluralismus statt KatholizitäGott, das Christentum und die Religionen*, (Regensburg: Verlag Friederich Puster, 2017).

grew throughout the centuries, is today faced with the reality of religious pluralism that the Church cannot ignore and from which it cannot escape. Christian communities, which, in Western countries, are often shrinking in number, must acquire full and deeper awareness of the richness of their own traditions, which they often ignore or do not fully know, and, at the same time, engage concretely in interfaith dialogue. In fact, although ignored for almost two millennia, Christian faith and dogma carry in their own DNA the capability of acting in dialogue with those who follow other religious traditions.[48] This commitment to dialogue has to accompany and be accompanied by witness on the part of the entire community. Dialogue is the guarantee that the Church of the third millennium will survive and avoid falling into a new religious colonialism with unacceptable forms of proselytism. Proceeding in this way, new paradigms, new ways of thinking and new symbols through dialogue with other believers, can emerge and be molded. As Christians, we are called to come closer to 'others', while recognizing them as truly 'others'.[49]

Dialogue does not imply that one's own identity be ignored or underplayed. It does not replace or cancel our Christian duty to witness and to proclaim the mission of the Church. The document '*Dialogue and Proclamation*' (1991) mentions that "the sincerity of interreligious dialogue requires that each enters into it with the integrity of his or her own faith".[50] In fact, a precise identity is the primary pre-condition of dialogue. Pope Benedict XVI and Pope Francis have both forcefully underlined this.

> [Both] parties to the dialogue remain consciously within their identity, which the dialogue does not place in question either for themselves or for the other.[51] True openness involves remaining steadfast in one's deepest convictions, clear and joyful in one's own identity, while at the same time being "open to understanding those of the other party" and "knowing that dialogue can enrich each side" (EG 251). The duty to respect one's own identity and that of others, because true dialogue cannot be built on ambiguity or a willingness to sacrifice some good for the sake of pleasing others.[52]

---

[48] See Ibidem, 23.
[49] See Ibidem, 148.
[50] Pontifical Council for Interreligious Dialogue, *Dialogue and Proclamation*, Rome, May 19, 1991, n. 48.
[51] Benedict XVI, *Address to the Roman Curia on the occasion of Exchange of Christmas Greetings*, Vatican City, December 21, 2012.
[52] Pope Francis, *Address to the International Conference on Peace*, Cairo, April 28, 2017.

Interreligious dialogue truly and successfully serves the purpose only when each partner openly expresses whatever he/she considers essential to his/her self-perception. Dialogue, in fact, has to be built on the awareness of the historical and theological diversity that each religion carries with itself. This diversity has to be accepted by people engaged in dialogue, as it represents the premise and presupposition of any serious commitment about religions.[53] Moreover, dialogue offers the unique opportunity to rediscover one's own tradition and faith. Engaging in dialogue, in fact, presupposes a clear identity, which is not destined to remain rigid and closed. Meeting people of another tradition compels both partners to be ready to answer questions posed on the respective faiths, traditions, doctrine and rituals. Often, one is taken aback and has to deepen aspects of his/her faith which he/she believed were clear and well rooted. Further to all this, on some occasions, the spiritual experience lived along with people of other faith traditions may be so strong that all reach the point of experiencing a presence of the Absolute. Everyone may describe it according to the respective faith and tradition, but the spiritual effects are the ones of God's presence. Pope John Paul II explained very clearly this experience while meeting a group of people of different faiths in Madras (today renamed Chennai), during his first visit to India in 1986.

> The fruit of dialogue is union between people and union of people with God, who is the source and revealer of all truth and whose Spirit guides men in freedom only when they meet one another in all honesty and love. By dialogue we let God be present in our midst; for as we open ourselves in dialogue to one another, we also open ourselves to God.[54]

Dialogue, therefore, helps to make us aware that God is at work, in a mysterious way in all religions. At the same time, a certain caution is required in order to avoid falling into a further temptation: the one of believing that Christianity has initiated dialogue singlehandedly. Although, it may be true and widely acknowledged that, inspired by prophetic figures like all the popes from John XXIII onward, the Catholic Church has taken a leading role in interreligious dialogue. Nevertheless, as Catholics, we cannot claim that we have the monopoly on dialogue. Also within the

---

[53] See G. Colzani, "Pluralismo, relativismo e dialogo. L'universalismo di Cristo e il ruolo della Chiesa", Euntes Docentes 59 no.1 (2005), 128.

[54] Pope John Paul II, *Address to Exponents of non-Christian Religions*, Madras (Chennai), 05 February 1986.

other religious traditions, in a variety of ways and to different degrees, the same process is taking place. For quite some time, clerics and scholars of different faiths have delved into the patrimony of their respective texts and millennia old traditions to rediscover those values where 'others' are acknowledged.[55] In fact, the ancient religious traditions are more and more aware that they would betray their rich patrimonies if they close themselves off from others.[56]

"To Become Artisans of Communion"

This appears to be in line with Pope Francis' perspective, which claims that Catholics are not the only men and women called to implement the change of paradigm we have explored so far. Already in *Evangelii Gaudium*, he underlined with conviction and clarity that "dialogue is a necessary condition for peace in the world, and so it is a duty for Christians as well as other religious communities".[57] At the basis of this statement lies a robust anthropological approach, which can be applied to all men and women, irrespective of their ethnic, cultural and religious background. It is a call to propose a positive and constructive alternative to "a distorted view of the person [...] that ignores [his/her] dignity and relational nature".[58]

> [In fact], at times we look at others as objects, to be used and discarded. In reality, this type of perspective blinds and fosters an individualistic and aggressive throwaway culture, which transforms the human being into a consumer good.[59]

---

[55] Already at the end of the last millennium, the engagement was active in other faith traditions. See, for instance, H. Fitte (ed.), *Fermenti nella teologia alle soglie del terzo millennio*, LEV, Città del Vaticano, 1997; especially, the two following contributions: David Rosen, "Presenza del dialogo interreligioso nello sviluppo del pensiero teologico. Prospettiva ebrea", 56–65 and Hmida Ennaïfer, "Presenza del dialogo interreligioso nello sviluppo del pensiero teologico. Prospettiva islamica", 66–75.

[56] See Erio Castellucci, *Annunciare Cristo alle genti. La missione dei cristiani nell'orizzonte del dialogo tra le religioni*, (Bologna: EDB, 2008), 166.

[57] Pope Francis, *Evangelii Gaudium*, Vatican City, November 23, 2013, n.250.

[58] Pope Francis, *Catechesis "Healing the world": 2. Faith and human dignity*, General Audience, Vatican City, August 12, 2020.

[59] Ibidem.

On the contrary, human dignity is an inalienable right, as men and women are created in the 'the image of God'.[60] This is not merely an individual element but the foundation of the entire social life. In fact, being "created in the image of God, One and Triune",[61] we all are social beings and, consequently, "we need to live in this social harmony".[62] Pope Francis effectively summarized this whole perspective, last September 2022, during his address to the "VII Congress of Leaders of the World and Traditional Religions" held at Nur-Sultan (Kazakhstan).

> We are creatures; we are not omnipotent, but men and women journeying towards the same heavenly goal. Our shared nature as creatures thus gives rise to a common bond, an authentic fraternity. It makes us realize that the meaning of life cannot be reduced to our own individual interests, but is deeply linked to the fraternity that is part of our identity.[63]

In practical terms, this will inspire us to look at all human beings as at our brothers and sisters. Each of them is a gift received from the love of the same Father.

In this way, the believer, contemplating his or her neighbor as a brother or sister and not as a stranger, looks at him or her compassionately and empathetically, not contemptuously or with hostility. Contemplating the world in the light of faith, with the help of grace, we strive to develop our creativity and enthusiasm in order to resolve the ordeals of the past.[64]

All religions, through their followers, are called to commit to 'others beings' in order to be promoters of respect, of appreciation and, ultimately, of fraternity. In so doing, they pave the way to peace. This path is the one chosen by those who commit to become 'artisans' of dialogue and peace. In fact, in Pope Francis' perception, dialogue is never a mere hermeneutical exercise but, rather, "a conversation about human existence or simply [...] a matter of "being open to them [others], sharing their joys and sorrows". In this way, we learn to accept others and their different ways of living, thinking and speaking.[65] All this can be summed up in the

---

[60] See Pastoral Constitution *Gaudium et Spes*, n.12, Vatican City, December 7, 1965.
[61] Pope Francis, *Catechesis "Healing the world"*: 2.
[62] Ibidem.
[63] Pope Francis, *Address to "VII Congress of Leaders of the World and Traditional Religions"*, Nur-Sultan, September 14, 2022.
[64] Ibidem.
[65] Pope Francis, *Evangelii Gaudium*, n.250.

existential concept of *'fraternal acceptance'*, which is crucial in this time of mass migrations, the world witness everywhere. Yet, *'fraternal acceptance'* should be the style of approaching whomever we encounter. Those who engage in this venture are *'artisan of communion'* contributing, each in his/her own way, to a *'culture of dialogue'*. Interestingly, in his journey to Kazakhstan, Pope Francis explained this process using typical categories of the local culture. In fact, he noted, in the Kazakh language, the expression 'to love', which is the key to dialogue, communion and peace, literally means *"to gaze kindly on someone"*.[66] Coherently, during this visit to the Central Asian Republic, the pope has shown a great appreciation for the local culture by using a typical local instrument (*dombra*) and the national poet (Abai) as references for explaining the key points of his official addresses. This appreciative attitude speaks by itself of the paradigm shift that has been taking place in the Catholic Church's attitude toward other cultures and religions.

Conclusion

For many centuries, the missionary vocation of the Church has at times gone hand in hand with colonial powers, oftentimes proselytizing by means of forced conversion; nevertheless, this does not detract from the fact that mission is part of our Christian identity and of our respective communities.[67] The Church cannot exclude anyone. Thus, it is called upon to set aside exclusivist ideas of membership: "The opening of the culture and the community to the salvific newness of Jesus Christ requires leaving behind every kind of undue ethnic and ecclesial introversion".[68]

In recent years, Pope Francis has drafted an excellent and challenging roadmap in the effort to pursue the missionary vocation of the Church along with its dialogical commitment with other cultures and religions. He has summarized this into three fundamental points.

> *The duty to respect one's own identity and that of others*, because true dialogue cannot be built on ambiguity or a willingness to sacrifice some good for the sake of pleasing others. *The courage to accept differences*, because those who

---

[66] See Pope Francis, *Address to "VII Congress of Leaders of the World and Traditional Religions"*.

[67] See Pope Francis, *Baptized and Sent: The Church of Christ on Mission in the World*. Message for World Mission Day 2019, Vatican City, June 9, 2019.

[68] Ibidem.

are different, either culturally or religiously, should not be seen or treated as enemies, but rather welcomed as fellow-travellers, in the genuine conviction that the good of each resides in the good of all. *Sincerity of intentions*, because dialogue, as an authentic expression of our humanity, is not a strategy for achieving specific goals, but rather a path to truth, one that deserves to be undertaken patiently, in order to transform competition into cooperation.[69]

In today's context, a final element of value for an effective and creative proclamation and dialogue is the central dimension of the community. This is one of the main highlights of Pope Francis' message for *World Mission Day 2022*. The missionary vocation—he argues—has been communitarian from the beginning and follows from Jesus words to the apostles that "[they] shall be my witnesses" (Acts 1:8). Mission, therefore, is not a solitary but a communitarian enterprise that has to "be carried out together, [and] not individually, in communion with the ecclesial community and not on one's own initiative".[70] In fact, "in carrying out the mission, the presence of a community, regardless of its size, is of a fundamental importance".[71] The real subject of Christian mission is the entire Church, as a people walking toward God and toward one another. Similarly, Paul VI mentioned that "evangelization is for no one an individual and isolated act; it is one that is deeply ecclesial".[72] And once again, keeping in mind that "modern man listens more willingly to witnesses than to teachers, and if he does listen to teachers, it is because they are witnesses",[73] something which can never be overemphasized enough. It is in such a context that dialogue acquires a new dimension that is crucial to avoid falling back into proselytism and forced conversions.

Today's problems which have been further complicated by the recent pandemic ask Christians to reach out to other men and women, their cultures and religions with the same esteem and respect that they have for their own. Appreciation and respect, when they become mutual, will help a great deal to create a positive disposition for constructive dialogue based on one's own faith and tradition while acknowledging the 'other'. We people of faith witness to our own believe in reaching out to the 'stranger'.

---

[69] Pope Francis, *Address to the International Peace Conference*.
[70] Pope Francis, "*You shall be my witnesses*". Message for the World Mission Day 2022.
[71] Ibidem.
[72] Paul VI, *Evangelii Nuntiandi*, Vatican City, December 8, 1975, n.60.
[73] Ibidem.

Religious zeal focused only on one's own religion is no longer the way for a true proclamation and a constructive dialogue.[74] All of us should be aware that today there are no ready-made or pre-defined formula for proclaiming the Gospel. Christians are invited to listen to the Spirit's whisper, while allowing the Spirit to shape us with ever-new creativity.

---

[74] See Stubenrauch, *Pluralismo*, 199.

CHAPTER 7

Decolonial Options for World Christianity: Thinking and Acting with Santa Teresa Urrea and Prophet Garrick Sokari Braide

Ryan T. Ramsey

BEYOND POLITICS TO EPISTEMOLOGIES

Though political colonialism continues to exist in many places, much of the discourse around decoloniality takes place in politically postcolonial contexts. Decolonial thought and work are necessary for the very reason that, as Boaventura de Sousa Santos states,

> [T]he term "decolonization" does not concern political independence alone, but rather an ample historical process of ontological restoration, that is, the recognition of knowledges and the re-construction of humanity. It

R. T. Ramsey (✉)
Baylor University, Waco, TX, USA
e-mail: ryan_ramsey2@baylor.edu

© The Author(s), under exclusive license to Springer Nature Switzerland AG 2023
R. C. Barreto, V. Latinovic (eds.), *Decolonial Horizons*, Pathways for Ecumenical and Interreligious Dialogue,
https://doi.org/10.1007/978-3-031-44839-3_7

includes, of course, a people's inalienable right to have their own history and make decisions on the basis of their own reality and experience.[1]

"Political independence alone" does not ensure epistemic or even economic independence. The modern world is replete with daily reminders that political independence is not enough. The recognition of formerly colonized peoples' complete humanity, epistemological insights, and ways of being in the world requires more than this. Decolonial thinking is a process to push past political independence. It seeks to "delink" from cultural ghosts and recalcitrant structures that colonize ways of knowing and being beyond what the modern west culturally and intellectually upholds.[2] While this process of decolonizing the mind—to borrow from Ngũgĩ wa Thiongo's book title[3]—ultimately has, I think, long-term *political* effects, the focus of decolonial discourse (in its current instantiation) often attends to the *epistemic* foundations of coloniality. Within the colonial matrix of power, humanity (colonized, colonizers, and the wide spectrum who operate as both) is restricted to modern western epistemological conventions.[4] For those of us in postcolonial contexts, decolonial thinking helps us step beyond politics to epistemologies—that is, to use de Sousa Santos's terms, beyond "political independence" to "ontological restoration."[5]

Decolonial thinking offers much to historiography. In particular, decolonial historians can try to identify, we might say, thinkers and actors who embodied decolonial thinking long before the modern theorizations. De Sousa Santos suggests especially that we need to look to practitioners and activists utilizing "artisanal knowledges": "practical, empirical, popular knowledges, vernacular knowledges," insights which only come from lived experience rather than free time and a comfortable chair.[6] Another

---

[1] Boaventura de Sousa Santos, *The End of the Cognitive Empire: The Coming of Age of Epistemologies of the South* (Durham: Duke University Press, 2018), 109.

[2] Walter Mignolo, "Delinking: The Rhetoric of Modernity, the Logic of Coloniality, and the Grammar of De-coloniality," *Cultural Studies* 21, nos. 2–3 (Mar/May 2007): 449–515.

[3] Ngũgĩ wa Thiong'o, *Decolonising the Mind: The Politics of Language in African Literature* (London: James Currey Ltd., 1981).

[4] Anibal Quijano, "Coloniality and Modernity/Rationality." *Cultural Studies* 21, nos. 2–3 (2007): 168–78.

[5] de Sousa Santos, *The End of the Cognitive Empire*, 109.

[6] Ibidem, 43.

theorist, Javier Aguirre, says clearly, "Decolonial studies of religion and theology ought to be open to research methodologies engaged in praxis."[7]

What happens when we turn away from our postcolonial age to a time—not long ago—before the decolonization[8] of Africa and when new republics like Mexico and the United States colonized the indigenous communities within their borders?[9] We can identify historical figures who, under colonial or otherwise oppressive modern regimes, utilized non-Western knowledges and practiced ways of being in the world which sought the flourishing of their local communities. Such figures have, moreover, long existed even within the Christian religion, so often a forceful node in the colonial matrix of power.[10] World Christianity has

---

[7] *"Los estudios decoloniales de lo religioso-teológico deben estar abiertos a metodologías de investigación comprometidas con la praxis."* Javier Aguirre, "Religiones, teologías y colonialidad: hacia la decolonización de los estudios académicos de las religiones y las teologías," *Revista de Estudios Sociales* 77 (2020): 87, italics original, my translation.

[8] Though both use the terms "decolonial" and "decolonization," I distinguish between African political decolonization and Latin American discourse on decoloniality. Both are important discourses, but their historical circumstances make them slightly different. Around the mid-twentieth century, many formerly colonized agents established independent nations, primarily in Africa. African discourse on these historical, political movements often is the former way of discussing "decolonization." The primarily Latin American *pensar decolonial* intellectual movement (though it has very practical *teloi*) is distinct yet related to both historical decolonization and postcolonialism. Here, it is important to remember that most (though certainly not all) Latin American nations gained independence in the nineteenth century. The development of *pensar decolonial* is much more recent. It responds not only to the political realities (and the need to reshape them) but to the underlying coloniality that undergirds the very minds which could imagine new political realities. Thus, this movement is more so focused on "de-linking" postcolonial epistemic, cultural, and institutional realities from the ghosts of historical colonialism. Though there are significant theoretical, historical, and political overlaps, the movements (mid-twentieth century African decolonization and *pensar decolonial*) have different foci (political history vs. epistemology) and points of departure (Africa vs. Latin America). The former is the history of specific events and the immediate postcolonial challenges, and the latter is a reaction to the limits of postcolonial theory and a desire for epistemic decolonization. The distinction I draw between the two discourses is not adequately recognized in the scholarship, but it is, I think, a distinction that can help these discourses better understand their own histories, ideas, and ultimately become more fruitful dialogue partners. Without proper recognition of the differences in the discourses, scholars easily "talk past" one another.

[9] Of course, especially in the United States, indigenous people are often still politically colonized.

[10] Walter D. Mignolo, *The Darker Side of Western Modernity: Global Futures, Decolonial Options* (Durham, NC: Duke University Press, 2011), 8.

performed much of the challenging and diligent work needed to historically recover subaltern Christian figures and communities.

Many of these figures, albeit often "crossed"[11] and complicated with various markers of coloniality, sought through their adoption and adaptation of Christianity the flourishing of their peoples and communities[12]—to build off de Sousa Santos' quote, the right to have their own *religious* history, make decisions on the basis of their own reality, and *religious* experience.[13] The two figures in this essay, Santa Teresa Urrea and Prophet Garrick Sokari Braide, responded to the needs of their communities through their religious experiences and using the religious histories of their communities. They took up Christ in their idiom and embodiment, weaving the gospel into their local knowledges and ways of being. Through examining the stories of these practitioners, we can glean insights to deepen and extend decolonial thinking within World Christianity.[14]

---

[11] Ibidem., 16.

[12] See, for instance, Lamin Sanneh's recognition of the complications in the process of Africans' search for flourishing within the missionaries' Christianity as well as the missionaries' obstructions to their flourishing. "Africans adopted the Christian path because they were led to believe that they would gain all that belonged with their welfare and future prospects. Surrounded by powers seen and unseen, and all too aware of the forces of the spirit world, Africans were predisposed to believe that the material world was connected to their spiritual interests, and their spiritual interests to the material world. Missionaries' selective use of Christianity to avoid addressing the crisis occurring in society as having spiritual significance looked like a deliberate obstruction of God's work for human flourishing." Lamin Sanneh, *Disciples of All Nations: Pillars of World Christianity* (NY: Oxford University Press, 2008), 166.

[13] de Sousa Santos, *The End of the Cognitive Empire*, 109.

[14] In addition to this volume, an emerging body of literature is attempting to think decolonially about Christianity. The Ecclesiological Investigations International Research Network's 2022 conference in San Juan, Puerto Rico theme, *Decolonizing Churches*, provided space and dialogue for this and several other presentations and ongoing projects. This essay, as well as the work of several other early career decolonial scholars in the inaugural cohort of the Graymoor Scholars, received support from the Graymoor Ecumenical and Interreligious Institute. These developments follow and build upon the growing number of monographs, edited volumes, and articles attempting to think decolonially about Christianity. For example, see Raimundo Barreto and Roberto Sirvent, eds., *Decolonial Christianities: Latinx and Latin American Perspectives* (Cham: Palgrave Macmillan, 2019); Oscar Garcia-Johnson, *Spirit Outside the Gates: Decolonial Pneumatologies of the American Global South* (Downers Grove: InterVarsity Press, 2019); Teresa Delgado, *A Puerto Rican Decolonial Theology: Prophesy Freedom* (Cham, Switzerland: Palgrave Macmillan, 2017).

Exemplars of what Enrique Dussel calls "Messianic Christianity," I contend that Urrea and Braide help us articulate how decolonial practices can inform and deepen World Christianity engagement with decolonial thinking and acting.[15]

Artisanal Knowledges: Santa Teresa Urrea

As the nineteenth century—the "Great Century" of Christian missions according to Kenneth Scott Latourette—drew to a close, the face of Christianity changed dramatically.[16] For Roman Catholics in Latin America, Jesuit missions' years of nuanced inculturation had established Christian communities with roots intertwined with precontact religious pasts. The papally ordained expulsion of the Jesuits during the late eighteenth century had only deepened the local roots and particularities of these indigenous churches. With decades of little official clerical oversight, they continued to move the Christian religion into their own idiom, practices, and religious cosmologies. For the Yaquis and Mayos of northern Mexico, their very soil and selves held Christ and the Virgin. The mother and child had walked among them.[17] In his detailed and admirable study of Yaqui culture, Edward Spicer refers to Yaqui Christianity as a "new religion" mixing Roman Catholicism and precontact Yaqui religion.[18] Urrea's "biographer," William Curry Holden, even referred to Yaqui people as "[h]ighly religious in a pagan-Christian kind of way."[19] Writing in the 1970s, Spicer (and Holden as well) did not have the benefit of World

---

[15] Dussel, "Epistemological Decolonization of Theology," in *Decolonial Christianities: Latinx and Latin American Perspectives*, eds., Raimundo Barreto and Roberto Sirvent, 25–42 (Cham, Switz.: Palgrave Macmillan, 2019).

[16] Kenneth Scott Latourette, *The Great Century in Europe and the United States of America, A.D. 1800-A.D. 1914*, A History of the Expansion of Christianity, vol. iv (NY: Harper and Row, 1941).

[17] Jennifer Koshatka Seman, *Borderlands Saints: The Worlds of Santa Teresa Urrea and Don Pedrito Jaramillo* (Austin: University of Texas Press, 2021), 25.

[18] Edward Spicer, *The Yaquis: A Cultural History* (Tucson: University of Arizona Press, 1980), 60.

[19] William Curry Holden, *Teresita* (Owing Mills, MD: Stemmer House, 1978), 113. In many ways, Holden's work is better described as historical fiction. Though he performed years of research, the book scarcely cites a source, fabricates dialogue, and clearly reflects his own paternalistic biases.

Christianity's insights. The field has since demonstrated the diversity of the Christian religion and its inherent propensity to "syncretize" in whatever contexts it finds itself. Such religious mixing is an essential part of the religion's translatability and "indigenizing impulse."[20] Indeed, Spicer's own description of Yaqui Lenten celebrations reveals the depth of the "indigenization" of Christianity within the Yaqui world.[21] Christianity had become as indigenous to Northern Mexico as it was to Northern Italy. Indeed, in some ways, the vivacity and particularities of their Christianity threatened the authority of official priests and a government desperately trying to modernize and push aside any "superstition" especially when associated with indigenous people.[22]

Into this world arose living saints like *la Santa de Cabora*, Teresa Urrea.[23] She was the illegitimate daughter of a *hacendado* and one of his workers,[24] raised within Yaqui and Mayo Christian worlds, and trained in

---

[20] Lamin Sanneh, *Translating the Message: The Missionary Impact on Culture* (Maryknoll: Orbis, 1989); Andrew Walls, *The Missionary Movement in Christian History: Studies in the Transmission of Faith* (Maryknoll: Orbis, 1996), 53.

[21] Spicer, *The Yaquis,* 60ff. There exist a couple recent notable ethnographic works as well as their Christian religious life: David Delgado Shorter, *We Will Dance Our Truth: Yaqui History in Yoeme Performances* (Lincoln, NE: University of Nebraska Press, 2009). Seth Schermerhorn, "Global Indigeneity and Local Christianity: Performing O'odham Identity in the Present," in *Handbook of Indigenous Religion(s),* ed. Greg Johnson and Siv Ellen Kraft (Leiden: Brill, 2017). The latter in particular utilizes some World Christianity discourse to locate Yaqui religion within the gamut of the world's largest faith tradition (albeit, to the disappointment of exoticizing tourists hoping to see indigenous "shamans" rather than Catholic pilgrims).

[22] Edma I. Delgado Solórzano, "Crusaders, Martyrs, and Saints: Representations of Christian Militancy in Mexico, 1850–2013" (PhD Diss: University of Kansas, 2015), 3, 56.

[23] For a broader understanding of folk saint devotion in Latin America, see Frank Graziano, *Cultures of Devotion: Folk Saints in Spanish America* (NY: Oxford, 2006). For *curanderismo*, see Seman, *Borderlands Saints.*

[24] Urrea refers to her mother in one place as a "Mexican" (Helen Dare, "Santa Teresa, Celebrated Mexican Healer, Whose Powers Awe Warlike Yaquis in Sonora, Comes to Restore San Jose Boy to Health," *The Examiner,* San Francisco, CA, July 27, 1900). Holden claims the woman was a mestiza of Tehueco (a smaller group related to Yaquis and Mayos) descent (Holden, *Teresita,* 7). Holden could be correct—indeed, most scholars refer to her mother as Tehueco—but he cites no source. Brianda Domecq is suspicious of Holden in this regard (as well as in regard to many of his other claims). Brianda Domecq, "Teresa Urrea: La Santa de Cabora," en *Tomochic: La Revolución Adelantada,* vol. 2, ed. Jesús Vargas Valdez (Ciudad Juárez: Universidad Autónoma de Ciudad Juárez, 1994), 48n3–4.

curanderismo.[25] As the stories are told, she emerged from her casket claiming to have seen God and the Virgin. She was no official saint; indeed, the far-off official priests, perhaps fearful of the superstition of grassroots religion and their own precarious place in the Mexican government of the day, denounced her.[26] In the late nineteenth century (and perhaps this has not changed), lines between "saint" or "prophet" and "witch" or "hypnotist" were thin.[27] Nonetheless, she was certainly a saint to the hundreds of pilgrims who came to her every day seeking healing. She was meeting the needs which the modern/colonial project—here, medical science of the day—often could not by utilizing her knowledge of local herbs and sincere prayers.[28] Hers was an artisanal knowledge—to use de Sousa Santos's term. It was a knowledge formed out of the daily life of struggling for ontological respect, personal and communal flourishing, and the needs of everyday life in contexts of patriarchal, political, economic, and religious oppression.[29] Urrea's artisanal knowledge formed literally from the very

---

[25] Though I am yet to be convinced there exists a complete historical study of Urrea, the best available *historical* works (with adequate citations) are Domecq, "Teresa Urrea" and Paul J. Vanderwood, "Santa Teresa: Mexico's Joan of Arc," in *The Human Tradition in Latin America: The Nineteenth Century*, eds. Judith Ewell and William H. Beezley (Wilmington: Scholarly Resources, 1989) as well as the relevant chapters in Robert McKee Irwin's *Bandits, Captives, Heroines, and Saints: Cultural Icons of Mexico's Northwest Borderlands* (Minneapolis: University of Minnesota Press, 2007) and Jennifer Koshatka Seman's *Borderlands Saints*. There are excellent historical fictions of Urrea available: Brianda Domecq's *La insólita historia de la Santa de Cabora* (Mexico City.: Planeta, 1990), in translation as *The Astonishing Story of the Saint of Cabora*, transl. by Kay S. Garcia (Tempe, AZ: Bilingual Press, 1998); Luis Urrea's *The Hummingbird's Daughter* (NY: Little, Brown, and Co., 2005) and its sequel *Queen of America* (NY: Little, Brown, and Co., 2011).

[26] After anticlerical regimes earlier in the century, they knew well how swiftly their tides could turn.

[27] See the relevant chapter in Irwin, *Bandits, Captives, Heroines, and Saints* for a detailed study of Urrea's newspaper depictions. Illustrative sources are, however, easy enough to find. Indeed, one US newspaper of her day printed, underneath an illustration, the words "Santa Teresa de Cabora, 'The Sonora Witch.'" Albert Cameron, "Powerful is Teresa Hidden," *The Topeka Daily Capital* (Topeka, KS), September 6, 1896, p. 11.

[28] For the place of *curanderismo* as an alternative medical practice within a world where physicians so frequently disappointed, see Seman, *Borderlands Curanderos* and Brett Hendrickson, *Border Medicine: A Transcultural History of Mexican American Curanderismo* (NY: NYU Press, 2014). Similar dissatisfaction likely gave rise to Protestant "faith healing" of the same era across the border. See Heather Curtis, *Faith in the Great Physician: Suffering and Divine Healing in American Culture, 1860–1900* (Baltimore: Johns Hopkins University Press, 2007).

[29] Mignolo, *Darker Side of Western Modernity*, 8.

ground upon which she stood. It formed from her indigenous Christian background and remarkable religious experience.

Not unlike the Virgin of Guadalupe, Urrea soon exemplified to her followers that God was indeed on the side of the sick and those removed from their lands. Yaquis, Mayos, and—famously in Mexican history—the obliterated town of Tomochic invoked her name as they fought federal troops.[30] The government therefore imprisoned this icon of indigenous Christianity and exiled her to the United States. She continued to receive pilgrims in the borderlands and may have lent her support for revolution from this vantage point (the historical details here are blurry).[31] Perhaps most significantly, Urrea continued her healing ministry despite changing land and cultures. Her knowledge of herbal medicines was literally rooted to the land she had known. Surely, this loss hindered her abilities, but she worked nonetheless. Moreover, though many in Arizona and California spoke her tongue, communication barriers arose as she traveled to Saint Louis and New York, and she was surely economically exploited by the medical company with whom she worked. She returned to Arizona to build a healing home in which she died from tuberculosis at the cruciform age of thirty-three.[32]

---

[30] See Heriberto Frías' classic novel, originally serialized anonymously in 1893, *Tomochic: Episodios de la Campaña de Chihuahua: 1892, Relacion Escrita por un Testigo Presencial* (Mexico City.: Oceano, 2002), in translation as *The Battle of Tomochic: Memoirs of a Second Lieutenant*, transl. Barbara Jamison (NY: Oxford University Press, 2006). For secondary sources, see Paul J. Vanderwood, *The Power of God Against the Guns of Government: Religious Upheaval in Mexico at the Turn of the Nineteenth Century* (Stanford: Stanford University Press, 1998); and Ruben Osorio, *Tomóchic en Llamas* (D.F.: Consejo Nacional para la Cultura y las Artes, 1995).

[31] See Lauro Aguirre [y Teresa Urrea?], "¡Tomóchic! ¡Rendición!" en *Tomóchic: La Revolución Adelantada*, vol. 2, ed. Jesús Vargas Valdez, 91–193 (Ciudad Juárez: Universidad Autónoma de Ciudad Juárez, 1994). Originally, *¡Tomochic!* Published serially in *El Independiente,* an imprint of "The Evening Tribune," El Paso, Texas, 1896. Though listed as a coauthor, it is uncertain as to whether Urrea actually contributed to Aguirre's polemical telling of Tomochic or if he simply utilized her name to reach his audience. The difficulty lies in the potentially contradictory statements in Urrea's own interviews: "I had nothing to do with the Yaqui revolution … I have cured the Indians and they love me for it, but I do not tell them to make revolutions" (Dare, "Santa Teresa"). "Do you wonder that the tribe fights the forces of such a government? My poor Indians! They are the bravest and most persecuted people on earth. They will fight for their rights until they win or are exterminated. God help them!" (*New York Journal,* March 3, 1901).

[32] In addition to Domecq ("Santa Teresa," 46–47), for details of Urrea's later US life, see Brandon Bayne, "From Saint to Seeker: Teresa Urrea's Search for a Place of Her Own," *Church History* 75, no. 3 (Sept. 2016): 611–31.

Urrea's was a kind of artisanal knowledge for practicing healing and knowing the divine. Her popular sainthood represented an epistemological delinking with modern medicine, "order and progress" under the rule of General Porfirio Diaz, and the collusion between the Mexican clergy and a government set against indigenous land rights.[33] Urrea's Christianity was set against structures of coloniality. Because of this, some refused to name her Christian. While failing to recognize her expression of Christianity as such colonizes her into limiting modern Western paradigms of who Christians are and what they can be, one could say she embodied both Christian and indigenous religious (namely, Yaqui and Mayo) worlds simultaneously. Yet, from the perspective of World Christianity, this is simply the normal way of being Christian. Christians across space and time draw upon their available knowledges, utilizing them to follow and embody Christ as best they can. Bound to the stories of Christ the healer and advocate for the poor, her artisanal knowledge led to a kind of "acting otherwise"—a topic I explore next through Braide.

Acting Otherwise: Prophet Garrick Sokari Braide

For Protestant missions in places such as West Africa, Henry Venn's and Rufus Anderson's ideal of the self-propagating, self-financing, and self-governing church moved rapidly toward its realization in the consecration of Bishop Samuel Crowther in the late nineteenth century.[34] These institutional developments in British colonial Africa—successful as they were in some ways—paled in comparison to the quick success of local prophet-healers like William Wadé Harris and the lesser-known Garrick Sokari Braide of the Niger Delta.[35]

---

[33] For a cross-reference on the inefficacy of nineteenth-century modern medicine, see Curtis, *Faith in the Great Physician*. For the Porfiriato, see Charles Hale, *The Transformation of Liberalism in Late Nineteenth-Century Mexico* (Princeton: Princeton University Press, 1989). For Yaqui politics, see Evelyn Hu-Dehart, *Yaqui Resistance and Survival: The Struggle for Land and Autonomy 1821–1910* (Madison: The University of Wisconsin Press, 1984).

[34] G.O.M. Tasie, *Christian Missionary Enterprise in the Niger Delta, 1864–1918* (Leiden: Brill, 1978), 88.

[35] Two of the most significant and accessible primary sources are from Braide's sympathetic catechist, M.A. Kemmer ("The Truth About Garrick Braide Lately Designated Elijah II," *The Lagos Weekly Record*, February 24, 1917, reprinted from *The Delta Pastorate Chronicle*, 1909), and his episcopal adversary, the complex and profoundly influential James "Holy" Johnson ("Elijah II," *The Church Missionary Review* 67 [Aug 1916]: 455–62).

Though the Niger Delta Pastorate was relatively well-supplied with clergy, they had been loath to ordain local Ijaw people like Braide, thus limiting the possibilities for the indigenization and local ownership of Christianity.[36] They often relied instead on Yorubans like assistant bishop James "Holy" Johnson, Crowther's successor (in duties if not title).[37] Around the time of Urrea's death in 1906, Braide was received as an eager catechumen and then began healing and working miracles.[38] Descended from a priestly line in service to the deity Ogu, Braide's ministry drew upon the religious imaginaries of the Niger Delta people to convert the region to Christianity far more swiftly than decades of plodding Church Missionary Society efforts. He smashed idols and, in the fashion of the prophet Elijah, held back the skies from the local rainmakers. Yet while these (what some might call) power encounters rejected local religion, they nonetheless required the backdrop of the Delta's en-spirited religious imaginary. His recent biographer, Chinonyerem Chijioke Ekebuisi, has contended historically that Braide's "power encounters" were more deeply

---

[36] Emmanuel Ayandele, *Holy Johnson: Pioneer of African Nationalism, 1836–1917* (NY: Humanities Press, 1970), 357–8.

[37] They also preferred to ordain Saro people. Ibidem, 357–8.

[38] Biographical details come primarily from Braide's definitive biography: Chinonyerem Chijioke Ekebuisi, *The Life and Ministry of Prophet Garrick Sokari Braide, Elijah the Second of Niger Delta, Nigeria (c. 1882–1918)* (NY: Peter Lang, 2015). The broad-strokes historiography on Braide can be generally traced through five scholars. First, Harold Turner ("Prophets and Politics: A Nigerian Test-Case," *The Bulletin for the Society of African Church History* 2, no. 1 [1965]: 97–118) interpreted that the colonial authorities had wrongly construed Braide's movement as political when it was, rather, primarily religious. His interpretation set a generally sympathetic agenda for later treatments of Braide. Second, Emmanuel Ayandele's biography of Assistant Bishop James Johnson (*Holy Johnson*) interprets Johnson's handling of Braide and his movement as a lowlight of an otherwise venerable ecclesial career. Johnson had spent his life advocating for African religious and political agency; Ayandele saw the irony in Johnson's rejection of Braide. Third, G.O.M. Tasie (*Christian Missionary Enterprise*) is, in the most recent biographer's words, "the main historian of the Braide movement" even though Braide is only a piece of Tasie's larger regional church history. Fourth, Frieder Ludwig ("Elijah II: Radicalisation and Consolidation of the Garrick Braide Movement 1915–1918," *Journal of Religion in Africa* 23 [1993]: 296–317), upon close review of the limited historiography, argued that Braide's movement is so difficult to interpret because it adapted to the shifting social, political, and ecclesial contexts of the British-controlled Niger Delta in the 1910s. Fifth, scholarly attention has met its zenith in Ekebuisi's biography which utilizes the above scholars, oral histories, and hagiographies. Albeit brief, the text attends to Braide's family lineage as priests of the local cult as well as stories of Braide still resonant among Delta Christians.

indebted to local ways of religious knowing than previously thought.[39] Earlier scholars had thought Braide had begun attending church in the 1890s.[40] Ekebuisi rejects this. As evident in the minutes of the later Niger Delta Pastorate board meeting concerning Braide, the pastor assigned to Bakana before 1905 was not personally acquainted with Braide. Given the generally low number of Christians, it is unlikely that Braide would have been inquiring without the notice of the local pastor.[41] Of course, some level of inquiry may have been possible without the pastor remembering it a decade or two later. Even then, Ekebuisi is right to think that Braide did not significantly enter the church until Kemmer's appointment in 1905. If true, Braide adopted Christianity no sooner than 1905 but was performing these miracles before 1909.[42] The influence of Braide's local religious upbringing would have been even more crucial. His world must have remained deeply attenuated to that religious cosmology.

Indeed, Braide's relationship with Delta indigenous religion reveals the complications of local peoples writing, in de Sousa Santos' words, "their own history and mak[ing] decisions on the basis of their own reality and experience."[43] Braide's rejection of his religious past in favor of a Christianity at once deeply reliant on the Hebrew and early Christian scriptures—he was called Elijah II[44]—and which nonetheless spoke to the religious needs of a people far away from Jerusalem reveals decolonial praxis addressing a community's needs and hopes for flourishing.

Perhaps more so than Urrea, Braide reveals the ways in which the nodes of coloniality run through and restrict decolonial possibilities. In his revivalistic fervor, Braide destroyed many indigenous religious artifacts. Perhaps such is the cost of a people writing their own religious history. One can at once act decolonially in one sense while violating and marginalizing others in another sense. Coloniality is rarely black and white, and even while acting decolonially, Braide's disdain for local religious alternatives demonstrates the ways in which he reproduced coloniality even while acting decolonially. History is rarely tidy.

---

[39] Ekebuisi, *Life and Ministry*, 85n21.
[40] Ekebuisi (ibidem., 85n21) claims this was due to Tasie's (*Christian Missionary Enterprise*) enduring influence.
[41] Ekebuisi, *Life and Ministry*, 85n21.
[42] The miracles occurred before Kemmer's 1909 report ("The Truth About Garrick Braide").
[43] de Sousa Santos, *The End of the Cognitive Empire*, 109.
[44] Johnson, "Elijah II," 455–62.

Nonetheless, the Niger Delta people named Braide a prophet, and he accepted the title. Though the evangelical-leaning Church Missionary Society initially supported his ministry, accepting his prophethood was a step too far.[45] They rejected him, and the British government—seeing his grassroots nationalism and his teetotaling movement's effect on the empire's lucrative gin trade—imprisoned him. He died soon upon release, but his followers established their own independent churches, namely the Christ Army Church, which counts Braide as its founder.

Braide's acting otherwise led, in some ways, to both political and epistemic delinking. His was a kind of artisanal knowledge derived from local religious ways of knowing yet joined with biblical narratives. He responded to the religious needs of a community deprived of religious authority from within their own people group, and he propelled forward a religion that spoke to the deeply set needs of the people. Ultimately, this decolonial way of practicing Christianity had political consequences for Braide and his followers. When it affected the empire's economic revenue and the continuance of its imperial reign (during the uncertainty of the First World War), it intervened.

Decolonial Options for World Christianity

Figures of religious vitality and epistemological possibility within Christianity during the late nineteenth and early twentieth centuries, Urrea and Braide exemplify the increasingly recognized reality that—whether knowingly or not—many Christians have long practiced decolonial thinking and acting. Yet in one sense, Decolonial thinking and Christianity are strange allies. Many locate the roots of coloniality within the history of Christianity, Christian theology, and missionary encounters. Walter Mignolo, for instance, argues that "the historical foundation of the colonial matrix (and hence of Western civilization) was theological."[46] In as much as early modern Europeans drew essential distinctions between the "blood" of Christians, Jews, and Muslims, they constructed categories of *ontological* difference.[47] Indeed, Max Harris' study of *Reconquista* festi-

---

[45] Johnson, "Elijah II," 456.
[46] Mignolo, *The Darker Side of Western Modernity*, 8.
[47] Ibidem, 8.

vals and performances in Spain and Mexico historically demonstrates how the logic of ontological difference translated within colonial missionary encounters.[48] Even in today's "enlightened" world, colonial specters persist in the guise of exclusionary social systems and prejudices— as alive in Christian churches as anywhere else.[49] Colonial epistemic frameworks were, most certainly, formed by Christian peoples and, often, even Christian theologians.

Yet at the same time, the study of Christianity has undergone a kind of decolonial internal shift of its own. As Raimundo Barreto has argued, the field of World Christianity has common roots with Decolonial thinking.[50] Politically and ecclesially, both discourses developed largely out of the experience of African and Asian decolonization. The Third World Movement attempted to bring solidarity for nations recovering from decades or centuries of political colonialism. The movement further sought to provide an alternative center of gravity away from the two dominating Cold War powers. Especially through the work of Lamin Sanneh, Andrew Walls, and Kwame Bediako (as well as crucial predecessors like John Mbiti and Harold Turner), World Christianity similarly sought to provide alternatives to Western-centric narratives of the history of Christianity. Together with organizations like the Ecumenical Association of Third World Theologians, World Christianity reckoned with the fact that "the very universality of the Gospel, the fact that it is for *everyone*,

---

[48] Max Harris, *Aztecs, Moors, and Christians: Festivals of Reconquest in Spain and Mexico* (Austin: University of Texas Press, 2000).

[49] Mignolo identifies a distinction between *humanitas* and *anthropos* formed through colonial encounter. This distinction is ontological (Walter Mignolo, *Habitar la Frontera* [Ciudad Juarez: Universidad Autónoma de Ciudad Juarez, 2015], 443). de Sousa Santos, furthermore, sees a "abyssal line" that determines the kinds of exclusions in modernity. He posits that, within the modern imaginary, some people are not accorded the status of humanity. In as much as these nonhuman humans are excluded from Modern consideration, it is an *abyssal* exclusion. That is, it is an exclusion of those who exist beyond the abyss of who counts as truly human. There are, however, exclusions which occur within the realm of humanity. Perhaps, the best example includes workers who advocate for their rights based on shared human dignity with their oppressors. This is an argument based on "non-abyssal" exclusion—they are indeed human, but they are not treated as such. (De Sousa Santos, *The End of the Cognitive Empire*, 19–24).

[50] Barreto, "The Epistemological Turn in World Christianity," 52.

leads to a variety of perceptions and applications of it."[51] Of course, Christianity's universality can be a problem for decolonial thinking. De Sousa Santos contends that "the superiority of the universal and global" is one of the "five monocultures that have characterized modern Eurocentric knowledge."[52] Elsewhere he calls these monocultures "modes of production of non-existence."[53] For de Sousa Santos, "the superiority of the universal and global" is a means through which some peoples are deemed lesser.[54] He claims that the West determines that the "universal" and the "global" ought to supersede the local and parochial. Whatever is universal or global trumps all other local forms of knowledge, steamrolling them into nonexistence.

Indeed, there is certainly a sense in which Christianity may adapt during intercultural transmission and yet refuse to change "essential" aspects of itself—such as catholicity, universality.[55] There is also a sense in which local religions are transformed and grafted into Christianity's universal gravity, falling prey to a globalizing religious steamroller. Certainly, this is a kind of colonial force. Nonetheless, it is hardly possible for Christianity to fully divest itself of its universal claims. It may, however, be an instructive paradox rather than a damnation of the Christian religion. Indeed, if we follow Walls to his idea that Christian universality lies in the diversity of its local instantiations, then theological claims of catholicity and universality actually defy Christian monoculture. As Walls' quote contends, Christianity—in its theological essence—must contain a rich variety of responses, appropriations, and adaptations. It must be full of *options*. Indeed, at least in World Christianity discourse, the religion critiques "the *monoculture of the logic of dominant scale*," another phrase de Sousa Santos used for "the superiority of the universal and global."[56] Walls' version of

---

[51] Walls, *The Missionary Movement in Christian History*, 46. For EATWOT and its decolonial bend, see Barreto, "The Epistemological Turn" as well as Stephen Di Trolio Coakley, "The First Conference of the Ecumenical Association of Third World Theologians (EATWOT) in Dar es Salaam, Tanzania 1976," *Global South Studies: A Collective Publication with The Global South* (2020), https://globalsouthstudies.as.virginia.edu/key-moments/first-conference-ecumenical-association-third-world-theologians-eatwot-dar-es-salaam.

[52] de Sousa Santos, *The End of the Cognitive Empire*, 25–26.

[53] Boaventura de Sousa Santos, *Epistemologies of the South: Justice Against Epistemicide* (Boulder: Paradigm, 2014), 172.

[54] Indeed, for de Sousa Santos, it is a means through which ontology is determined. They are markers of the abyssal line (see fn49).

[55] Walls, *The Missionary Movement in Christian History*, 8–9.

[56] de Sousa Santos, *Epistemologies of the South*, 173, emphasis original.

universality highlights and celebrates the local, incarnated forms of Christianity which so often fall outside the bounds of the typical narrative. It invites those typically outside the bounds to dialogue about what Christianity has been, is, and could become. Indeed, Urrea and Braide fall outside the typical narratives and, because of their indigenous religious negotiations, are hardly able to be neatly integrated into the typical narrative of Christian history. They exemplify realities which World Christianity often encounters. Largely drawn from the on-the-ground lives of diverse Christian communities, World Christianity often suggests that the very shape of Constantinian and otherwise imperial Christianities are not the most proper reflections of Christianity. Indeed, this is precisely how Enrique Dussel understands Christianity.

According to Barreto, Dussel is a crucial interconnecting figure between World Christianity and Decolonial thought.[57] For Dussel, the Christian religion has often uncomfortably swung back and forth between coercive elite power and voluntary grassroots adoption.[58] It is far too easy, in surveying the religion's history, to identify eras in which the former or the latter proliferated. The Ante-Nicene church, for instance, is often portrayed as truly grassroots, noncoercive, and a church of the poor. Constantinian Christianity, on the other hand, is a colonial coercive movement married to power and military might. Dussel, one of the great liberationist thinkers, distinguishes the two types as *messianic Christianity* versus *Christendom*. The key for Dussel is that regardless of its form—Constantinian, Crusader, Conqueror, or Commercial—Christendom has developed a way of being Christian that is, indeed, counter-Christ. "It," for instance, "crucified the indigenous in the name of the one who was crucified."[59] Such religion, it would seem, has very little to do with the anointed one.

---

[57] Barreto, "The Epistemological Turn in World Christianity," 53.

[58] Dussel, "Epistemological Decolonization of Theology." Admittedly, I hesitate to follow Dussel's dichotomy whole cloth. Many Christians arguing for kinds of primitivism (i.e., return to early church) present similar arguments. As World Christianity demonstrates, Christendom and Messianic Christianity live together, inhabit the same times and places, and—sometimes—even the same individuals. The wheat and the chaff grow up together. Nonetheless, Dussel's model provides an axiological framework for viewing expressions of Christianity, and it is certainly helpful for understanding Urrea's and Braide's Christianities amid expressions of Christendom.

[59] Ibidem, 32.

Clearly, in both Mexico and West Africa at the turn of the twentieth century (Urrea's and Braide's contexts), there existed simultaneously "Christendom" and "messianic Christianity."[60] The official church structures maintained close ties to government powers which recognized these grassroots messianic leaders as threats. In Mexico, nearly a century of anticlericalism demonstrated to clergy the tenuousness of their positions within the for-now favorable reign of Porfirio Diaz.[61] Indeed, the federal law by which the government stole indigenous land was originally designed to federalize church lands.[62] In West Africa, even nationalist leaders like assistant bishop James "Holy" Johnson believed that revolutionary movements could crush future hopes for gradual decolonization.[63] Though Church Missionary Society figures themselves discouraged gin-drinking, the empire required it economically. In disrupting the gin trade through his mass conversions, Braide indeed fulfilled the desires of the CMS yet at the chagrin of their sponsoring empire.[64] In these precarious situations, many clergy understood popular lay leaders as threats to the church and their own political interests. The success of popular leaders like Urrea and Braide developed out of the ground rather than the church. It built upon the local knowledges, religious worlds, and concerns of their communities. As official Roman Catholic structures waned in the face of Mexican anticlericalism, Urrea's decolonial work blew fresh life. Decolonial politics, in this way, offered a way forward for the Christian religion in a world where colonial structures finally faltered. In his decolonial politics, Braide too attracted far more Christian believers than coloniality could. Nonetheless, forces of Christendom remained so fixed to their structures that they could not imagine Christian politics without them and sought to colonize them—both epistemically and by government force.

---

[60] Dussel, "Epistemological Decolonization of Theology," 28.

[61] Paul J. Vanderwood, *The Power of God Against the Guns of Government,* 188–9.

[62] Gregorio L. de la Fuente Monge, "Clericalismo y anticlericalismo en México, 1810–1938," *Ayer* 27, (1997): 46. For a more detailed and particular study of the confiscation of indigenous lands, see Jean Meyer, "La Ley Lerdo y la Desamortización de las Comunidades en Jalisco," in *Jean Meyer: de una revolución a la otra: México en la historia. Antología de textos* (México, D.F.: El Colegio de México, 2013).

[63] Johnson, "Elijah II." While he recognizes how popular and nationalistically significant Braide is, he sees him and his Christianity as deficient, lacking proper catechesis and sacraments and moving far too quickly to destroy local religion.

[64] Ibidem. Of course, Johnson himself saw Braide's discouragement of gin-drinking as positive.

Christianity is and was always a political religion; indeed, Urrea and Braide had their own politics—albeit decolonial, I suggest. Yet when Christianity colludes—even if only for its own perpetuation amid uncertain political situations—it tends to turn a blind eye to the plight of the poor, disenfranchised, exploited, and religiously derided. Christendom cannot fulfill the mission of Christ.

Earlier, I suggested that Urrea and Braide utilized "artisanal knowledges," ways of knowing that are drawn from the lived experienced of practitioners seeking the flourishing of their communities on their own terms. The key is that the knowledges are *emplaced*, socially and geographically bound to land and peoples like the Yaqui and Kalibari. This does not mean that the religions are static. To the contrary, Urrea's and Braide's religious practices and knowledges evidence the fact that religion changes, integrates indigenous knowledge and knowledge gained from missionary encounters. Of course, those encounters have their own histories and asymmetries of power, but oftentimes local actors can and do utilize the received Christianity for decolonial purposes. The key is that the knowledges are local; they represent what people value, think, and practice. Urrea and Braide, as popular leaders, embody and further these ways of knowing. Their practices were a kind of religious integration and innovation in service to, in Dussel's words, messianic Christianity, and they further demonstrate the role of migration and grassroots diffusion in the development of decolonial Christian movements.

Urrea and Braide both seamlessly integrated their indigenous religious backgrounds with Christianity. They "drank from their own wells" to provide for the religious needs of their communities.[65] Whether they realized it or not, utilizing indigenous practices and cosmologies for Christianity demonstrated to their communities that God—even the Christian God worshipped by their oppressors—can speak to them in their own idiom. Unlike the forces of Christendom, they embodied ways of practicing religion that do not require people to abandon their histories or cultures but instead invite people to write their own religious histories and take seriously their own religious experiences—their divine calls, healing practices, rituals, and miracle-working. These were, it seems to me, kinds of messianic Christianity, in service of the ontological restoration of their local communities in the face of Christendom and empire.

[65] Gustavo Gutierrez, *We Drink from Our Own Wells: The Spiritual Journey of a People* (Maryknoll: Orbis, 2003).

Their faith, however, were mobile missionary movements. Messianic Christianity as seen in Urrea and Braide is not "indigenous" in the sense in that it stays rooted in one particular culture or people. Urrea and Braide themselves were formed in migrancy. In her youth, Urrea moved with all the indigenous people serving her father from Sinaloa to Sonora. It was only after this that her father recognized her and adopted her into his home.[66] Braide likewise underwent a traumatic move in his youth when a diviner saw "evil lumps" in his head and recommended he be put to death.[67] His family chose instead to move villages, serving in the home of Braide's uncle essentially in servitude for several years.[68] Urrea again migrated—though internationally—upon her exile and had to refashion herself in a foreign land. Formed in migration, it may be helpful to think of Urrea's and Braide's Christianities as kinds of border thinking, formed in the experiences of movement. Their wells of knowledge formed at intersections of shifting identities, religious experiences, and even trauma.

Not only did Urrea and Braide migrate, but their movements migrated far beyond them. Though deeply embedded in their places cosmologically and even ecologically, Urrea and Braide ought not to be seen as parochial leaders. Both had broad interethnic and even international appeal. Urrea drew a variety of indigenous, Mexican, and US audiences to her, and these audiences developed their own cross-ethnic solidarities rooted in recognition of her sainthood. Both Yaquis and Mayos approached her, the sick traveled miles to visit and took their memories with them, and skeptical reporters pushed her story abroad.[69] Braide's sweeping "revival" likewise stretched across Ijaw, Igbo, Saro, and Yoruban ethnic lines and contributed to the formation African nationalism in the face of the British Empire in the midst of the First World War.[70] His movement "extended beyond the Niger Delta frontiers"[71] during his life, and then, even when Braide

---

[66] Dare, "Santa Teresa."
[67] Ekebuisi, *Life and Ministry*, 78.
[68] Ibidem, 78–80.
[69] For reporters, consider the syndicated article originally from a correspondent with the *New York Sun*, "Miracles of a Mexican Maiden," *The New York Sun*, December 20, 1891, p. 16. Heriberto Frías (*Tomochic*) highlights the Tomochic figures who brought their memories of Urrea to the village and, according to Frías, used it to whip the town into religious and revolutionary fervor.
[70] See Ekebuisi, *Life and Ministry*, 7, 83–4. Ludwig, "Elijah II," 300. Tasie, *Christian Missionary Enterprise*, 12–6.
[71] Ekebuisi, *Life and Ministry*, 112, 143–182.

refused to serve as bishop of the group breaking away from the Anglican Niger Delta Pastorate, the Christ Army Church moved beyond him to found itself as, what we would now call, an African Initiated Church.[72] Urrea and Braide were themselves formed in migration. It is no wonder that their movements were dynamic, diffusing cross-culturally and creatively, outliving them, and even pushing beyond them. Like a flourishing plant, messianic Christianity grows out of local soil, but because of its vitality, it spreads abroad, both replicating and changing.

Conclusion

Mexican folk-saint Teresa Urrea and Niger Delta prophet-healer Garrick Braide, both popular leaders at the turn of the twentieth century, provide models for resisting forces not only of colonialism but of coloniality. For contemporary purposes, that distinction is crucial. They were not merely historical figures resisting empires and regimes now seen as horribly destructive. They embodied epistemological alternatives—creative, grounded, and practical artisanal knowledges formed in migration and then diffused through grassroots movements—that speak as much to contemporary contexts of epistemic coloniality as to their own. Crucially, these were not primarily political revolutionaries—though many understood them as such, and they inspired revolution. They were popular Christian leaders, indebted to their divine calls, gifts, and experiences. Indeed, it was their locally derived, decolonially oriented Christianities that were so dangerous to the Porfiriato's positivistic goal of "order and progress" and British economic colonialism. In faith, Urrea and Braide exhibited the terrifying realities of local lay leaders with divinely given authority—healing, performing miracles, and even baptizing without clerical license. They embodied Christianities which had grown up from beneath the purview of colonial powers, seeking not only political recognition but ontological restoration. For contemporary churches and communities struggling in the face of colonialism's ghost, coloniality, Urrea and Braide are exemplars for practicing decolonial Christianity. And if Dussel is correct, then this practice is simply the Christianity of the Messiah himself.

---

[72] Ibidem, 143–182.

PART III

Decolonizing History and Theological Education

CHAPTER 8

Decolonizing the Reformation: Centering Ethiopian Christianity, Decentering the Eurocentric Narrative

David Douglas Daniels III

Reformation narrative can be expanded to include Ethiopian Christians and Ethiopian Christian texts since they played a role during the sixteenth-century Reformation in Europe. By including these Christians and their texts, the Reformation narrative can become crafted in a way that portrays the Reformation as more than an event among Europeans exploring solely European concerns and replying on solely European texts; the Reformation becomes an exchange between Ethiopians and Europeans in addition to an exchange between Europeans among themselves. Ethiopian Christianity became a source of Christian knowledge for European reformers during the Reformation.

The chapter will explore how Ethiopian Christians and their texts played a significant role during the Reformation. In the encounters between Ethiopian and European Christians, leading European Catholics

---

D. D. Daniels III (✉)
McCormick Theological Seminary, Chicago, IL, USA
e-mail: ddaniels@mccormick.edu

© The Author(s), under exclusive license to Springer Nature Switzerland AG 2023
R. C. Barreto, V. Latinovic (eds.), *Decolonial Horizons*, Pathways for Ecumenical and Interreligious Dialogue,
https://doi.org/10.1007/978-3-031-44839-3_8

and Protestants learned from Ethiopian Christianity. In order to encourage decolonizing the Reformation narrative, this chapter seeks to demonstrate that Ethiopian Christianity was among the topics discussed during the Reformation, and that these Christians were interlocutors of both Catholic and Protestant reformers. The chapter also shows how Ethiopian-European exchange served as an alternative to the European colonizing model of engaging the Global South; it was a collaborative model that promoted peership between Ethiopian and European Christians.

Decolonizing the Reformation Narrative: Key Issues

Decolonizing takes seriously how knowledges of the global South within the vice of coloniality are discredited, devalued, erased, or outright, denied ever existing. The aim of coloniality is to make Europe the primary agent of history-making in order to legitimate European dominance and the subordination of the people of the global South through colonialism, imperialism, or neo-imperialism. A Eurocentric narrative does the intellectual work that "naturalizes" or justifies the geo-political maneuvers. As Enrique Dussel contends: "The effect of Eurocentrism is not merely that it excludes knowledge and experiences outside of Europe, but that it obscures the very nature and history of Europe itself." In this case, in the history of Europe, colonialism is constitutive of the later Renaissance, the Reformation, and the Enlightenment. The decolonizing project exposes these Eurocentric processes.[1]

By discrediting, devaluing, erasing, or denying the existence of the knowledges of the global South, Eurocentric narratives presuppose a hierarchy of peoples and knowledges, adopt a center-periphery schema with Europe at the center and the maker of history, deem Europe the authority and arbiter of truth, and recognize Europe as the repository of knowledge as well as the zenith of all civilizations. Eurocentric narratives promote European exceptionalism.

In the words of G. W. F. Hegel's characterization of Africa:

> For it is no historical part of the World; it has no movement or development to exhibit. Historical movements in it-that is in its northern part-belong to the Asiatic or European World. Carthage displayed there an important

[1] Enrique Dussel, "Eurocentrism and modernity (Introduction to the Frankfurt Lectures), *Boundary 2* [1993] 23 (3): 65–76.

transitionary phase of civilization; but, as a Phoenician colony, it belongs to Asia. Egypt will be considered in reference to the passage of the human mind from its Eastern to its Western phase, but it does not belong to the African Spirit. What we properly understand by Africa, is the Unhistorical, Undeveloped Spirit, still involved in the conditions of mere nature, and which had to be presented here only as on the threshold of the World's History.

Within Hegel's narrative, Africa lies outside "the real theatre of History," to use his phrase, supplying warrant for the subjugation of Africa and Africans. Eurocentric narratives tell their stories based on "texts" located in archival collections that forefront material which advance the Eurocentric argument and bracket sources, for example, that illustrate African Christian knowledge which offer a counter-narrative, a non-Eurocentric narrative; alternative African Christians sources, then, are "buried" in the archive and rendered nonexistent in the Eurocentric narrative.[2]

In the words of Steed Davidson,

decolonization is a set of practices that challenge coloniality which is a structured system of thought that results in various forms of unequal domination such as racial discrimination, class exploitation, including the theft of resources land from indigenous peoples. The aim of decolonization is a clear delinking through theory and practice, through thought and politics from colonial networks of power. As a liberation project, decolonization draws upon Marxist thought but represents the unique contextual aspirations of formerly colonized and presently colonized peoples.[3]

Decolonizing histories liberate the knowledges of the global South from the grip of coloniality by excavating, resuscitating, and making legible this range of knowledge in order to reconstruct the past in a robust manner. To best understand the present and envision the future, the past must be reconstructed from the perspective of these knowledges and communities.

As a historical analysis of the Reformation, decolonizing the Reformation narrative can pursue at least three approaches. First, the narrative can be decolonized by exposing how the colonial project serves as a scaffold of the Reformation narrative. How does the Reformation narrative

[2] Georg Wilhelm Friedrich Hegel, The Philosophy of History (New York: Cosimo, Inc., 2007), 99.
[3] Steed Davidson, email to David Daniels on 12 November 2022.

legitimize the colonial project? And, how does the Reformation narrative reproduce coloniality (colonial matrix of power)? Second, the narrative can be decolonized by incorporating how the Reformation dealt with colonialism and slavery. How topics of colonialism became topics of the Reformation? How the Reformation legitimated and rejected colonialism and slavery? Third, the narrative can be decolonized if it is reframed from the perspective of Christians of color, specifically Ethiopian Christians and their Christianity. How do the role of Ethiopian Christians and Christianity shape the Reformation, revealing the European engagement of Christian knowledge from the global South? How does this history offer a counter-narrative to the Eurocentric one and subvert the colonial matrix of European domination and the subjugation of the people of the global South? How does this history decenter Europe, provincializing, and recenter African Christianity in the narrative?

In decolonizing the Reformation narrative, this chapter will employ the third approach of decolonizing the narrative by making legible and audible the African Christians of the Reformation and demonstrating the role that African Christianity, especially Ethiopian Christianity, in co-constructing the Reformation. This chapter, then, challenges the Eurocentric narrative with its portrayal of the 16th Reformation as solely a European event about European religious concerns which were only engaged by European actors. This study focuses on Ethiopia as a site of generating Christian knowledge employed by Ethiopians residing in Europe who participated in the Reformation. According to recent research by Matteo Salvadore, Samantha Kelly, James DiLorenzi, Sam Kennerley, Jennifer McNutt, Stanislau Paulau, myself and others, Ethiopian Christians and Christianity played different roles in the Reformation.[4]

---

[4] See Matteo Salvadore, Matteo. *The African Prester John and the Birth of Ethiopian-European Relations, 1402–1555* (New York: Routledge, 2017); Samantha Kelly, "The Curious Case of Ethiopic Chaldean: Fraud, Philology, and Cultural (Mis)Understanding in European Conceptions of Ethiopia," *Renaissance Quarterly*, 68:4 (Winter 2015); Sam Kennerley, "Ethiopian Christians in Rome, c.1400–c.1700" in *A Companion to Religious Minorities in Early Modern Rome*, edited by Matthew Coneys Wainwright and Emily Michelson (Amsterdam: Brill, 2020), 142–168; Jennifer Powell McNutt, "From Codex Bezae to La Bible. Theodore Beza's Biblical Scholarship and the French Geneva Bible of 1588" in *Theodore Beza at 500: New Perspectives on an Old Reformer*, edited by Jon Balserak, Jennifer Powell McNutt et al. (Gottingen: Vandenhoeck & Ruprecht Verlage, 2021), 157–176; Jennifer Powell McNutt, "An Unsung Inspiration for the Protestant Reformation: the Ethiopian Church," *Christianity Today* (Oct. 2020) online; and Stanislau Paulau, "An Ethiopian Orthodox Monk in the Cradle of the Reformation: Abba Mika'el, Martin Luther, and the Unity of the Church" in *Ethiopian Orthodox Christianity in a Global Context*, edited by Stanislau Paulau and Martin Tamcke (Leiden & Boston: Brill, 2022), 81–109.

Foregrounded in this study are not the voices of the oppressed nor the colonized, although these deserve to be heard, but this study "unmutes" the voices of Ethiopians as peers to Europeans which were heard by Catholic and Protestant reformers. This chapter ponders whether a theological trajectory informed by the Ethiopian-European exchange was being charted during the Reformation that was an alternative to the European imperial trajectory which legitimated colonialism and the slave trade.

In decolonizing the Reformation, the goal is to identify Ethiopian Christianity as a topic of the Reformation, Ethiopian Christians as interlocutors of Catholic and Protestant reformers, and the Ethiopian-European exchange as an alternative to the European colonizing model of engaging the Global South. Does an Ethiopian-European collaborative model emerge during the Reformation? Did a collaborative model parallel the colonial model? Whereas the colonial model fostered European dominance and Global South subordination, the collaborative model promoted Christian Ethiopian-European collegiality. The goal here is to prove that the collaborative model existed.

In decolonizing the Reformation narrative, this new narrative presented in this chapter seeks to dislodge the Reformation narrative from coloniality as an imperial/Western ideology that legitimates racial hierarchies and white supremacy. By dislodging the Reformation narrative from the matrix of coloniality, the Reformation story can resist legitimating the colonial project and its logic by provincializing rather than universalizing and normalizing European Christianity.[5]

As noted above, a decolonized Reformative narrative replaces the Eurocentric framework with Christian knowledge generated outside of Europe. The Ethiopian Christianity is the site of that knowledge. The Reformation should be depicted as an intercontinental Christian exchange between Ethiopia and Europe.

---

[5] Walter D. Mignolo, Local Histories/Global Designs: Coloniality, Subaltern Knowledges, and Border Thinking (Princeton: Princeton University Press, 2000).

Ethiopian Christian Scholars During the Reformation Era

Ethiopian scholars were theologians, teachers, authors, editors, translators, librarians, advisors, priests, abbots, and bishops. Tomas Walda Samu'el, an Ethiopian Orthodox priest from Jerusalem, instructed Johannes Potken, a German Roman Catholic priest, in the reading of Ge'ez; thus, Samu'el launched the linguistic study of Ge'ez in Europe. With Potken's syllabary written under the "supervision" of Samu'el, Europeans began to learn Ge'ez without an Ethiopian as the teacher. Printed in Rome in 1513 and later in Cologne, the *Psalterium David et cantica aliqua in lingua Chaldea* was co-edited by Samu'el and Potken. The Ethiopic Psalter with its 151 Psalms included also the Song of Moses and the Song of Hannah in addition to the Prayers of Hezekiah, Manasseh, Jonah, Azariah, and the Three Children as well as the Song of Solomon. The Ethiopic Psalter of 1515/16 edition was an Ethiopianized text in that it followed the Ethiopian sequencing, with the Psalter, as noted above, including the Psalms, two biblical hymns and five prayers from the Old Testament, and the Song of Solomon. This was the Ethiopian text both in terms of script and sequencing. By the production of the Ethiopic Psaltery, the Ethiopian reader would have recognized the text, and the European reader would be introduced to a new way of reading the songs of the Scripture.[6]

Five years later, Potken published a polyglot of the Psalms in Cologne, *Psalterium in Quatuor Linguis: Hebraea, Greca, Chaldaea, Latina*; this assisted Europeans in learning to read Ge'ez by placing the Ethiopic Bible in parallel with three other versions of the Bible, specifically Hebrew, Greek, and Latin.

The *Testamentum Novum* cum *Epistola Pauli ad Hebreos Tantum*, cum *Concordantiis Evangelistarum Eusebii et Numeratione Omnium Verborum Eorundem. Missale* cum *Benedictione Incensi Cerae* etc. *Alphabetum in Lingua [...] Gheez [...] Libera Quia a Nulla Alia Originem Duxit, & Vulgo Dicitur Chaldea, Quae Omnia Fr. Petrus Ethyops*, was printed in Rome between 1548 and 1549. The editors were Tasfa Seyon (Petrus),

---

[6] Matteo Salvadore and James DiLorenzi, "An Ethiopian Scholar in Tridentine Rome: Täsfa S̱eyon and the Birth of Orientalism," *Itinerario*, Vol. 45 (2021), No. 1, 22–23; Ge'ez is an ancient Ethiopian language that became the liturgical and theological language of the Ethiopian Orthodox Church.

Tanse'a-Wald (Paulus), and Za-Sellase (Bernadus). According to Fentahun Tiruneh, Area Specialist for Ethiopia and Eritrea (African & Middle Eastern Division) of the Library of Congress, "the Ethiopic New Testament was published in Rome under the auspices" of Pope Paul III, and the emperor of Ethiopia, Gelawdewos. As the printers lacked knowledge of Ge'ez, Tasfa also had to supervise the mechanical part of the printing and so served as the chief editor and supervisor of the printing process. Having these responsibilities, according to Tasfa, meant that "typographical errors" were in the printed Ethiopic New Testament. According to Metzger, Tasfa expressed his chagrin with these words: "Fathers and Brethren, be pleas'd not to interpret amiss the faults of this edition; for they who compos'd it could not read [viz. Ethiopic]; and for ourselves we know not how to compose. So then we help'd them, and they assisted us, as the blind leads the blind; and therefore we desire you to pardon us and them."[7]

The Ethiopian collection of New Testament books opened with the Eusebian canon tables within the Epistle of Eusebius to Carpianus as a guide to reading the New Testament, according to James DeLorenzi, and the along with the Anaphora of Our Lord and that of Our Lady. DeLorenzi suggests that this might mean that Tasfa had an Ethiopian audience as his target with his "specifically Ethiopian mode of reading" with "the common Ethiopian practice of introducing the Gospels with the Eusebian canon tables."[8]

The 1548 edition included the canon tables and the anaphoras as well as the Catholic recognized New Testament canon, save thirteen letters of Paul which were printed the next year. In addition to the difference in the collection of the Ethiopian New Testament, the Ethiopian ordering of the New Testament followed a different sequence than the West. The Ethiopian ordering placed the Apocalypse (Book of Revelations) earlier in the canon rather than at the end. 1548 edition as "the Gospels, Apocalypse,

---

[7] Bruce M. Metzger, *The Early Versions of the New Testament: Their Origins, Translations and Limitations* (Oxford: Clarendon Press, 1977), 229; Metzger used J. P. Gent.'s translation of Ludolf's *A New History of Ethiopia* (London, 1682), 263.

[8] Metzger, 228–229; James De Lorenzi, "Red Sea Travelers in Mediterranean Lands: Ethiopian Scholars and Early Modern Orientalism, ca. 1500–1668," in *World Building and the Early Modern Imagination*, edited by Allison B. Kavey (New York: Palgrave Macmillan, 2010). 179 f.

Catholic Epistles (in the order of 1,2, and 3 John, 1 and 2 Peter, James, Jude), Hebrews, Acts," and the two Anaphoras.[9]

Tasfa possessed an incomplete book of Acts. He warned the readers that he translated the missing sections: "these Acts of the Apostles, for the most part, were translated from the Latin and the Greek by reason of the imperfection of the [Ethiopic] archetype; for what we have added or omitted, we beg your pardon, and request you to amend what is amiss." The second publication, printed in 1549, included thirteen letters of Paul, which came from an Ethiopian manuscript that had been in Cyprus.[10]

In this author's estimation, the 1548 edition was Ethiopian in terms of language, collection, ordering, and narrative arc. For example, instead of the narrative arc of the New Testament beginning with the creation of humanity in the genealogy of Matthew's first chapter to the incarnation to the ministry, crucifixion, resurrection, and ascension of Jesus to the birth of the church and, then, to new heaven and earth in the last chapter of Revelations, the Ethiopian narrative began with the canons as a reading guide to Matthew's genealogy and incarnation with the ministry, crucifixion, resurrection, and ascension of Jesus to an eschatological focus of apocalypse and the last churches, and, then, the "global" churches before concluding with the history of the birth of the church at Pentecost through Paul's arrival at Rome. In the last chapter of Acts, the Ethiopic book adds the story of Nero. This story underscores the important lesson that sequence matters in Biblical narrative.

The European printing of select manuscripts of the Ethiopic Bible "produced," then, the Ethiopic Bible during the Reformation era. In Ethiopia, the Ethiopic Bible consisted of a collection of manuscripts; throughout the Reformation era, only manuscripts of a select group of books of Bible existed in Europe. During this era, the only printing of any books from the Ethiopic Bible occurred in Europe. With a couple of books from the Old Testament and most of the books from the New Testament printed from Ethiopic manuscripts, a printed volume of the Ethiopic Bible was made but since not all the manuscripts of the Ethiopic New Testament were available in Europe during this era, substitutes needed to be utilized. With the replication of the written script into a printed script not being exact, there were errors. To summarize, the Ethiopic Bible was "produced" in three distinct senses: production of the physical printed

---

[9] Metzger, 228.
[10] Metzger, 228.

collection, printed texts with Ge'ez script, and a New Testament that was missing sections. While resembling the Ethiopic Bible of manuscript form with approximate script and mostly based on Ethiopian manuscript, it was quite different from the Ethiopian manuscript sources. The Ethiopic Bible as a printed text, then, was a creation of the Reformation.

A line of Europeans readers of Ge'ez and the Ethiopic Bible between the 1510s and 1700 emerged out of the above-mentioned Samu'el education of Potken. While this European company of readers first "learned" from Samu'el through Potken's scholarship, they eventually expanded to include Konrad Pellikan, Sebastian Munster, Gualtieri, Mariano Vittori (future bishop of Rieti), Justus Scaliger, Jacob Wemmers, Edmund Castell, Dudley Lofton, Anna Van Schurman, Hiob Ludolf, John Michael Wansleben, Louis De Dieu, Thomas Erpenius, Johan Georg Nisselius, Theodorus Petraeus, Peter Heyling, Louis de Azevedo, and Louis de Cardeira. Some like Vittori and Ludolf were taught by Ethiopians such as Tasfa Seyon and Abba Gorgoryos, respectively.[11]

The first editors of the Ethiopic Bible called the Ethiopic script Chaldean instead of Ge'ez, and Chaldean was identified as a dialect of Aramaic, the language spoken by Jesus and other first-century Palestinian Jews and Christians. Consequently, the language of the Ethiopic Bible was included among the sacred languages of Scripture along with Hebrew, Greek, and Latin. Given this identification, the Ethiopic Bible was pertinent to early modern arguments regarding Biblical authority, texts, and translations. The sacredness of Ge'ez as well as the antiquity of the Ethiopic Bible added to its status and authority during the early Reformation era; the proper classification of Ethiopic would be a continuing topic of discussion during the Reformation.[12]

Samantha Kelly noted the Potken stated that his Ethiopian contemporaries in Rome believed that Ge'ez as Chaldean or Chaldaic as the native language of Abraham and, probably, the original language of Adam. Thus, Ge'ez as Chaldean would be classified as the first human language. Therefore, the Ethiopic version of the Bible was in the original language of humanity or the native language of Abraham. Either option added to the status and authority of the Ethiopic Bible within the broader Humanist

---

[11] A list compiled by the author.
[12] Samantha Kelly, "The Curious Case of Ethiopic Chaldean: Fraud, Philology, and Cultural (Mis)Understanding in European Conceptions of Ethiopia," *Renaissance Quarterly*, 68:4 (Winter 2015), 1253.

debates on language, human origins, and human taxonomies that would be racialized. In these ways, the Ethiopian text also played a significant role in the Biblical and the broader Humanist debates on the unity and diversity of the human family.[13] By 1527, Sebastian Münster challenged the classification of Ethiopic as Chaldean or a dialect of Aramaic. Yet, Ge'ez continued to be called Chaldean. For Ethiopians, Ge'ez was only a liturgical, theological, and classical language; in fact, they spoke other languages such as Aramaic or Oromo. Therefore, during the Reformation, only select books and sections of books from the Ethiopic Bible were printed.[14]

The Ethiopic Bible and its tradition of biblical interpretation was printed, translated, circulated, cited, and debated. Ethiopians participated as editors, co-editors, translators, and interpreters of the Ethiopic Bible during the Reformation in Europe. In these ways, the Ethiopic Bible and its tradition of Biblical interpretation concerned several key debates during the Reformation era. The Ethiopic text was a site of the confessional debate on the European continent about the ancient Church and the future Church. Rather than being nonexistent, inconsequential, or ancillary to the Reformation, the Ethiopic Bible and its tradition of biblical interpretation was prominent and contributed to the confessional debates of the era.

ETHIOPIAN CHRISTIANITY IN REFORMATION DEBATES AND THE DECOLONIZED NARRATIVE

The Ethiopian interpretations of some New Testament texts were circulated within Europe by Ethiopian Christians during the Reformation of the 1500s. Ethiopian Orthodox and Portuguese Roman Catholics offered competing interpretations of Act 10, for instance. Their interpretations exposed major theological differences that had implications for living the Christian life and for the boundaries of the respective Christian identity of each communion. For Catholic reformers, Jewish dietary laws were abolished in Acts 10 when Peter was instructed in his dream "to slay and eat," deeming all meats as clean. The abolition of dietary laws paralleled the instruction to enter the "unclean" house of the gentile, Cornelius, and baptize Cornelius and his household, registering that Jesus's message of

---
[13] Kelly, 1253.
[14] Kelly, 1229.

salvation extends beyond the Jewish people. The Ethiopian interpretation of Acts 10 limited the mandate of the text only to the evangelization of Gentiles; dietary laws were not the topic of Acts 10, according to them; the reference to dietary laws was an analogy and not an ecclesial directive or ruling in the Ethiopian interpretation to the pericope.[15]

For Ethiopian Christians, dietary laws still had a role to play in Christianity because they continued to be practiced by Jesus and the first Christians. At the council presented in Acts 15, dietary laws were retained for Jewish Christians and scaled down for Gentiles but not abolished. Consequently, the Ethiopian interpretation of Acts 10 and the dietary laws in Scripture followed the council in Acts 10 in which dietary laws were an option in the Christian faith and not abolished; by being optional, they were not essential to salvation, according to the Ethiopian Christians. Therefore, different Christian communions possessed the right to choose whether to include dietary laws as a feature of their Christian witness. European Christianity was not universal nor the norm.[16]

Similarly, in the Roman Catholic–Ethiopian Orthodox debate about initiatory practices such as circumcision, each tradition likewise followed its respective logic regarding the law. According to the Roman Catholic reading of Paul, circumcision as required for Jews ceased to be mandatory for Christian males because it was nonessential to salvation and deemed unadvisable because of its association with Judaism and Islam. The absence of circumcision served as a Christian marker for Portuguese Catholics. In the Ethiopian Orthodox reading of Paul, circumcision also ceased to be essential for salvation but local customs could continue circumcision as a form of contextualization. As in regards to dietary laws, the Ethiopian viewed themselves as being consistent with the practice of the first Christians. Again, in the spirit of the council recorded in Acts 15, according to Ethiopian Christians, circumcision was an option in the Christian faith and neither obligatory nor abolished; different Christian communions possessed the right to select it in accordance with local customs. Similarly, the observance of Saturday and Sunday as Sabbath days was practiced in Ethiopian Christianity because the early church practiced both, according to the Ethiopian scholars. Since Sabbath-keeping

---

[15] Andreu Martinez D'Alos-Moner, "Paul and the Other: The Portuguese Debate on the Circumcision of the Ethiopian," in *Ethiopia and the Missions: Historical and Anthropological Insights*, edited by V. *Boll* et al. (Munster: LIT Verlag, 1984), 32, 34–37.

[16] D'Alos-Moner, 32, 34–37.

encompasses both days, Ethiopians affirmed that Christian communions possessed the right to observe both Sabbaths. The two topics shaped Reformation debates.[17]

Portuguese Roman Catholics vehemently critiqued and denounced these Ethiopian Orthodox practices as Judaic and Islamic. These practices showed that Ethiopian Christianity was tainted by Judaism, and possibly, Islam or worse heterodox and in need of reformation along Catholic standards. The differences in how Acts 10 and 15 were interpreted according to an Ethiopian Orthodox or Roman Catholic perspective set markers for the respective Christian identify of each communion such as the practice or non-practice of dietary laws and of circumcision. Polemically, these differences in Christian identities either supplied ecclesial space or erased ecclesial space for Jewish and Muslim converts and their descendants, the New Christians, regarding dietary laws and circumcision. For Roman Catholics, eating pork and the non-circumcision of males were indicators of the authenticity of the conversion of Jewish and Muslim families. If the Ethiopian Orthodox reading of Acts 10 and 15 were permitted as optional, New Christians could openly follow key practices of Judaism or Islam and "pretend" to be Christian without engaging what they ruled as abominable practices such as eating pork. To Roman Catholics, the Ethiopian Orthodox reading of Acts 10 and 15 undermined their apparatus of distinguishing true converts from false ones. As noted earlier, it erased these particular Roman Catholics boundaries that distinguished Christians from Jews and Muslims. For Roman Catholics, the Ethiopian Orthodox reading of Acts 10 and 15 was dangerous, subversive, and, as stated above, heterodox.[18]

Ethiopian Christianity fell, then, along the shifting fault-lines of the Reformation between Catholics on one hand and Jews and Muslims on the other. Ethiopian Orthodox and Roman Catholics differed in the use of circumcision and dietary laws as boundaries between Christians and non-Christian monotheists. As noted above, Ethiopian Orthodox, based on their reading of Acts 10 and 15, were willing to adopt these as Christian practices, albeit they held that these are nonessential for salvation, while

---

[17] D'Alos-Moner, 34–37; Afework Hailu, *Jewish Cultural Elements in the Ethiopian Orthodox Tawahedo Church* (Piscataway, NJ: Gorgias Press, 2019); Leonardo Cohen, *The Missionary Strategies of the Jesuits in Ethiopia, 1555–1632* (Wiesbaden: Harrassowitz Verlag, 2009); Verena Krebs, *Medieval Ethiopian Kingship, Craft, and Diplomacy with Latin Europe* (Cham, Switzerland: Palgrave Macmillan, 2021).

[18] D'Alos-Moner, 34–37; Krebs.

Catholics refused to tolerate these practices, deeming them as religious markers of Judaism, Islam, and heterodox Christianity.

The Ethiopian interpretation of these biblical texts, then, played a role in key theological debates of the Reformation. In the Catholic polemic against Judaism and Islam as well as the New Christians, Catholics read Paul as rejecting the law, specifically circumcision, Sabbath-keeping, and dietary codes; to them, Paul recognized a break with Judaism within Christianity. Therefore, according to Catholicism, Christianity broke with Judaism, Christians were to be uncircumcised, permitted to work on Saturday, and free to eat pork. The Ethiopian interpretation of Paul read Paul as calling for the fulfilling the law. While this reading saw the practice of the "law" as nonessential to salvation, it saw the first Christians as observant Jews; Ethiopian Christians recognized themselves as following the New Testament and the first Christians.[19]

Scholars such as Luis Filipe F.R. Thomaz and Francisco Bethencourt have proposed that for some Catholic reformers Ethiopian Christianity offered a way to overcome an important component of the Catholic-Protestant divide prior to the Colloquy of Regensburg in 1541. Thomaz argued that for some Catholic reformers, Ethiopian Christianity could be a third way as an ancient Church, serving as a potential way to bridge the Catholic-Protestant division.[20] Instead of a third way, Bethencourt argues that Ethiopian Christianity could be a bridge between Protestant and Catholic. Based on the Saga Za Ab's interpretation of the Ethiopian Christianity, it could be "a source of inspiration for tolerance concerning different rituals and manners of being Christian."[21] This tolerant posture could replot divided European Christianity from being toxically polemical to an "irenic vision of the universal Christian church in which all tendencies coexist," in which ecclesial space exists for differences in Christian practices and theologies to coexist amicably.[22] In Saga Za Ab words: "Treat

---

[19] D'Alos-Moner, 34–37; Gretchen Starr-LeBeau, *In the Shadow of the Virgin: Inquisitors, Friars, and Conversos in Guadelupe, Spain* (Princeton, NJ: Princeton University Press, 2003); Lee Palmer Wandel, *The Reformation: Towards A New History* (New York, NY: Cambridge University Press, 2011), 187–188.

[20] Luis Filipe F.R. Thomaz, "Damião de Góis e o cristianismo oriental," in Damião de Góis na Europa do Renascimento, 779–816; cited in Francisco Bethencourt, "Early Modern Cosmopolitanism and Imperialism" in Cosmopolitanism in the Portuguese-Speaking World, edited by Francisco Bethencourt (Brill, 2017), 89, 90.

[21] Bethencourt, 89, 90.

[22] Bethencourt, 90.

them [the Ethiopians] with kindness and charity and suffer them to live and converse with other Christians, for we are all baptized with the same baptism and subscribe unanimously to the same belief." According to Bethencourt, then, the ecclesial aim of Saga Za Ab's "text was to intervene at a particular period when several members of the Catholic Church were engaged in dialogue with exponents of the Protestantism, trying to build bridges and effect a reconciliation, before the failure of the Colloquy of Regensburg in 1541."[23]

Ethiopian Orthodox Christians, then, entered firmly into the Reformation context. The Ethiopian interpretation of the Bible framed the law as "boundary markers" rather than as entries to or means of salvation. During the sixteenth century, Roman Catholics differentiated themselves against New Christians, casting them as equivalents to first-century Judaizers and imposters. Protestants casted the Roman Catholics as equivalents of first-century Judaizers who promoted work righteousness salvation rather justification by faith alone. Catholics casted Protestants as schismatics, disengaging themselves from the one true church, the mother church. Ethiopian Christianity entered this ecclesially contested space of European Reformation.[24]

Ethiopian Christianity in the Reformation Archive

According to Michel Foucault, the archive was a "system of statements" and the law that governs "what can be said."[25] In the Reformation archive, Ethiopian Christian texts were a subject and set of texts. There was the European project of defining, explaining, and interpreting difference between European Catholic, European Protestant, and Ethiopian Orthodox Christians; there was the Ethiopian project of engaging difference with Christianity in Europe. It resulted in the negotiation of Ethiopian Christianity within Catholic knowledge and identities as well as the reappropriation of Ethiopian Christianity within Protestant knowledge and identities. Since the Reformation Archive provided space for the Ethiopian Christian texts, specifically, how did it govern what Ethiopians and

---

[23] Saga Za Ab; See Giacomo Baratti, *The Late Travels into the Remote Countries of the Abissines, or of Ethiopia...Confirmation ... de Goes and Jos. Scaliger* (Benjamin Billingsley, 1670), 180.
[24] D'Alos-Moner; Starr-LeBeau; Lee Palmer Wandel.
[25] Michel Foucault, *Archaeology of Knowledge* (London: Routledge, 1972), 128–129.

Europeans said about Ethiopian Christianity as a tradition? Did Ethiopian texts and interpretations of these texts open space within Reformation for other voices? Did the scholarship of Ethiopian Christians in Europe particulate within the European community of interpreters of Christianity? How did Ethiopian and European interpreters serve as sources for the early modern invention of Ethiopia and Europe?

Three African migrations to Europe marked the Reformation archive. The voluntary migration of a limited population of Ethiopians to Europe often from Ethiopia, Cairo, Jerusalem, and Cyprus contrasted with the forced migration of a vastly larger population of Africans from the Africa's Atlantic coast into slavery in Europe, especially Portugal, Spain, and the Italian peninsula. Though, a small voluntary migration of Africans from the African Atlantic coast did occur, especially from the Kongo. From all three migrations, an estimated 100,000 or more Africans lived in Europe, including England, during the Reformation.[26]

The "arrival" of the ancient Ethiopic Bible in Europe was preceded, accompanied, and followed by Ethiopian monks and pilgrims from Ethiopia and the Ethiopian diaspora who voluntarily migrated to Europe.[27] Rather than being solely deemed as outsiders, Ethiopian Christians in Europe functioned as peers to their European counterparts. They were Ethiopian Orthodox bishops, priests, monks, editors, translators, and teachers; specifically, they were teachers of European students and these pupils were Catholic as well as Protestant clergy. Without being under the auspices of European colonial or the transatlantic slave trade, they and the Ethiopic Bible introduce another narrative into the emerging modern world, traversing the eastern Mediterranean, and signally the Christian world beyond Europe.

Countering the early modern European translation circuit of ancient to vernacular languages initiated, the Ethiopic Bible and other Ethiopian Christian texts, for instance, navigated the trajectory of ancient to ancient language: Ge'ez to Latin. These texts migrated from being housed in an ecclesially bound and classical language to being lodged in the pan-European and global elite language of Latin as the language of the

---

[26] David D. Daniels, "Will African Christians Become a Subject in Reformation Studies?" in *Subject to None, Servant of All: Essays in Christian Scholarship in Honor of Kurt Karl Hendel*, edited by Peter Vethanayagamony and Kenneth Sawyer (Lutheran University Press, 2016), 104.

[27] Salvadore; Salvadore and DiLorenzi; Kennerley.

Republic of Letters. These Ge'ez to Latin translated Ethiopian Christian texts functioned differently from Europeans texts in the German, Dutch, or English, for instance. German, English, or Dutch translations of Latin texts made Latin Christian texts national and not pan-European nor global; these translations participated in the forming of specific vernacular languages and literatures. In addition to creating vernacular literatures, these vernacular texts played a key role in constructing national identities and nation-building of the German states, the Netherlands, and Britain during the Reformation. While the English, Dutch, German, and other vernacular Christian texts were bound by linguistic boundaries and accessible to national or ethnic readerships, particular Latin translated Ethiopian Christian texts became accessible to a pan-European readership, albeit an elite readership literate in Latin.[28]

Within the Reformation archive, the Ethiopian narrative of its Christian origins found a place. Grounding its origins in Acts 8, Ethiopian Christianity emerged decades prior to the Church in Europe, according to this historical account.[29] This narrative was chronicled in ancient texts as well as sketched in the writings of Martin Luther and other Protestant reformers.[30] To the Christian origins story, Ethiopians added the story of the Ethiopian queen of Sheba traveling to Israel, meeting Solomon, and bearing him a son. The queen and her son would return to Sheba or Ethiopia, introducing Judaism to the kingdom. In both these narratives, the Ethiopians supplied the names of the central characters in these two

---

[28] On the Ge'ez Bible, see Bruce Metzger, *The Bible in Translation: Ancient and English Versions* (Grand Rapids, MI: Baker Academic, 2001), 44–46; Adrian Hastings, *The Construction of Nationhood: Ethnicity, Religion, and Nationalism* (Cambridge: Cambridge University Press, 1997), 58; Christopher Hill, *The English Bible and the Seventeenth-Century Revolution* (Harmondsworth: Penguin, 1993); translations also went from Latin to Ge'ez.

[29] Kelly; for Ethiopian attendance at the Day of Pentecost, see John Chrysostom, *Homily on Pentecost*; for the evangelization of Ethiopia by the Apostle Matthew, see Rufinus, *Church History*, 18; both cited in Keong-Sang An, *An Ethiopian Reading of the Bible: Biblical Interpretation of the Ethiopian Orthodox Tewahido Church* (Cambridge, UK: Lutterworth Press, 2016), 87.

[30] David Daniels, "Luther and Ethiopian Christianity" in *Reformation in the Context of World Christianity: Theological, Political and Social Interactions Between Africa, Asia, the Americas, and Europe* (Wiesbaden: Harrassowitz Verlag, 2019); Stanislau Palau, *Das Andere Christentum: Zur transkonfessionellen Verflechtungsgeschichte von äthiopischer Orthodoxie unde europäischem Protestantismus* [The Other Christianity: Towards an Entangled Transconfessional History of Ethiopian Orthodoxy and European Protestantism] (Gottingen, Germany: Vandenhock & Ruprecht, 2020); McNutt.

chronicles: Makeda as the queen; Menelik I as the son; Indich as the Ethiopian captain; and Judith or Lacasa as the queen in Acts 8 (Kandake or Candace for the word queen). The Ethiopian naming of these "unnamed" biblical figures found its way into the Reformation archive.[31]

Within the Reformation archive, Martin Luther was part of the debates on Ethiopian Christianity. Luther recognized the Ethiopian Church as an ancient Church. Ethiopian Christianity, according to Luther, possessed apostolic practices which were absent in the Catholic Church; Protestants would "adopt" these practices prior to becoming aware of their practice by Ethiopian Christians: communion in both kinds, vernacular Scripture, and married clergy. Absent, meanwhile, within the Church in Ethiopia were Catholic practices then under critique by various Protestant reformers: the primacy of the Bishop of Rome, indulgences, purgatory, and marriage as a sacrament.[32]

By 1534, Luther welcomed to Wittenberg a new voice into his ecumenical dialogue: Michael the Deacon, an Ethiopian cleric. Recalling his dialogue with Michael, Luther stated: "We have also learned from him, that the rite which we observe in the use of administration of the Lord's Supper and the Mass, agrees with the Eastern Church." Luther expressed his approval of the Church of Ethiopia along with his embrace of Deacon Michael in a letter dated July 4, 1534: "For this reason we ask that good people would demonstrate Christian love also to this [Ethiopian] visitor." According to Luther, Michael responded positively to his articles of the Christian faith, proclaiming: "This is a good creed, that is, faith." In quoting the Ethiopian cleric, Michael the Deacon, Luther stated that Michael persuaded him on some theological matters.[33]

According to the twentieth-century scholar, Tom Hardt, Luther extended full communion to Deacon Michael and the Ethiopian Church,

---

[31] Names from Saga Za Ab in *The manners, lauues, and customes of all nations collected out of the best vvriters by Ioannes Boemus ...; with many other things of the same argument, gathered out of the historie of Nicholas Damascen; the like also out of the history of America, or Brasill, written by Iohn Lerius; the faith, religion and manners of the Aethiopians, and the deploration of the people of Lappia, compiled by Damianus à Goes; with a short discourse of the Aethiopians, taken out of Ioseph Scaliger his seuenth booke de emendatione temporum; written in Latin, and now newly translated into English,* by Ed. Aston (London: G. Eld, 1611), 557, 560. Accessed.

[32] David Daniels III and Lawrence Anglin. "Luther and the Ethiopian Deacon." *Lutheran Quarterly* 32 (2018): 428–434; *Luthers Werke: Kritische Gesamtausgabe: Briefwechsel*, 18 vols. (Weimer: H. Bohlau, 1930–1985) 7:85–86.

[33] Martin Luther, Table-Talk, November 17, 1538 [WA, TR 4:152–153, no. 4126].

an invitation that Luther notably withheld from the Bohemian Brethren (Hussites) and Reformed Churches connected to Huldrych Zwingli. Luther acknowledged theological "equivalency" with Ethiopian Christianity, and in his 1534 dialogue with Michael, Luther finally had the opportunity to find out whether his attractive theological portrait of Ethiopian Christianity was historically credible. Although Hardt's interpretation of Luther extending full communion to the Ethiopian Church appears not to be widely known among scholars today, however, if he were correct, this would be a major ecumenical development in the Protestant Reformation.[34]

As part of the Reformation archive, Ethiopians and Europeans cited Ethiopian texts as reliable Christian sources. In some instances, Europeans preferred the Ethiopian position over European ones. The citing of Ethiopian sources, positions, and perspectives in texts authored by Europeans shaped these European texts as well as created new meanings, revealed cross-cultural affinities, and established affiliations between Ethiopian and European Christianity. Citations, according to Daniel Hack, possess the capacity to "shape texts, create meanings, reveal affinities, and establish affiliations." Rather than a hierarchical "cultural traffic" or exchange wherein European Christian knowledge was superior to Ethiopian Christian knowledge, the act of citing Ethiopian Christian sources as viable and, in some instances preferred over European sources, demonstrated the cultural exchange as symmetrical. During the Reformation, Ethiopian Christian source possessed equal status in various cases and vaulted status in others. Published Ethiopian-authored texts circulating at the time included 1509 Letter of Elleni [Helena], grandmother of the emperor; a 1521 Letter and three 1524 Letters of Emperor Lebne-Dengel [David]; Tasfa Seyon's 1548 Preface to the Ethiopic New Testament; Saga Zabo's Confession; and the Confession of Galawdewos. When Europeans devalued Ethiopian sources, it was primarily about European confessional warfare than about Ethiopian Christianity per se.[35]

Within the Reformation archive of the sixteenth century, Ethiopian Christian sources or persons were cited by Erasmus, Martin Luther, Philip Melanchthon, Martin Bucer, Damiao Gois, and others. In his

---

[34] Hardt, Tom G. A. "The Confessional Principle: Church Fellowship in the Ancient and in the Lutheran Church," *Logia: A Journal of Lutheran Theology*, Vol. 8, No. 2 (1999): 27.

[35] Daniel Hack, *Reaping Something New: African American Transformations of Victorian Literature* (Princeton: Princeton University Press, 2016), 9, 22.

correspondence to Gois, Erasmus referred to a book "that tells of the obedience displayed by the king of Ethiopia to the pope." Luther and Melanchthon quoted Michael the Deacon whom they dialogued with in Wittenberg. Damiao Gois cited Ethiopian sources and published the treatise of Saga Za ab.[36]

Here the Ethiopian Orthodox tradition represented a different pillar of Christianity, a pillar beyond the control of Rome and Roman Catholicism, offering a counterpoint to the Church in Europe. For Protestant reformers like Luther, the interpretation of Matthew 16:13 (*upon this rock*) as the basis of the primacy of the bishop of Rome was a misinterpretation of Scripture. Also, the designation of the successor to Peter as the ecclesial basis of the unity of the church was historically inaccurate. Communion with the Church of Rome was not the basis of unity for the ancient church. In Luther's reconstruction of the history of the ancient church, there were three original co-equal patriarchates: Ethiopia, Antioch, and Rome. Although Luther conferred on Ethiopia a higher status within the ancient church than it claimed for itself, the Ethiopian interpretation of Scripture did not argue for the primacy of the Roman pontiff as the successor to Peter; communion with the Church of Rome was not essential for the authenticity of every Christian communion; ancient Christian authors recognized the Ethiopian Church as authentic or canonical. Ethiopian Orthodox and some European Protestants read this history similarly in a non-Catholic way. Ethiopian Christianity and Christians occupied a place in the Reformation.[37]

---

[36] "Letter 2914 Erasmus to Gois" in Desiderius Erasmus, *The Correspondence of Erasmus Letters 2803 to 2939*, translated by Clarence H. Miller with Charles Fantazzi (Toronto, Ontario: University of Toronto Press, 2020), 250; Daniels and Anglin; [Damiao de Gois] Damianus a Goes, "The Faith, Religion, and Manners of the Aethiopians..." (1540), translated by Edward Aston, in *Manners, Lawes and Customes of all Nations* ... (London: George Eld printer, 1611). 502–589.

[37] David D. Daniels, "Luther and Ethiopian Christianity" in *Reformation in the Context of World Christianity: Theological, political and social interactions between Africa, Asia, the Americas and Europe*, edited by Ludwig Frieder et al. (Wiesbaden: Harrassowitz Verlag, 2019).

Conclusion

In this chapter, I sought to prove that Ethiopian Christians and Christian texts played a meaningful role in the Reformation. As stated above, it ranked as the second Bible ever printed in a Semitic language after Hebrew and the first text of an African language ever printed or translated in Europe. The Reformation shaped the Ethiopian production and, later, European "production" of the Ethiopian Christian texts as printed books, framing the editing, functioning, translating, and interpreting of these texts. These texts played a myriad of roles during the Reformation. They were an ancient source, an ancient vernacular translation, a key text in comparative Biblical studies, a potentially broader canon, and new books as a printed text. Ethiopians and Europeans forged partnerships in Europe around these texts, fostering ecumenical and intercultural exchanges.

Countering the Latin-to-vernacular trajectory of translation, the Ethiopian Christian texts were printed in Ge'ez and translated into Latin, becoming accessible to a pan-European readership. Intersecting with the humanist, Reformation, and anti-colonial archive, Ethiopian-authored theological essays participated in the debates of the Reformation and introduced or, at times, re-introduced narratives of Ethiopia's Christian origins. Leading European Christians heard, respected, and learned from Ethiopian Christians.

Ethiopian Christianity possibly pointed to a third way for the Church in Europe, a pathway beyond the Catholic-Protestant divide with its posture of tolerance and, in Bethencourt's words, an "irenic vision of the universal Christian church," cultivating amicable co-existence amidst Christian difference. As the Ethiopian Christian texts were printed, translated, circulated, cited, and debated, they played a significant role in the life of the "divided" Church in Europe during the era of the Reformation.[38]

In decolonizing the Reformation narrative, this chapter demonstrated that Ethiopian Christianity was a topic of the Reformation, Ethiopian Christians were interlocutors of Catholic and Protestant reformers, and the Ethiopian-European exchange was an alternative to the European colonizing model of engaging the Global South. The main argument is that an Ethiopian-European collaborative model did emerge within the Reformation which challenged the colonial model of European dominance and Global South subordination. The collaborative model advanced Ethiopian-European Christian collegiality. Ethiopian Christianity became a source of Christian knowledge during the Reformation.

---

[38] Bethencourt, 90; see footnote 20.

CHAPTER 9

Race, Theology, and the Church: A Transatlantic Conversation, and a Model for a Church in Productive Tension

R. Ward Holder and Cynthia Holder Rich

What is racism, and how does it affect the church? Is racism a subversive power that undercuts all efforts to realize the spotless bride of Christ that earlier generations of Christians considered to be possible? Is racism a factor which can never be escaped, but for which systems of amelioration can be devised? Is racism the wrong consideration to bring to the consideration of ecclesiology—should theorists instead be considering colonialism,

R. W. Holder (✉)
Saint Anselm College in Manchester, Manchester, NH, USA
e-mail: WHolder@Anselm.Edu

C. H. Rich
Faculty of Theology of Tumaini University Makumira, Arusha, Tanzania

Trinity Lutheran Seminary at Capital University, Columbus, OH, USA

© The Author(s), under exclusive license to Springer Nature Switzerland AG 2023
R. C. Barreto, V. Latinovic (eds.), *Decolonial Horizons*, Pathways for Ecumenical and Interreligious Dialogue,
https://doi.org/10.1007/978-3-031-44839-3_9

or class/caste,[1] or colorism, or incarnational possibilities that seek to rise above the question of race?[2] All of these questions (and many more) were the fuel that drove the project that took on the joint educational enterprise that brought three researchers, thirty-eight students, and two institutions on two different continents together in the spring of 2021.[3]

Context frames the reality humans experience and provides crucial elements of its meaning. The context of 2020–2021 was significant in this investigation. On February 23, 2020, Ahmaud Arbery was murdered in Brunswick, Georgia. Most people knew nothing about this case until the *New York Times* made a video that went viral available on May 7.[4] This was because the district attorney had cleared Travis McMichaels, who had shot Arbery, and his father Gregory McMichaels who accompanied him. Ahmaud Arbery was a young black man who was out jogging. The McMichaels followed him in their pickup truck and murdered him. The reason they gave was that they believed he was stealing, though he had neither a weapon nor possessed any material. District Attorney Jackie Johnson refused to consider the case, possibly because Gregory McMichaels had worked as an investigator for her office.[5] On March 14, 2020, police

---

[1] Cf Isabel Wilkerson, *Caste: The Origins of our Discontents* (New York: Random House, 2020).

[2] The authors note that they are pursuing one approach out of a variety of possibilities. The literature from possible approaches is vast and growing. See, among others, Ada Maria Isasi-Diaz, *En La Lucha: Elaborating a Mujerista Theology* (Minneapolis: Fortress, 2004), J. Kameron Carter, *Race: A Theological Account* (New York: Oxford, 2008); Ada María Isasi-Díaz and Eduardo Mendieta, eds., *Decolonizing Epistemologies: Latina/o Theology and Philosophy* (New York: Fordham University Press, 2012); Roberto Goizueta, *Caminemos Con Jesus: Toward a Hispanic/Latino Theology of Accompaniment* (Maryknoll: Orbis, 2013); Orlando Espin, *The Faith of the People* (Maryknoll: Orbis, 1997, 2013), Eddie S. Glaude, Jr., *An Uncommon Faith: A Pragmatic Approach to the Study of African American Religion* (University of Georgia Press, 2018); Vincent W. Lloyd and Andrew Prevot, eds., *Anti-Blackness and Christian Ethics* (Maryknoll: Orbis Books, 2017); and Raimundo Barreto and Roberto Sirvent, *Decolonial Christianities: Latinx and Latin American Perspectives* (Palgrave, 2019).

[3] See Laura Lemire, "Course Intertwines Race and Theology," May 6, 2021. https://www.anselm.edu/news/course-intertwines-race-and-theology, accessed 23 January 2023.

[4] "Ahmaud Arbery's Final Minutes: What Videos and 911 Calls Show." https://www.nytimes.com/video/us/100000007142853/ahmaud-arbery-video-911-georgia.html?searchResultPosition=2, accessed 17 January 2023.

[5] Martin Savidge and Angela Barajas, "Conviction of Ahmaud Arbery's Killers Puts New Focus on First Prosecutor." CNN, December 5, 2021. https://www.cnn.com/2021/12/05/us/jackie-johnson-brunswick-da-charges-arbery/index.html, accessed 23 January 2023.

in Louisville, Kentucky, executed a no-knock warrant on the home of Breonna Taylor, a young black emergency medical technician, and when her companion fired at persons he believed to be burglars, the police killed Taylor and shot the companion. On May 25 of that same year, a black man in Minneapolis, George Floyd, would be videoed begging to breathe while police officer Derek Chauvin murdered him, with a knee on his neck for eight minutes and forty-four seconds. Again, the video went viral, bringing his agonizingly slow murder into homes across the nation.

These notorious killings were not, of course, the only police killings of Black or Brown or Asian people in the spring of 2020. The *Washington Post* keeps a database, and between February 23 and May 25, police in America shot and killed 102 Black, Hispanic, and Asian people.[6] Ironically, that database does not contain either Ahmaud Arbery, who was murdered by citizens who occasionally worked for the police, or George Floyd, as it only counts fatal shootings. But in those three months, over 100 Black, Hispanic, and Asian men and women were killed by police in the US. In those 92 days, over one person a day was killed by police in the nation. These tragic atrocities, and many more, brought about the conversations that resulted in the development of a joint learning experience on race and theology. Far too frequently, these efforts do not engage serious dialogue between the privileged and the colonized.

We designed a course in New Hampshire, which would be a special reading group for interested students in Tanzania. Because of the strictness of the curriculum mandated by the government in Tanzanian universities, where all the courses are prescribed, adding a course in Tanzania was unworkable. So, for the New Hampshire students, this was a course, with credits and a grade. For the Tanzanian students, it was a reading group, without credit. That was not the only difference between the two populations. There were 18 Saint Anselm College students. They averaged 21 years of age. They were all undergraduates. Most identified as White. All were taking the class to fulfill some sort of either distribution or theology requirement. The 12 Tumaini Makumira University students averaged 39.5 years of age. Most were undergraduate Theology majors, and a few were Masters and Ph.D. candidates in Theology. All students in Tanzania were Protestant, and the majority of them were Lutheran; a

---

[6] Washington Post database, Fields 5061–5337, only counting B, H, and A identified people. https://www.washingtonpost.com/graphics/investigations/police-shootings-database/, accessed 12 May 2022.

majority of Saint Anselm students were Roman Catholic. Additionally, all Saint Anselm students spoke English as their native language; English is at least the third language for all Tumaini Makumira University students.

We planned the experience around two exciting, though at times (possibly terrifying) factors. First, through Zoom, both groups of students would meet some of the figures whose works we were reading. Five African and African American scholars of international repute agreed to address the classes, for about 75–90 minutes each. These were J. Kameron Carter from Indiana University, Angela Sims from Colgate Rochester Crozer Divinity School, Elieshi Mungure from the Lutheran World Federation where she serves as the secretary for Africa, Emmanuel Katongole from Notre Dame University, and M. Shawn Copeland from Boston College.

The second new issue was having and facilitating conversations between students at Tumaini Makumira University and Saint Anselm College. Perhaps in part because of these differences, misunderstanding between students proved significant. Many North American students turned their cameras off, and many did not speak in joint sessions. Both of these actions had become normalized in many online classrooms in North America by term 3 of the pandemic. However, participating African students speculated that these were potential signs that racism was something these silent, invisible students enjoyed—or, at least was not of concern to these students. Additionally, evidence on the screen that all North American students had their own computers and access to reliable Wi-Fi was noted and commented on by African students.

North American students wondered at the use of the chat function in Zoom by professors—used to bridge understanding barriers due to difficulties in comprehending English spoken at a normal pace with a variety of accents. Some African American guest lecturers' pace and accents proved particularly problematic for African students, as British English is spoken and learned in many regions of Africa, and some guest lecturers' accents were impacted by southern US accents and phrasing.

In the research phase of the project, we engaged in a process of ethnographic study to determine some of the educational outcomes produced by what for all involved was a unique experience.[7] In this project, some of our basic pedagogical challenges were recognized and made explicit to the participants. When teaching about race, racism, and colonialism, the racial,

---

[7] We enlisted another experienced ethnographic researcher, Aubrey Scheopner-Torres, Professor of Education at Saint Anselm College, to assist with our work.

cultural, and linguistic background of those teaching matters. Both participating lecturers were White native English-speakers, and one was in mission service. Both are active in communions that took primary roles in the missionary enterprise of the nineteenth to twentieth centuries, churches that continue to engage in global mission efforts, in whose mission efforts colonial strategies can even today be identified. Thus, both lecturers operated from an identity of privilege and a system from which we continue to benefit. Naming this upfront was an important pedagogical strategy, and we found visiting and revisiting what it meant that we are White essential.

In early class sessions, African students shared that because of their past experiences with racism from White Christians, including from some representatives of mission societies and churches that had offered them scholarship to come to university, they were both startled and interested in the invitation from a White lecturer to talk about race and racism. In the North American course, the ability of the lecturer as a White Christian to name from personal experience the difficulty and discomfort—often rising to an extraordinary level that might even evoke shame—of the conversations needed to discuss course materials about the impact of racism on Christianity was important. Our experiences have been echoed in research, which has found that those who teach anti-racist pedagogies from a place of privilege need to experience being unsettled or "acknowledge settler colonialism and recognize their own colonial blinders to resist decolonization", admit the limitations of their own understandings, and even "unlearn" by accepting that race/gender/class intersectional perspectives for explaining social inequalities are "insufficient for comprehending the oppression and resistance of people of color."[8]

The response from both groups of students to the chance to hear and speak to figures whose works they were reading was overwhelmingly positive. One of the professors remarked that he had thought the centerpiece of the course was the chance to consider the texts and ideas—but learned that the students thought it was the chance to dialogue with the thinkers and their fellow students in another country. While the experience was positive, it was rarely easy. The students read M. Shawn Copeland's "White Supremacy and Anti-Black Logics in the Making of U.S. Catholicism."[9]

---

[8] Cynthia Fabrizio Pelak. "Teaching and Learning about Settler-colonial Racism: A Case for "Unsettling" Minoritizing and Multicultural Perspectives," *Sociology of Race and Ethnicity* 5 (2019): 294–304.

[9] M. Shawn Copeland, "White Supremacy and Anti-Black Logics in the Making of U.S. Catholicism," in *Anti-Blackness and Christian Ethics*, edited by Vincent W. Lloyd and Andrew Prevot (Maryknoll: Orbis, 2017), 48–54.

The clarity of Copeland's argument, and the theological anthropology that had argued that Black people were less human than their White masters, provided a stark reminder that all of the people who committed sins against Black people before, during, and after the US Civil War were not people we can assign to the "monster" category and then dismiss, but people who participated actively in the church and saw themselves as upstanding members of the Roman Catholic Church in the United States. The appropriately professional detachment of a scholar making a carefully researched argument fell away, however, when students were faced with this reality. African students were infuriated, and immediately elided the historical distance between the antebellum South and their own lives. "They believed we were not fully human? Do they still believe we are not fully human?!?"

Responses in the New Hampshire classroom were different, but no less jolting. Many of the Catholic students had been raised with a sense that the church was the spotless bride of Christ. Reading Copeland and Shannen Dee Williams' "'You Could Do the Irish Jig, But Anything African was Taboo': Black Nuns, Contested Memories, and the 20th Century Struggle to Desegregate U.S. Catholic Religious Life," demonstrated to them that the historical record did not accord with their idealism.[10] Some reported being "heartbroken," "stung," and "in pain" after considering these texts and the responses of their African counterparts. That was in stark contrast to how Catholic students had viewed texts such as Carolyn Renée Dupont's *Mississippi Praying: Southern White Evangelicals and the Civil Rights Movement, 1945–1975*.[11] The analyses of Catholic practices removed the psychic defenses of defining the problem either as regional—not a New England problem, or as denominational—not a Catholic problem since it was a problem that happened among Evangelicals in the South. Instead, these investigations by Black Catholic theologians destroyed inherent psychological defensive strategies and caused real emotional and mental turmoil.

While the course and readings were not set up to investigate ecclesiological issues specifically, the material did inevitably cause a series of

---

[10] Shannen Dee Williams, "'You Could Do the Irish Jig, But Anything African was Taboo': Black Nuns, Contested Memories, and the 20th Century Struggle to Desegregate U.S. Catholic Religious Life" *Journal of African American History*, (2017): 125–156.

[11] Carolyn Renée Dupont, *Mississippi Praying: Southern White Evangelicals and the Civil Rights Movement, 1945–1975* (New York: New York University Press, 2015).

conversations about ecclesiologies for all students. These topics could be broadly grouped into three topics. First, race and approaches and understandings of race have influenced the church's self-understanding—whether Lutheran or Roman Catholic. Second, racism, or its first cousin colonialism—these have exerted a historically demonstrable effect on the actions of White priests, religious, ministers, superintendents, missionaries, and bishops; this has caused an extraordinarily corrosive consequence on present day communities of faith, and their sense of whether race should even be problematized. Additionally, the actions of White religious leaders have had significant and ongoing impacts on the ministry, belief systems, and understandings of God and the church among Black religious leaders and members of Christian faith communities. Finally, we found that race and racial considerations are and will be a necessary component in ongoing ecclesiological conversations to come.

Lutheran and Catholic Senses of the Church

Whether Lutheran or Catholic, missionary or established church, race has influenced any sense of the church and its mission. Shannen Dee Williams' work established that for White Catholics, whether secular or religious, treatment of Black women seeking to take religious vocations was starkly racist, including shouts of the N-word at the ceremony of first profession.[12] Williams pointed out that of the eight known African American women to join White orders between 1900 and 1942, seven passed for White.[13] These historical facts, as well as work by Copeland and Bryan N. Massingale, were forceful for Catholic students.[14] They wrote that they saw that racial prejudice had been an important force in Catholic orders and churches, and that writers like Jay P. Dolan were seeking to whitewash a racist history.[15] A Catholic student wrote, "Over the past 500 years of

---

[12] Shannen Dee Williams, "'You Could Do the Irish Jig, But Anything African was Taboo': Black Nuns, Contested Memories, and the 20th Century Struggle to Desegregate U.S. Catholic Religious Life," 126. "At her first profession ceremony in 1964, for example, five of the sisters with whom Adams entered the order loudly yelled "Nigger" in unison and snickered as she walked down the back path of the motherhouse to join her cradle Catholic family that had come to celebrate the sacred occasion."

[13] Williams, Irish Jig, 130.

[14] Bryan N. Massingale, *Racial Justice and the Catholic Church* (Maryknoll: Orbis Books, 2010).

[15] SA-M-2, Response paper, 4.

history, the Church has played an intrinsic role in perpetuating racial injustice and catering to a white dominated congregation. It was primarily through the examples of leaders of the faith that continued to drive the Church away from racial justice and desegregation."[16] Another Catholic student, reflecting on a reading from Erin Rowe's *Black Saints in Early Modern Catholicism*, asked a series of rhetorical questions.[17] "For myself, I realized that I can only name a few black saints that I know of or have thought of developing a relationship with. On the other hand, I can name a multitude of white saints. This led me to ask myself hard questions like: Why have I never sought to develop a relationship with or devotion to a black saint? Why can I name so many white saints? How would I feel if growing up every saint I learned about did not have the same color skin as me?"[18]

Students in Tanzania shared thoughts on these issues as well. A student reflected on religious art he had viewed at a church building in Europe that depicted God as White and Satan as Black—and how these depictions impact understandings of God, and also of people.[19] Students noted the close ties between racism and colonialism[20] and explored the meaning of Whiteness (as the concept is described by Willie James Jennings), seeing it as strongly related to power. A student reported that missionaries and mission organizations have used Whiteness to achieve their mission goals, often using oppression of local leaders and congregations as a strategy. This history continues to operate today in international Christian relationships and ministries. Students also noted that powerful African tribes can exhibit some features of Whiteness in their relationships with less powerful tribes.[21] Students noted that these ways of using power either echoed or were learned from colonizers and missionaries, almost all of whom were White.[22]

---

[16] SA-M-2, Response paper, 4.

[17] Erin Rowe, *Black Saints in Early Modern Catholicism* (Cambridge: Cambridge University Press, 2020).

[18] SA-F-5, Response paper, 2.

[19] TUMA-M-1, Interview on May 11, 2021.

[20] TUMA-M-2, interview on May 22, 2021.

[21] Willie James Jennings, "Can White People be Saved? Reflections on the Relationship of Missions and Whiteness", in Love L. Secrest et al., eds., *Can "White" People be Saved? Triangulating Race, Theology, and Mission* (Downers Grove IL: IVP Academic, 2018).

[22] TUMA-F-3, Interview, May 11, 2021.

Corrosive Effects of Racism on the Church

All of the students surveyed and in class that had home churches reported that they grew up in and were nourished in parishes or congregations that were predominantly either White or Black. None reported significant integration in their communities of faith. One student noted, "The problem, then, is not that racism is not a theological concern; rather it is that the dominant Eurocentric theological narrative does not view racism as a concern. In fact, by excluding other viewpoints, it perpetuates racism. One need only to look at the Church's struggle to take a uniform position in the Black Lives Matter movement."[23] The students, after reading texts like Dupont's *Mississippi Praying*, and Martin Luther King Jr.'s *Letter from Birmingham Jail*,[24] had grasped the manner by which the lack of equity and diversity in their parishes was not simply a matter of parish demographics that could be shrugged off as representative of communities. Instead, they are part of a system that sought and seeks to draw a color line between the good purity of whiteness and the evil sinfulness of blackness.

This was recognized by every student in the research group at Saint Anselm College. One student noted that racism's effect on the church had led to "a theology, particularly Christianity and Catholicism kind of being white-washed and then weaponized to be used as a way to assert superiority over people who are different."[25] Another shared, "For me, I think something is definitely the idea of Jesus and Catholicism being very white-washed, especially in the United States. I think it can be easy, as we learned in class, to think of white Christianity as the only type of Christianity and the impact that race and racism has had on that idea and the people that it's effected in a harmful way."[26]

Race has not generally been addressed in theological education in Tanzania—or, indeed, across the African continent outside South Africa, whose racialized history rendered conversations about race distinctly different than those elsewhere. It took students in East Africa, then, some time to see race as it relates to theology and the church as a valid subject for study. Conversely, many courses at Tumaini University Makumira explore the impact of colonialism and what it means to live and minister in

---

[23] SA-F-7, Final examination.
[24] Martin Luther King, Jr., "Letter From Birmingham Jail", originally published April 16, 1963; in Martin Luther King, Jr., *Why We Can't Wait* (New York: Signet Books, 1963), 76–95.
[25] SA-M-8, Interview on May 7, 2021.
[26] SA-F-5, Interview on May 7, 2021.

post-colonial contexts. Bringing race and racism together with the pain wrought and damage done through the partnership between mission and colonial activity brought latent understandings about the relationship between Black and White Christians into the foreground, where it could be studied more intentionally. Most students had not considered race as an ecclesiological or theological issue prior to this learning experience. The African students were particularly impressed with the research of Emmanuel Katangole on the ongoing impact of brutal colonial strategies in communities in Congo.[27] Having African theologians address the class—both of whom greeted the students in Kiswahili—and having both speakers name the issue of race and racism in their own experiences in ministry, teaching, and research was very powerful for African student participants.

ECCLESIOLOGICAL INVESTIGATIONS THAT TAKE RACE SERIOUSLY

Race and racism represent necessary components of the present reality that must be considered in the any ecclesiology that consciously seeks to be meaningfully contextual. Emilie Townes wrote that churches need to think deeply and broadly about the "why" of discipleship and the "how" of mission in a chaotic world. "For in times of chaos, we often look for safety and comfort and assurance – or we think that is what are doing-rather than to step out as pilgrims on a journey that must be wrapped in the bold strokes of faith and perhaps not at all sure about where we will end up. But our faith and God's grace will hold us (even when our courage wanes) if we dare to tackle large issues, hard issues, arresting issues. For this, I argue, is the way of Jesus and the hope of salvation."[28] Townes recognizes that the effect of racism and racialized discourse creates a desire in the churches—all churches—for a flight toward security. But she argued that model was neither faithful nor trusting in God's grace. While the church could not know exactly where it was going because God's providence, while certain, is also opaque

---

[27] See Emmanuel Katangole, *The Sacrifice of Africa: A Political Theology for Africa* (Grand Rapids, MI: Eerdmans Publishing Company, 2011) and *Born from Lament: The Theology and Politics of Hope in Africa* (Grand Rapids, MI: Eerdmans Publishing Company, 2017).

[28] Emilie Townes, "Memory, Identity, and Hope: Reflections for American Baptist Ecclesiology in the 21st Century," *American Baptist Quarterly* 30 (2011): 186–200. (186)

behind this mortal veil, that trust reflects both the truth of faith and the recognition that salvation in Jesus Christ is not only an eschatological reality, but a living out of the kingdom in the present.

Jessica Wormley put it differently, noting that the present time presents a critical point for the church. She wrote, "We in the American church are at a critical point, poised between a crisis of relevancy and credibility on the one hand, and a weary broken world desperately in need of a prophetic voice and transformative acts of healing on the other."[29] Wormley identifies the vital nature of the present time in history, illustrating this with stories from her own family's efforts to live in a predominantly white Catholic parish, while maintaining a sense of their own Catholicism. This was not easy, as she relates accounts of bluntly racist attitudes, from people being unwilling to pass members of her family the peace of Christ to men in the Knights of Columbus making sure to let her father know that he was not truly welcome.

Akbonkhianmeghe E. Orobator's account of being verbally assaulted by a policeman who shouted at them "Africans, go back to Africa! You don't belong in this country. Black people, go back home!" is a searing memory that wounds the spirit while endangering the body.[30] If police officers act as agents of racist systems and ideologies, their victims have little recourse in a judicial system that reflexively grants police wide latitude to engage in a variety of dangerous practices.[31] While the claims of necessity for public safety ring loud and clear from the bench, these are hollow—providing nothing more than the echo of attacks on Martin Luther King, Jr.[32] Orobator's critique of Bryan N. Massingale's claim that racism is the context for the United States of America asserts only that

[29] Jessica Wormley, "A Small Island in a Vast Sea: Theological Reflections on African American Catholic Experience," *Chicago Studies* 42 (2003): 142–152 (142).
[30] Agbonkhianmeghe E. Orobator, "The Struggle against Racism and the Global Horizon of Christian Hope," in *Ecclesiology and Exclusion: Boundaries of Being and Belonging in Postmodern Times*, edited by Dennis M. Doyle, Timothy J. Furry, and Pascal D. Bazzell (Maryknoll: Orbis Books, 2012), 125.
[31] This wide latitude enjoyed by police in the United States is supported by Qualified Immunity, "a judicially created doctrine that protects government employees or those acting with state authority from being held personally liable for constitutional violations." Legislation has been and is being considered both by the US Congress and by individual states to change or eliminate Qualified Immunity and its role in protecting police from prosecution. https://www.congress.gov/bill/117th-congress/house-bill/1470.
[32] Martin Luther King, Jr.'s "Letter from Birmingham City Jail" was in response to the public letter from eight white clergymen who had raised the issue of public safety.

Massingale has failed to be broad enough. Orobator argues that, "in light of my experience, it is safe to assert that racism is alive not only in America but also elsewhere in the world as well. Simply put, racism is a global phenomenon. It may be socially active, economically prevalent, and historically contextualized in the U.S. society, but it is a reality that is present in the world."[33] This global characteristic necessitates dialogical work that transcends national boundaries, as well as denominational borders.

While many analysts surveyed offer up the same analysis—that racism and racialized ideologies have set the framework for all Christian confessions around the world—few postulate practical solutions to the issue at hand. Orobator's consideration of Bryan N. Massingale's argument in *Racial Justice and the Catholic Church* that Catholic social teaching's intersection with race has been its "best-kept silence."[34] Orobator adopts an increasingly prevalent frame, that the "church's concern for racism pales in comparison to its passion for abortion/pro-life issues and sexual ethics. Racism does not yet appear as a theological and ethical priority for the church."[35] A fine example of the dynamic of which the Jesuit writes can be found in Archbishop Cordileone's open letter to Speaker of the House, Nancy Pelosi. Cordileone excommunicates her until she repents from her support of the pro-choice position. But there is no balancing letter, from any American bishop, excommunicating those who would reject the stranger at the gates.

Orobator suggests a variety of options as resources for addressing the problem in Catholicism. He advocates "a radical conversion via a self-emptying (*kenosis*) of sinful attachments, the baptismal incorporation into the body of Christ where all are recognized as equal, and the inclusion of all at the Eucharistic table of fellowship."[36]

However, it is difficult to accept these are serious options for addressing racism in Catholicism or any other Christian confession. First, there is nothing new about these—if they are going to work, one must generate some kind of argument for why they have not already done so. Second, the Eucharistic table has already become a site for political dialogue. It would be too extreme to argue that it has been weaponized against those politicians who will not toe the church's doctrinal line concerning access

---

[33] Orobator, 125–126.
[34] Orobator, 126.
[35] Orobator, 126.
[36] Orobator, 127.

to abortion. However, it is instructive to note that Archbishop Cordileone's letter to Speaker of the House Nancy Pelosi enforced Catholic doctrine with a severe mercy.[37] A far different standard has been applied to Governor Ron DeSantis of Florida, though he trafficked immigrants by plane from Texas to Massachusetts for political gain.[38] Believers are left to wonder why some politicians are disciplined and others are not. The idea that the Eucharistic meal would draw all in an eschatological vision of believers seated together at the table of their God regardless of their race or class, remains an unrealized hope at best. Third, the baptismal incorporation has already occurred! The majority of immigrants in the United States' southern border are Catholics—whom other Catholics happily reject. Here, one can see the manner in which Orobator's point about global realities gets traction. The rejection of the immigrant is a problem not only in the United States but in Europe, Africa, and Oceania.

The Nigerian Jesuit is hardly the only theorist who does not offer a meaningful praxis for addressing racism in the Christian church. Shannen Dee Williams' jeremiads are powerful in the manner that they reframe the manner in which Catholics, especially White Catholics, should view the church's history of dealing with African Americans. Her consideration of Jay P. Dolan's efforts at describing the history of race and racism in American Catholicism illustrates the manner that dominant groups, in this case White American Catholics, whitewash their history to tell the progressive story that they wish was historically accurate. But this does not provide a roadmap, other than actually telling the truth about the church's history, for a model of reconciliation.

Bryan N. Massingale's work runs into some of these same problems. While his *Racial Justice and the Catholic Church* has become a modern classic and contains excellent diagnostic work on the manner in which systemic racism has taken over the church—he provides less in the way of a way forward to solve the situation. Orobator argues that the kind of problems Massingale identifies are impossible to address without

---

[37] "Full text of Archbishop Cordileone letter to Nancy Pelosi banning her from Communion," *Catholic World Report*, May 20, 2022. https://www.catholicworldreport.com/2022/05/20/full-text-of-archbishop-cordileone-letter-to-nancy-pelosi-banning-her--from-communion/, accessed 23 January 2023.

[38] Edgar Sandoval, Miriam Jordan, Patricia Mazzei and J. David Goodman, "The Story Behind DeSantis's Migrant Flights to Martha's Vineyard," *New York Times*, October 4, 2022. https://www.nytimes.com/2022/10/02/us/migrants-marthas-vineyard-desantis-texas.html, accessed 23 January 2023.

reimagining the church without the "connection that ties together racial difference, power, privilege, and prestige."[39] While Orobator finally agreed with Massingale that to be a theologian was to be possessed by a "powerful vision of an alternative and possible world," there is too much of the prophetic task of hope and proclamation and too little of a practical program for changing things in such a vision.[40]

Necessity of Racial Dialogue for the Future of the Church

We argue that a different possibility exists. This is to engage in intentional racial dialogue to reform the church, to reach the Vatican III or the church reformed, always being reformed of the Reformations, that tears down the present realities and fulfills Isaiah's proclamation.[41] The prophet wrote, "Behold, I am doing a new thing. Now it springs forth, do you not perceive it?" In that same manner, the possibilities exist to take the broken pieces of the church's relationship with people of all races and to achieve a new thing that all will see.

We began this article with a reminder of the cases of Ahmaud Arbery, Breonna Taylor, and George Floyd. The furor over the blatant injustice, and the incalculably small value of Black and Brown life in the United States, led to riots. On May 26, 2020, protests began in Minneapolis, Minnesota. These were followed by organized protests against police violence against Black and Brown people in Los Angeles, California; Memphis, Tennessee; and Louisville, Kentucky. The movement quickly became a national movement, and on May 29, 2020, President Trump tweeted the notorious words, "When the looting starts, the shooting starts."[42] Trump was quoting Miami Police Chief Walter Headley, who had used this phrase

---

[39] Orobator, 128.
[40] Orobator, 129.
[41] Agbonkhianmeghe E. Orobator, *The Church We Want: African Catholics Look to Vatican III* (Maryknoll: Orbis Books, 2016). The church reformed, always being reformed, is the English translation of the Dutch description of the Reformations' ecclesiology, *ecclesia reformata, semper reformanda*.
[42] Hatewatch Staff, "Trump Tweets 'When the Looting Starts, the Shooting Starts', Extremists Will Respond," Southern Poverty Law Center, May 29, 2020. https://www.splcenter.org/hatewatch/2020/05/29/trump-tweets-when-looting-starts-shooting-starts-extremists-will-respond, accessed 10 October 2022.

in testimony about crime, justifying the killing of protesters.[43] When Trump used the phrase, he intentionally hearkened back to a time of unfettered police action against protests. Two days later, Trump would go further. Though there were protesters in the streets of Washington, Trump had declared a 7:00 PM curfew. Prior to 7:00, National Guard units and police attacked the protesters with flash-bang grenades and tear gas. Trump then paraded to St. John's Episcopal Church for a photo opportunity with a Bible. In the words of the Most Reverend Mariann E. Budde, presiding Episcopal bishop of Washington, "He did not pray. He did not mention George Floyd, he did not mention the agony of people who have been subjected to this kind of horrific expression of racism and white supremacy for hundreds of years. We need a president who can unify and heal. He has done the opposite of that, and we are left to pick up the pieces."[44]

The results, for those who have studied racial struggles in America, were predictable. While those supporting rights of BIPOC people expressed horror over the treatment of Arbery, Taylor, Floyd, scores of other people of color killed extrajudicially by agents of the state, and the treatment of protesters, conservative supporters of the status quo voiced their belief that the protesters were far worse than the police whose behavior they sought to ameliorate, and drew equivalence between property damage and the killing of people of color by the state without trial. This has always been the strategy of dominant groups, as noted by Reinhold Niebuhr, and Martin Luther King, Jr.[45]

Thus, we arrive at a familiar state. People of color and their allies who see the injustice of racism and its effects, clamoring for change—and adherents of the dominant models of power who caution against abrupt

---

[43] Barbara Sprunt, "The History Behind 'When The Looting Starts, The Shooting Starts,'" *National Public Radio*, May 29, 2020. https://www.npr.org/2020/05/29/864818368/the-history-behind-when-the-looting-starts-the-shooting-starts, accessed 10 October 2022.

[44] Katie Rogers, "Protesters Dispersed With Tear Gas So Trump Could Pose at Church," *New York Times*, June 1, 2020. https://www.nytimes.com/2020/06/01/us/politics/trump-st-johns-church-bible.html, accessed 11 October 2022.

[45] Reinhold Niebuhr, *Moral Man and Immoral Society: A Study in Ethics and Politics*. Introduction by Langdon B. Gilkey (New York: Charles Scribner's Sons, 1932). Reprint (Louisville: Westminster John Knox Press, 2001), Chapter 5, "The Ethical Attitudes of Privileged Class." Martin Luther King, Jr., especially in his "Next Stop: The North," and "The Drum Major Instinct," in *A Testament of Hope: The Essential Writings of Martin Luther King, Jr.*, edited by James M. Washington (San Francisco: Harper & Row, 1985), 189–194, 259–267.

change, and argue for a gradual approach. Normally, this is where progress grinds to a halt. But what if we examined this in a better framework, one that is actually available? Such a model comes about in the reception of the theories of Thomas S. Kuhn, in the work of Mark Massa.[46] Massa explicitly examined the model of a paradigm shift, taken from Kuhn's theory of the manner in which science makes progress.[47] Kuhn argued that scientific progress is not evolutionary, advancing by accretion, but revolutionary. In other words, the idea that science, or any particular field of science, slowly built up by the cumulative observations and minor break-throughs over the years to reach ever more perfect descriptions of the world is wrong. Instead, in Kuhn's theory, a particular model or construct organizes scientific research and observation until it is mature. Then, in an unforeseeable revolution, a new model or paradigm replaces the old one, allowing new observations and progress. For Kuhn, it is important to note that the paradigms are incommensurable despite a shared language basis. Mass in Newtonian physics is not the same as mass in Einsteinian physics, though the signifier remains the same. But that paradigm will eventually be replaced by another.

Kuhn argued that the process leading up to a revolution would begin with scientists recognizing the problems with the present model. Research would appear that demonstrated its inability to explain observed phenomena. This could lead to a period of "crisis," in which extraordinary science begins. That would eventually be resolved in one of three manners. First, ordinary science could resolve the questions at hand. Second, problems resist all approaches and were set aside for a future generation. Third, the crisis would end with the emergence of "a new candidate for paradigm and with the ensuing battle over its acceptance."[48]

Mark Massa, a Jesuit theological historian working at Boston College, used Kuhn's theory to examine the progress of the natural law tradition within Roman Catholicism, especially as an explanation of its history in the late twentieth century in America. Massa reasoned that as traditionally theology had been the "queen of the sciences," it might be an interesting

---

[46] Mark Massa, SJ, *The Structure of Theological Revolutions: How the Fight Over Birth Control Transformed American Catholicism* (Oxford: Oxford University Press, 2018).

[47] Thomas S. Kuhn, *The Structure of Scientific Revolutions, 50th Anniversary edition with introductory essay by Ian Hacking* (Chicago: University of Chicago Press, 1962, 2012).

[48] Kuhn, 81–84.

test case for the application of Kuhn's theory.[49] He argued that this model might help provide a framework and an ideologically neutral method of considering the "micro-tradition of natural law in the Catholic moral theology community."[50] Just as Kuhn had argued against the theory of a continued and linear progress of science, so too Massa was arguing against the theories of John Henry Newman and John Noonan. Further, he rejected them for the same reason that their ideals of development of Catholic thought were "linear" or based on a notion of "organic extrapolation."[51]

Extrapolating from Massa's work on the "micro-tradition of natural law," this is a significant application of Kuhn's theory to the history of theology. Following this model would suggest that the tradition is not static, that it does not always change in manners that are predictable or linear, or even organic, and that any revolution would generate a variety of new traditions or at least candidates to become the new paradigm. The possible application to an era of civil rights agitation seems obvious. If Massa's theory is correct, then churches and societies and the global community should expect, rather than dread, upheavals as part of paradigm shifts.[52] Historical examples abound. This happened in the Jesus community, in the beginnings of the monastic movement, in the Reformations, and in the Great Awakenings.

Other thinkers support this path. In 2001, Terrence Tilley argued about tradition and its authority that tradition was far more a verb of handing down than it was a noun of the material being handed down. Tilley argued, "Authority in the Church does not have its foundation outside the Church but arises in the relationships between the communion of saints, the people who practice discipleship, seeking to live a holy life and die a holy death. The Church is not founded on an external authority, whether Jesus or the scriptures."[53] While this is about ecclesiology and not

---

[49] Massa, 47. Theology as the "queen of the sciences" was a medieval notion, in which theology was frequently seen as the highest science, and that one which required the greatest preparation.

[50] Massa, 47.

[51] Massa, 179.

[52] David Bosch also takes this on in a chapter on "Paradigm Changes in Missiology," in which he posits that missiological paradigms shift and each carries part of the former paradigms forward, sometimes in twisted or transformational ways. Bosch, *Transforming Mission: Paradigm Shifts in Theology of Mission* (Maryknoll: Orbis, 1991), 185–194.

[53] Terrence W. Tilley, *Inventing Catholic Tradition* (Maryknoll: Orbis Books, 2000), 181.

tradition per se, his insight is significant. The relationships between authors and readers, between people who studied theology in the United States and Tanzania, and between Black and White people changed what people saw, and how they viewed the church. James Kenan, depending on Vincent Lloyd who was drawing on Kierkegaard, noted that it was necessary for Whites to see the thing that Whites might actually hope for, instead of hold in their hands, is despair. Despair throws us back on God, rather than ourselves. Kenan noted that the shocks of the pandemic and Black Lives Matter movement had shocked him out of his complacency.[54]

John De Gruchy, writing in 2016, argued that the Kairos document from thirty years earlier, still held promise for the church.[55] De Gruchy linked the tradition of the Hebrew prophets, who did not speak in "balanced theological propositions," but instead spoke to the concrete realities of their situation, providing Israel with new visions of reality that were "subversive to the status quo."[56] De Gruchy linked this subversive model of prophecy to the Kairos documents, both the original and the 2009 Kairos-Palestine document. For the South African theologian, true ecclesiology would also have to be prophetic. It would have to allow the space to hear the prophetic words of those who experienced the present realities institutional churches would rather ignore. Anything else, he wrote, would be nothing other than a "false church theology," one that sought a cheap reconciliation.[57]

All three of these white theologians who were taking up the task of thinking about ecclesiology and the church's ministry were echoing Martin Luther King, Jr. In his celebrated *Letter from Birmingham City Jail*, enumerated four steps in a campaign of nonviolence. These were "(1) collection of the facts to establish the existence of injustice; (2) negotiation; (3) self-purification; and (4) direct action."[58] King was clear that the point of all this was to create tension, so that the situation of injustice

---

[54] James F. Keenan, SJ, "The Color Line, Race, and Caste: Structures of Domination and the Ethics of Recognition," *Theological Studies* 82 (2021): 69–94.

[55] John De Gruchy, "Kairos Moments and Prophetic Witness: Towards a Prophetic Ecclesiology," *HTS Teologiese Studies/Theological Studies* 72 (2016).

[56] De Gruchy, 1.

[57] De Gruchy, 6.

[58] Martin Luther King, Jr., "Letter from Birmingham City Jail," in *A Testament of Hope: The Essential Writings of Martin Luther King, Jr.*, edited by James M. Washington (San Francisco: Harper & Row, 1985), 290.

could no longer be ignored.[59] The point of a theological revolution, the effort at recognizing God's kairos moment, the laying of oneself in harm's way to make brutality, and injustice so obviously heinous all come to the same thing—to create situations that dominant groups (read White people) can no longer tolerate.

Conclusion: Dialogue Between the Voices We Hear and Those We Ignore Is Key

The greatest impact for the students was the engagement in interracial and intercultural dialogue. In research interviews, time and time again, students in New Hampshire identified the opportunity to discuss racial constructs with African and African American writers, as well as the chance to exchange views with Tanzanian students, as the most influential moments of the course.[60] Students identified White people's dominance of Christianity and rejection of either integration or of the recognition of the value of Black people's spirituality, religious personhood, and spiritual gifts as outcomes that stemmed from acceptance of racialized constructs.

And while some North American students expressed fatigue with online coursework, African students were excited by the potential for expanded opportunities for learning through online learning strategies. "This is how we should study *everything*," opined one student.[61] The opportunity to talk to students and lecturers who were physically on another continent opened African students' eyes to how their educational outlook and perspectives could change and grow, despite the lack of resources that hamper many educational initiatives across Africa and in other less-resourced contexts.

The course and reading group in which we participated was fantastic—one of the most rewarding and also draining experiences of our pedagogical experiences. Several unexpected insights arose out of the experience—awareness of the necessity of different pedagogical techniques, the possibilities inherent in the use of Zoom to break down previously uncrossable barriers, and the growth in understanding of the other. These were some of the gifts that came from a wonderful opportunity.

---

[59] King, 291.
[60] SA-F-4, SA-F-3, Interview on May 5, 2021. SA-F-1, SA-F-5, SA-F-6, SA-F-7 Interview on May 7, 2021.
[61] TUMA-M-6, Interview on May 10, 2021.

But another was the broadening sense that students on both sides of the Atlantic had of their churches. While students all rated the chance to speak with writers and other students as the high point of the course that did not simply give them warm feelings. Instead, these caused them to consider factors that were missing in their own churches. Why were their congregations racially segregated? Why had the powerful white men in their communions not led toward a fuller vision of the children of God that would reflect the diversity of God's human creation? Why were mission societies and churches active in East Africa always or nearly always led by White Christians, and why do these continue to employ colonial and racist strategies in their relationships with African churches and Christians? Why did the churches that sent missionaries to Africa insist on exclusively male leadership and teach that women in ministry leadership, which was common in many regions before the continent was colonized, was not of God? African students were quite aware that the missionaries brought a patriarchal view of God with them and spread this view as the Good News; after this educational project, students stated that patriarchy and racism were inextricably linked in mission efforts, and that these encouraged Africans to see themselves as created lesser than those who brought this patriarchal, racially hierarchical interpretation of the Good News. African students then asked: how do we repair the damage that has been done to us and to our churches?[62]

These intentional dialogues, between people of privilege and those who have lived colonized lives, can be a crucial tool to bring the church to that creative tension that can produce a new thing, one that springs forth so that all will perceive it. As we consider how to engender further discussions on how ecclesiology will bring life to and decolonize the church, these conversations, because they de-center White experience and expose real pain, are a crucial place to start.

[62] TUMA-F-2, interview on May 9, 2021.

CHAPTER 10

Nuevo Mundo Theology as a Latinx Decolonial Response to the Global Crisis in Theological Education

Oscar García-Johnson

INTRODUCTION

I will use two conclusive works to help us frame the crisis of theological education in the American Global South. The first work, "*El Pacto Educativo Global en América Latina: Documento de Trabajo*," is a self-reflective Roman Catholic review of theological education that registers the various episcopal conferences happening in Latin America since the

O. García-Johnson (✉)
Fuller Theological Seminary, Pasadena, CA, USA
e-mail: ogarcia-johnson@fuller.edu

© The Author(s), under exclusive license to Springer Nature Switzerland AG 2023
R. C. Barreto, V. Latinovic (eds.), *Decolonial Horizons*, Pathways for Ecumenical and Interreligious Dialogue,
https://doi.org/10.1007/978-3-031-44839-3_10

1960s. These conferences include Medellin, Puebla, Santo Domingo, and Aparecida. I summarize its conclusions as follows[1]:

1. Medellín (1968) criticizes the deficiency of educational efforts in the face of the excessive number of people marginalized from culture, especially indigenous populations. The educational systems seemed more determined to maintain social and economic structures than to solve their inconsistencies.
2. Puebla (1979) further extends the criticism of Medellin by noticing the challenges of the secularization of culture, poverty of a large part of the population, lack of structured forms of education for indigenous peoples, political criteria in the distribution of resources, and the abandonment of religious education by the population.
3. Santo Domingo (1992) classifies as "pastoral challenges" the difficulties that surround education: excessive illiteracy still in existence, the crisis in the family as the first educator, the divorce between the Gospel and culture, the high prices for Catholic education, the religious ignorance of the youth, and the inappropriateness of education to certain cultures (such as indigenous and Afro-Latinos/as).
4. Lastly, Aparecida (2007) affirms that there is a delicate educational emergency in the Latin American context, due to a clear marketing approach to the region. For this reason, educational reforms appear predominantly focused on the acquisition of knowledge and skills and denote a clear anthropological reductionism—since they conceive education predominantly in terms of production, competitiveness, and the market.

The second document, *Otra Educación Teológica es Posible*, edited by Nicolás Panotto and Matthias Preiswerk, is an ecumenical conversation convened by Servicios Teológicos y Pedagógicos that registers a two-day encounter of theological educators working in the Latin American context.[2] The encounter took place in Medellin, Colombia, in 2014. This work highlights a number of institutional deficiencies inherited from the

---

[1] P. Luiz Fernando Klein, *El Pacto Educativo Global en América Latina: Documento de Trabajo* (Consejo Episcopal Latinoamericano y Caribeño/Centro de Gestión de Conocimiento Observatorio Socio-antropológico Pastoral, 2019), 10–12.

[2] Nicolás Panotto y Matthias Preiswerk eds., *Otra Educación Teológica es Posible: Nuevos Sujetos y Campos* (Buenos Aires, Argentina: Libro Digital, 2017).

educational business model of representative theological institutions planted by western missions in Latin America. There are numerous categories of the educational business model that serve as examples of deficiencies:

1. An attraction problem: how several institutions have difficulty in marketing their academic offers and recruiting new students.
2. A retention problem: how various institutions have been impacted by student dropout.
3. A mission problem: how little commitment or relationship of churches with seminaries and faculty (and vice versa) have made formal education dispensable for the church.
4. A scholarly production problem is due to the fact that there are few interdisciplinary and distinctive faculty contributions.
5. A sustainability problem: how financial problems in the educational business model have led institutions to lose faculty and face bankruptcy.

Panotto and Preiswerk write the following conclusion:

All of these events are symptomatic of a larger cause: the lack of theological relevance—from its role to rethink practices and worldviews to the need for academic production—for the church, religious institutions, and societies in general, which affected theological education itself in its scope, importance, institutionality, and sustainability.[3]

The two sources we have reviewed suggest two types of theological education crises in Latin America. On the one hand, *El Pacto Educativo Global* situates the crisis of theological education in the education system itself, judged as unable and incompetent to meet the challenge of structural and systemic oppression affecting the population of Latin America. On the other hand, Servicios Teológicos y Pedagógicos, situates the cause of the problem in the lack of relevance of the theological work itself. In other words, the former points to an external deficiency, namely, the failure to shape the structures of continental life with a life-giving (self-developmental) version of Christianity. And the latter points to an internal incoherence,

---

[3] Panotto y Preiswerk, *Otra Educación Teológica es Posible*, 6.

that is, a lack of incarnational and indigenous vision of the Evangel as part of the Americas.

Interestingly enough, these two conclusions echo the critical observations made decades ago by two notable Evangelical theologians of Latin America: The Latino missiologist Orlando Costas and the Latinamericanist systematic theologian Juan Stam. In the 1970s, Costas critiqued the westernized academic model of theological education by saying: "With few exceptions, the missiological literature of the North is still oriented to the questions before the church 'there' [North] rather than 'here' [South]."[4] Some years later, Juan Stam critiqued the lack of relevance of the theological work by the evangelical church in Latin America:

> Although our evangelical church now spans several generations in most of our countries [...] and it has been predominately conservative in its theology, the truth is that it has not produced mature fruits in its theological development. It has produced practically no evangelical, popular, or technical [works], it has not developed an adequate set of high-level seminaries, it has not produced enough national leaders capable of interpreting the significance of the Gospel in the Latin American context and finding forms of expression that are adapted to the native language and customs.[5]

CONTRADICTION IN CATASTROPHE: THE GLOBAL CRISIS IN THEOLOGICAL EDUCATION

I suggest that the problem of theological education in the context of the American Global South is a reflection of the problem of theological education in the West. The global space has become a mirror through which we recognize our theological faces and shadows. This goes for the West and the rest.

The fundamental crisis defining the task of doing theology today can be described in one word intertwined with another: contradiction in the midst of catastrophe. Whatever attempt at doing theology today will be faced with this contradiction. What I mean by "contradiction" is how a designated group of ideas, statements, systems of beliefs, hierarchical structures, and institutionalized practices—arguably originated in the

---

[4] O. E. Costas, *Theology of the Crossroads in Contemporary Latin America: Missiology in Mainline Protestantism, 1969–1974* (Amsterdam: Editions Rodopi, 1976), 20.

[5] Juan Stam, *Un Teólogo del Camino*, vol. 1 of *Haciendo Teología en América Latina*, ed. Arturo Piedra (San José, CR: Universidad Bíblica Latinoamericana, 2006), 21–22.

West and communicated worldwide as indisputably normative, canonical, and universal templates of the Christian faith and identity—are faced with a radically opposing new situation. That is, "the teaching, curriculum, and paradigmatic core of their theological disciplines continue to be centered on the West while the Christian church has gone global and is going native; Christianity is no longer predominantly a Western religion; and the most rapid growth today is outside of the West."[6]

This contradiction, if taken seriously, can help us realize how fundamentally displaced westernized theological discourse is in the world. The displacement we are referring to is multidimensional: (1) westernized theological discourse is displaced in terms of spatiality, its social location is co-opted by the episteme of coloniality,[7] (2) it is displaced in terms of temporality, which is co-opted by the rhetoric of modernity,[8] and (3) it is displaced in terms of teleology, which is co-opted by the grammar and metaphysics of Occidentalism.[9] This triadic matrix (coloniality/modernity/Occidentalism) disables westernized theological discourse from offering a corporeal imagination with a theological capital that can give global hope in the midst of global catastrophe (bodily, political, ecological, and apocalyptic).[10]

The Harvard Divinity School Puerto Rican theologian, Mayra Rivera, has recently been researching coloniality, race, and ecology through the lens of catastrophe in the Caribbean. Her findings are beginning to show how political practices codify political policies that have impacted Caribbean ecology. In her own words: "these political-economic policies leave a material imprint in particular regions, making them more vulnerable, but also at the forefront of experiences and awareness of ecological catastrophe."[11]

---

[6] Oscar García-Johnson, *Spirit Outside the Gate: Decolonial Pneumatologies of the American Global South* (Downers Grove: IVP Academic, 2019), 1.

[7] George Tinker, *Missionary Conquest: The Gospel and Native American Cultural Genocide* (Minneapolis: Fortress Press, 1993).

[8] Walter Mignolo, *The Darker Side of Western Modernity* (Durham: Duke University Press, 2011).

[9] García-Johnson, *Spirit Outside the Gate*.

[10] For a helpful discussion on the problems of the incarnational imagination of Western Christianity in light of Chalcedon, see Eboni Marshall Turman, *Toward a Womanist Ethic of Incarnation: Black Bodies, the Black Church, and the Council of Chalcedon. Black Religion, Womanist Thought, Social Justice* (New York City: Palgrave Macmillan, 2013).

[11] Mayra Rivera, Alison Jasper, and Fiona Darroch, "An Interview with Mayra Rivera: Postcolonial Women's Writing and Material Religion," Literature and Theology 35, no. 4 (2002): 383–95. doi:10.1093/litthe/frab025. Accessed January 7, 2023.

When one looks through the lens of catastrophe and asks (like Latin American Liberation theologians did in the 1970s) how westernized discourse has mobilized theological themes for populations living in catastrophic times and places, then, the multi-matrix displacement we are alluding to becomes obvious. On this point, the critical observation of Michael Welker is a good defining statement, from within western theologizing:

> In many parts of the world, churches deriving from the Reformation and Counter-Reformation seem paralyzed. Bad moods-characterized by helplessness and fatigue—are spreading. Faith seems empty and incapable of articulation. Love is taken back into the private sphere, where it often suffocates in the struggle for self-assertion. Hope has no goal, no clear perspectives, and has even become extinct. Many worship services are sterile, joyless, and poorly attended. Scholarly theology has the reputation of being either elevated and incomprehensible or banal and boring.[12]

I have argued in *Theology Without Borders* that, "any attempt at doing theology in today's globalized contexts, whether by westerners or non-westerners, must begin by taking into account [...] that the western ways are no longer considered 'unique, superior, or unsurpassed.'"[13] In the same breath, a number of avant-garde theologians of the "third world" that subscribe to the New Paradigms approach believe the global displacement we are discussing is irreversible because we have come to face today "an axial age characterized by an epistemic rupture; a crisis experienced as a fracture between traditional conceptualizations/categorizations and the emergence of new perspectives."[14] This rupture generates the epistemic and social conditions for intellectual capital emerging from the outside, at the borders, of normative and hegemony structures of knowledge and power of the West. In other words, subaltern communities sharing colonial/modern/imperial subjugations around the world are becoming agents of cultural, theological, ecological, and political innovation.

---

[12] Michael Welker, "Christian Theology: What Direction at the End of the Second Millennium?" in *The Future of Theology: Essays in Honor of Jürgen Moltmann*, eds. Miroslav Volf, Carmen Krieg, and Thomas Dörken-Kucharz (Grand Rapids: Eerdmans, 1996), 73.

[13] William Dyrness and Oscar García-Johnson, *Theology without Borders: An Introduction to Global Conversations* (Ada: Baker Academic, 2015), 7.

[14] García-Johnson, *Spirit Outside the Gate*, 49.

The irruption of the new theological paradigms signals the inefficaciousness of westernized theological discourse in the context of the Global South (the displacement). At the same time, it signals an indispensable global activity of resistance and re-existence by way of achieving epistemic autonomy through the experiments of self-theologizing, self-missioning, and self-emancipation.

Nuevo Mundo Theologizing

It is at this juncture—where the displaced westernized theological discourse faces an emerging new world that resists it—that I want to introduce to the *reader Teología del Nuevo Mundo* as a Latinx response to the global crisis in theological education.[15] Expectedly, aware readers may be intrigued by the name of this theological articulation. A name imposed on ancient lands and peoples by outsiders on the eve of the doctrine of discovery, *nuevo mundo* (new world) offers an opportunity to access theology and americanity indigenously, from another epistemic place.

There are three main motivations for the elaboration of this project.[16] These three motivations are teleological in character, on the one hand, and geopolitical on the other. The former situates our theological imagination in transmodernity as a hermeneutics of in-between times on the underside of modern history. The latter situates Christian knowledge, experience, and action in the colonial difference, at the erasures of coloniality/modernity/Occidentalism. The global space where we do life and theology today can no longer be occupied by a single narrative claiming universality and totalitarian Christian utopias: western Christianity.

---

[15] The literary shape of Nuevo Mundo theology is being proposed as a series of seven theological volumes written in Spanish and configured into five doctrinal monographs and two practitioner's manuals. Volume 1 was published by Editorial CLIE (Barcelona, Spain) in November of 2022. The other volumes are in production. Here is a brief description of the seven titles: *1. Introducción a la Teología del Nuevo Mundo* (theology of place); 2. *Doctrina del Re-Conocimiento de Dios* (a theology of the Bible, creation, and sin); 3. *Doctrina de la Iglesia: Testimonio Público Sin Fronteras* (a public theology of the church); 4. *Doctrina de Jesús Descolonial en el Poder del Espíritu* (a decolonial Spirit Christology); 5. *Doctrina del Mundo Nuevo desde el Mañana de Dios* (is eschatology in plurucelular tones); 6. *Manual para Lideres Cristianos del Nuevo Mundo* (offers models for church administration and discipleship from the perspective of women and emerging gens); and 7. *Manual de Teología y Liturgia desde la Niñez* (offers liturgical and missional models from the perspective of children and other abilities).

[16] Oscar García-Johnson, *Introducción a la Teología del Nuevo* (Barcelona: CLIE, 2022).

One could consider these three motivations as epistemic-geopolitical portals leading us into a journey, in faith, by which we enter into a narrative of the evolution of the Christian itinerary as it transitions from the old (Mediterranean) Europe to the new colonial Europe and the American post-colony until reaching us, the post-COVID-19 American Global South. This narrative that informs the design of our theological project, however, is never told in lineal and leveled tones but more so in irregular ones and, even, labyrinthic rhythms that invite postmodernist/postcolonial anachronisms at times. The American Global South abides, as we Latinx theologians usually say, in *tiempos mixtos* (mixed times).

The first motivation has to do with "new world" as a categorical name given to *Abya Yala* when the colonizing enterprise carried out its colonial function. It was a colonial invention of a Europe that discovers the route to the Atlantic and reaches land and people that could not be found on its maps or in its philosophical and theological imaginations. Not knowing what to do with this new knowledge, because there were only three continents in pre-modern European knowledge (Europe, Africa, and Asia), a new cartographic and theological category "new world" is invented to indicate several things: (1) a world that has no [western] history (no past, no language, no knowledge), (2) a world that is empty, unoccupied, and free to be occupied and possessed, and (3) a world that has no religion and therefore its inhabitants have no soul/spirit and consequently they are not entirely human but savages, bestial beings, and monsters. But later, thanks to the efforts of missionaries defending indigenous rights (Montesinos and Bartolomé Las Casas), they came to be presented as "barbarians" who should be civilized and Christianized.

The second motivation has to do with the invented and colonized "new world" of Europe which, in fact, provoked the emergence of a non-European new world. The Indigenous nations then transformed into cities, metropolises, and nation-states until they became the mestizo/a American republics governed by the Creole castes to this day. Our mestizajes and own creations arose in the midst of Western domination, hence, creating a mixed time and living: we have lived occidentally in our indigenous world, that precedes (pre-modern) the colony and modernization, but at the same time, we have lived resisting Occidentalism.[17] As Octavio

---

[17] For more on this see: García-Johnson, *Spirit Outside the Gate*; Oscar García-Johnson, "Retheologizing Las Américas: A Transoccidental Approach," *Journal Of Hispanic/Latino Theology* 19 (Spring 2014): 9–24; Dyrness and García-Johnson, *Theology without Borders*.

Paz illustrates in *The Labyrinth of Solitude*, "the Mexican does not want to be neither Indian nor European [...] thus he becomes a son of nothing, an abstract being."[18] This depiction gives voice to the identity crisis with which we have been raised as colonized Americans. Children, not so much of nothing (here I criticize Octavio Paz), but children of our own de-creations. We are, at least partially, our own creations, cultural–religious–political characters that still have no proper name but live in our new world as nameless and landless peoples with aspirations, utopias, and quixotism.

Finally, there is a third "new world" (a worldwide world, not just a westernized world) that irrupts into the twenty-first century, during the global COVID-19 pandemic in 2020. Some world intellectuals of the stature of Boaventura de Sousa Santos argue that the twenty-first century's true beginning is 2020, during the global pandemic.[19] This new post-COVID-19 world evidences the transformation of various local and global spaces of public life through an ungovernable health crisis, a series of protests and world revolutions against racism, sexism, colonialism triggered by the systemic abuses of the United States police and legal apparatus against the black community, Latinxs, Middle Easterners, women, LGBTQAI+, and Asian Americans. The new post-COVID-19 world has forced the state, the private sector, and the religious sector to place themselves squarely on the virtual platform and solidify once and for all the informational society and informational capitalism (info-capitalism). The technocrats of Silicon Valley (California) came to show their great world power, even over the rule of law, when in January 2021 companies of the stature of Apple, Google, and Twitter prohibited the use of their platforms to no less than the president of the United States, Donald Trump, accused of sedition and agitating the violent masses to raid the Capitol in Washington, D.C., on January 6, 2021.[20]

In summary, during the global pandemic, the academy, the church, and the public space improved their operations in virtual platforms and social networks to do business, ministry, life, and revolution in new ways. Theology and ministry, hitherto rooted in an enlightened West fossilized

---

[18] Octavio Paz, *The Labyrinth of Solitude* (New York: Grove Press, 1994).
[19] Riboca, "*Boaventura de Sousa Santos 'The Future Begins Today,'*" YouTube, June 11, 2020, https://www.youtube.com/watch?v=JjPOgxd2KrQ.
[20] For an intriguing article addressing the power of tech billionaires see Scott Galloway, "America's False Idols," The Atlantic, September 23, 2022.

in temple-centered worship experiences, textbooks, classrooms, sermons, and hymns, were forced to respond by transforming their liturgical and cultic forms as well as their operations and infrastructures to demonstrate a much more fluid, versatile, domestic, popular and prophetic witness. We have now landed in the world of the millennial generation and *Zetas*. They dominate these digital spaces and have different social imaginaries, less faithful to the past and more deconstructive. Faced with a new and changing world in its most fundamental forms and structures, a minority conservative elite around the world in the fields of politics, economy, culture, education, religion, and ministry continue to cling to a nativist and Western/US-centric restoration ideology that combines ideologies of race, economic nationalisms, and fascist Christian fundamentalisms in order to keep the old world alive in the face of a new post-COVID-19 world.

Nuevo Mundo theology seeks to walk through the multidimensional conduits of this new post-COVID-19 worldwide world that is collapsing with the old, westernized world. *Nuevo Mundo* Theology is certainly not a systematic theology, but more so a rhizomatic system of *thinking-doing* and *doing-thinking*[21] that seeks to map the faith of the people who walk with God and of the God who walks with the peoples of this new post-COVID-19 world. In short, *Nuevo Mundo* theology seeks to rebuild an autochthonous faith language and an artisan theological framework that, from inside, outside, and across borders, accompanies and evokes the experiences, traditions, visions, and desires of the peoples of the American Global South. It is a new cartography of faith of those who for five centuries have lived captive between two worlds, but who today find a third world that opens their horizons in a new time and from a new place.

How to Speak of Christian Doctrine in a Time of Contradiction and Catastrophe?

Nuevo Mundo theology offers a series of theological articulations in Spanish and uses the language of Christian doctrines to refer to biblical theological framing themes. However, the use of doctrine is not dogmatic or credal, or normative (*regula fidei*). Doctrine, in *Nuevo Mundo* Theology, has an intersectional and insurgent character rooted in God's revelatory

---

[21] For the use of the praxiological model of decoloniality see: Walter D. Mignolo and Catherine E. Walsh, *On Decoloniality: Concepts, Analytics, Praxis* (Durham: Duke University Press Books, 2018).

transit around the world and God's liberative activity within creation and community. Doctrinal expressions in *Nuevo Mundo* Theology dialogues with western Christian orthodoxies when appropriate, but also with the orthodoxies of original Christianity's in the American Global South and other latitudes of world Christianity. Hence, the dialogue is pluri-doxical in a way that critically engages multiple traditions with a degree of equitable and inclusive epistemic attitude.

One must admit *that Nuevo Mundo* theology finds its place in an unprecedented time for world Christianity. Anywhere on our planet, where Christianity has left a footprint, the most significant challenge to date for Christian theology is to demonstrate in which way the social location that informs (a) its conceptual production, (b) the gospel message it seeks to communicate, and (c) the missional agenda guiding its vision of Christian formation, church planting, and social action in the world is no longer oriented by the core logic of western colonial modernity.

In response, *Nuevo Mundo* theology argues that the most significant problem in Christian discourse today is not only the captivity of its social location and history by a self-nominated sacred culture living in a sacred geography and suffering from western hyperlocalism. But the most significant problem is how this Christian exceptionalism is instrumentalized by dangerous epistemic cartographies that continue to map the itinerary of theology and mission in today's new world.

Today's new world, I propose, is the collapsing and succession of colonizing projects and liberating efforts coming together again and again under the utopias (left and right) of modern Christian theology and mission. This collapsing and succession dynamic in western theology is mediated by an expiatory epistemic machine embedded in popular doctrines, influential institutions, and normative scriptural reasonings.

Expiation, here, refers to the self-imposed obligation of westernized subjectivities to atone for the sins of the old world, not with their own bodies and means, but with the bodies and lands of "the wretched of the earth."[22] This was well captured by the theological judgment of Fray Bartolomé de Las Casas in the sixteenth century:

---

[22] Frantz Fanon, *The Wretched of the Earth* (New York City: Grove Press, 2005).

> In the Indies I leave Jesus Christ, our God, being whipped and afflicted, and buffeted and crucified, not once but thousands of times, as often as the Spaniards assault and destroy those people.[23]

The concept "*Nuevo Mundo*," I propose, has been used as an eschatological cartography, not merely as an accidental one. Continuing to do Christian theology today by hiding this theological conceptuality only perpetuates the violent possibilities of appropriating biblical narratives for the sake of self-preservation and land acquisition.[24] *Nuevo Mundo* theology proposes, instead, to continue to struggle with Scriptural meanings and their confrontations to our humanity in real time and place as an act of biblical obedience to "love the Lord your God with all your heart and with all your soul and with all your strength and with all your mind, and your neighbor as yourself" (Luke 10:27, ESV). To put it bluntly and borrowing from the argument of Zakiyyah Iman Jackson on matters of blackened bodies:

> The humanity of indigenous, enslaved African and mestizos/as in the New World was not denied by European humanity, but appropriated, inverted, and ultimately plasticized in the methodology of abjecting animality [...].[25]

Here the so-called universal humanity of the western character self-imposes violently and imperially on the other, while ignoring the human reality as a place of contestation, and therefore, a place of divine redemption.

Nuevo Mundo theology seeks to deactivate this expiatory epistemic mechanism by de-creating the fictional stories generated by colonizing methodologies of adjecting animality; a methodology that creates western missionaries and teachers as heroes and worshippers of God while creating the Indian and the African and the mestizo/a character as monsters and

---

[23] Gustavo Gutiérrez, *Dios O El Oro en las Indias: Siglo XVI*, (Salamanca: Ediciones Sigueme, 1989), 156.

[24] For a diverse and globally distributed number of essays arguing in this direction see K. K. Yeo and Gene L. Green, *Theologies of Land: Contested Land, Spatial Justice, and Identity* (Eugene: Wipf and Stock Publishers, 2020).

[25] Adapted from Zakiyyah Iman Jackson, *Becoming Human: Mattes and Meaning in Antiblack World*, (New York: New York University Press, 2020), 26.

worshippers of Satan.[26] It follows that the soteriological rhetoric of western missionizing, modernization, and democratization emerges as a modern civilizing apparatus justifying conversion, torture, or extermination as a globalizing process needed to advance progress, democracy, and the kingdom of God.[27]

Nuevo Mundo theology provides a biblical-theological framing of life and meaning at the erasures of colonial modernity. In this sense, it points to a Christian doctrine of de-creation as an act of biblical retraditioning. The biblical vision of life is one of living faithfully in Christ, which means, inhabiting spaces and identities de-created from colonial modernity in an effort to debestialize the wounded American persona, inscribed in the lands and bodies of the peoples of the American Global South.

THE TRANSOCCIDENTAL CHRISTIAN MATRIX

When articulating *Nuevo Mundo* theology, we acknowledge and value the insurgence of the New Paradigms.[28] We see, however, the need to move a step forward by focusing on the task of re-signifying theology based on an original American transoccidental imagination. The act of reimagining Christianity in the context of the American Global South is closely related to the act of reimagining Americanity, which requires the repositioning of our ourselves and our methodologies and epistemologies on a different theological horizon—before and beyond colonial modernity. This transoccidental repositioning inevitably enacts a theological rerouting that seeks to (1) track the activity of God in places and with peoples negated by

---

[26] Although I have elaborated in particular ways to suggest atonement imperialism as a form of cultural imperialism, there are some works that can help readers situate this conversation in the context of doctrine, history, and power. See for instance: Miguel A. De La Torre and Albert Hernandez, *The Quest for the Historical Satan*, Illustrated edition (Minneapolis: Fortress Press, 2011); Ramón Grosfoguel, *De la Sociología de Descolonización al Nuevo Antiimperialis*, 1st edition (Ciudad de México: AKAL, 1900); Ramón Grosfoguel, "The Structure of Knowledge in Westernized Universities: Epistemic Racism/Sexism and the Four Genocides/Epistemicides of the Long 16th Century," *Human Architecture: Journal of the Sociology of Self-Knowledge* 11, no. 1 (2013).

[27] See for instance David P. Gushee, J. Drew Zimmer, and Jillian Hickman Zimmer, *Religious Faith, Torture, and Our National Soul*, 1st ed. (Macon, Ga.: Mercer University Press, 2010).

[28] These paradigms are: modern, liberationist, pluralistic, ecofeminist, postreligionist, posttheistic, new axial-epistemological, and new archeological-biblical. See García-Johnson, *Spirit Outside the Gate*, 50–58.

colonial modernity and (2) re-tradition the relationship of God with creation on the basis of a liberative and decolonial cosmology.

A major framing argument of *Nuevo Mundo* theology is that colonial modernity, through its expiatory epistemic machine, has operated theologically by disassembling bodies and consciousnesses from Mother Earth as a living creature and neighbor. Recapitulating, this disassembling is made possible by the creation of fictional characters helped with skewed biblical hermeneutics that holds a rhetorical-soteriological agenda: to tell the story of pious Western (Christian) heroes in a land of evil non-Western monsters. The global-colonial effect of this fiction is the promotion of western modern characters and civilized ways of life as the model of finished humanity, self-sufficient individuals, salvation history, and embodied truth, beauty, and good.[29]

Transoccidentality seeks to de-create these genocidal stories by telling other stories from a different life-giving horizon. Transoccidentality offers three intersectional operations in the making of *Nuevo Mundo* Theology, that is, in the making of doctrinal expressions. As a de/reclassifying devise, the first operation focuses on themes and categories that organize knowledge, power, and life at the erasures of colonial modernity. As a critical epistemology, the second operation focuses on theological sources, religious traditions, and traditioning communities carrying legacies both ancestral and received from other contexts. As a grammar and syntax of a new theological language, the third operation focuses on language and meaning making in correspondence with indigenous sign systems and their evolution as a result of intercultural and interpolitical encounters.[30]

Transoccidentality provides a framing of life and meaning from the borders (erasures) of colonial modernity. In this sense, transoccidentality is part of an imaginative and neo-American traditioning effort that is rooted in ancestral and contemporary legacies and aspirations. Transoccidentality aims at enabling *Nuevo Mundo* Theology to retradition Christianity

---

[29] This is clear point made by the notable African American theologian Willie Jennings. See Willie James Jennings, *After Whiteness: An Education in Belonging*, Illustrated edition (Grand Rapids, Michigan: Eerdmans, 2020).

[30] For my use of "intercultural and interpolitical" translation see Boaventura de Sousa Santos, *The End of the Cognitive Empire: The Coming of Age of Epistemologies of the South* (Durham: Duke University Press Books, 2018), chapter 10.

otherwise and recovering/uncovering the *Other America*[31] (José Martí), Transamericanity that is.[32]

Transoccidentality points to Transamericanity as a way of inhabiting spaces and identities de-created from coloniality in an effort to debestialize the wounded American persona (liberative ontology and biopolitics), inscribed in the lands and bodies of the American peoples. To achieve this goal, *Nuevo Mundo* theology exercises four transoccidental-experimental processes as a way of reconstructing four wounded theological domains in the American Global South: ontology, epistemology, missiology, and ecclesiology.

Each process aims at providing the sociohistorical condition for achieving concrete transformation (reforms). Hence, while the three intersectional operations are framing devices internal to each process (re-sourcing, knowledge-making, and retraditioning) in the making of Christian concepts and praxis, the following four processes are domains of a Christian ecology of knowledge (Transoccidental Christian matrix) that hope to deactivate the western epistemic machine (Matrix of Colonial Power) so far informing normative Christianity in the world.

1. *Mestizo(a)logy as a Transoccidental Reason.* This ontological moment points to a *Latino/a/x/e* intelligence that seeks to create the cultural conditions to recover and revalue the subjectivities of the American Global South denigrated by the Matrix of Colonial Power (colonial modernity). It seeks a theoretical and practical *cultural re-form* based on a theological process in which all cultures and peoples fit.
2. *Traditioning Narratology.* This epistemological moment seeks to create the epistemic conditions to recover lost knowledge, brings hidden knowledge to light (including Occidental knowledge epistemicided by colonial modernity) and imagines potential knowledge in the context of the American Global South. It seeks an *educational re-form* that starts with learned ignorance (*Docta Ignorantia*) and enables an ecology of knowledge that does not waste knowledge,

---

[31] See Jose Martí, *Nuestra América*, https://www.sausd.us/cms/lib/CA01000471/Centricity/Domain/433/18_Nuestra%20America.pdf.

[32] Although I reconstruct the concept theologically, I use Transamericanity informed by José David Saldívar, *Trans-Americanity: Subaltern Modernities, Global Coloniality, and the Cultures of Greater Mexico*, (Durham: Duke University Press Books, 2011).

fertilizing the indigenous imagination. It affirms that *all indigenous wisdom and contextual knowledge* are valid and must be engaged with critically and constructively for the sake of Transamericanity.
3. *Transnational Faith Geography*. This missio-political moment seeks to develop the cartographic conditions to retrace the maps of *Our [indigenous] Faith*, instead of replicating the maps of the Western faith in the Americas. It seeks a *religious and geopolitical reform*, where *all lands* [living spaces] are granted self-worth and their people belong to them.
4. *Border Ecclesiogenesis*. This ecclesiological moment seeks to create the theological conditions for a decolonial re-churching of Christianity in the world. It seeks to de/reclassify the colonial modernity codes encrypting the modern church for the last five centuries. At the same time, it seeks a *structural prophetic re-form* of the modern institution (public, private, and religious) by which all public space is considered sacred and all sacred space is considered public. Grounded in an ecclesial-base-community revival, this moment seeks to reconfigure social life, the dominant establishment, the public sphere, and the vision of Theotopia—an alternative pluriversal life and living as the preferred future of God for New Creation, as supposed to the future proposed by the global designs of colonial modernity.

Epilogue

Undoubtedly, much has been left unsaid in this chapter on *Nuevo Mundo* theology. For instance, how does *Nuevo Mundo* theology offer a less ethnocentric vision of world Christianity than that experienced in dominant hyperlocal western theology? Also, how do non-westernizing expressions of Occidental Christianity participate, with equity and agency, in the construction of *Nuevo Mundo* Theology? Is there a vision, or even a desire, for non-westernizing expressions of occidental theology to join efforts against the seemingly invincible global domains of colonial modernity? These subjects and more are the reason to develop *Nuevo Mundo* theology in several treatises in the minoritized Spanish theological language and in multiple conversations and languages across the world.

So far, I have framed this presentation by suggesting a dual process of *unlearning* and *relearning* theological knowledge in the context of the American Global South. This dual process takes us on a journey where deconstruction happens on the other side of constructive energy. Hence, *Nuevo Mundo* theology is an exercise in unlearning everything that we have learned as fundamental, valuable, universal, and indispensable for life and living that is linked to western colonial modernity. In a sense, *Nuevo Mundo* theology includes *a-theology* as a self-critical mechanism, that is, a theological discourse where the very concept of God and God's knowledge of creation is interrogated and delinked from colonial modernity.

I am ending this chapter with an *atheological* composition I wrote inspired by two very different thinkers, of two very different western contexts, writing in two very different times, and yet addressing a very similar problem: how the Christian character in the public space has been occupied by political economies and geopolitics of knowledge. On September 1, 2022, Michael Gerson, a conservative columnist of evangelical background, wrote an article in *The Washington Post* titled "Trump should fill Christians with rage. How come he doesn't?" Some called it a masterpiece for being able to speak critically, broadly, concisely, imaginatively, and boldly to white Christian nationalism under the influence of Trumpism. Others called it a flawed and hurtful mischaracterization of conservative Christians. Whatever the case, Gerson's article disclosed a brilliant self-critical articulation of how the Christian public character of today seems to be occupied by a sinister version of white evangelical (US) nationalism.[33] I think he has a point.

On January 16, 1916, Karl Barth delivered a church lecture titled "The Righteousness of God" and was later published as a journal article in *Neue Wege* (April 1916) and as chapter 1 of Barth's seminal book *Das Wort Gottes und die Theologie* in 1924 (Eng. Trans. *The Word of God and The Word of Man*). Barth's theological sentiment reacted to how industrial capitalism, religious nationalism, and war transformed the public Christian character (Christian nationalism) by shepherding Christian knowledge and Christian commitment to the point of confusing the *imago dei* with the *imago civilis*. Hence Barth's summoning in *theological atheistic tones*: "It is high time for us to confess freely and gladly: this god, to whom we have built the tower of Babel, is not God. He is an idol. He is dead."[34]

[33] Michael Gerson, "Trump Should Fill Christians with Rage. How Come He Doesn't?" The Washington Post, September 1, 2022, https://www.washingtonpost.com/opinions/2022/09/01/michael-gerson-evangelical-christian-maga-democracy/. Accessed January 10, 2023.

[34] Karl Barth, *The Word of God and The Word of Man,* trans. Douglas Horton (Gloucester: Peter Smith Publishing Inc., 1958), 22.

And, of course, Friedreich Nietzsche is somewhere in the background of my composition, as he is in Barth's manuscript as well.

Nuevo Mundo theology may sound at times as *atheology*, calling us to declare ourselves atheist regarding our colonial-modern god. But the Good News is that the Spirit of Abundant Life, out of the piles of accumulated dead in the valley of wounded humanity and Mother Earth, like the bones in the book of Ezekiel, speaks a breath of life causing flesh to heal the human imagination and hope to determine a new history for a New World of those for five centuries chained by nonpersonhood, servility, coloniality, modernity, and extermination.

I live in a Christian nation
Oscar Garcia-Johnson

I live in a Christian nation where the "boundless tolerance and group rights," a mark of its cosmopolitan progress, find a curious expression in "perverse and dangerous liberties [...][such as] white national populism [...]and liberal multiculturalism" [...]

—.—

I live in a Christian nation where embracing conservative religious values translates into defending conservative people's right to their own God-given land and freedom, perceived as being occupied by liberal "modernity, big businesses, media, academia," and waves of hostile immigrants [...]where embracing progressive values translate into defending people's right to freedom and liberal white privilege, perceived as being endangered by "confederate nostalgia, white nationalism, antisemitism, [Islamophobia], replacement theory and QAnon" [...]

—.—

I live in a Christian nation where current republicanism has been fueled by religious "apocalyptic rhetoric" and in turn has offered a medication, Christian nationalism and popular fascism to mitigate the pain of those "boiling with righteous resentment," and a promise of healing: to make America faithful again [...]

—.—

I live in a Christian nation where the democratic spirit today has become a cynical portrait of common good, God's truth and shared patriotism proclaiming "God remains dead! And we have killed him!" Extreme polarization has killed him. "How shall we console ourselves, the most murderous of all murderers?"

—.—

I live in a nation where Baptism comes schooled by "imperious ignorance"; the eucharist is served at the table of "untamed egotism and reflexive bigotry";

the homily exalts "villainy as virtue"; the prophetic witness is demonstrated as an assault on vain civic altars and the reconquest of the holy of holies with signs of the cross mixed with icons of white supremacy [...]

—.—

Oh, infamous Karl Barth, how clearsighted you were for a hundred years, when becoming an atheist [...]

"we have made ourselves a god," you declared, "in our own image and must now own him [...]"[35]

It is clear that such a god is not God. He is not even righteous.
He cannot prevent his worshipers,
all the distinguished Europeans and American apostles of civilization,
welfare and progress, all zealous citizens and pious Christians,
from falling upon one another with fire and sword
to the amazement and derision of the poor heathen in India and Africa [...]
[and the forsaken American Global South]
This god is really an unrighteous god,
and it is high time for us to declare ourselves thorough-going doubters,
sceptics, scoffers and atheists in regard to him [...]"

---

[35] Barth, *Word of God and Word of Man*, 22.

PART IV

Worship, Rite and Sacrament as Decolonial Events

CHAPTER 11

Toward a Decolonial Liturgical Theology

Laurel Marshall Potter

In the 1960s and 1970s, Latin American liberation theology opened Christianity in the region to questions of faith, justice, and politics—to the reality of the majority experience of material poverty and to the damning judgment that the God of Christian scripture makes on the structures of sin that produce such suffering. In his July 1968 address in Chimbote, Peru, Gustavo Gutiérrez proclaimed that "[...] faith tells us that God loves us and demands a loving response. This response is given through love for human beings, and that is what we mean by a commitment to God and to our neighbor."[1] Jon Sobrino echoes by stating that "[...] the current and foreseeable historical situation continues forcing theology to direct itself according to the reign of God."[2] This "irruption of the poor"

---

[1] Gustavo Gutiérrez, "Toward a Theology of Liberation," in *Liberation Theology: A Documentary History*, ed. Alfred T. Hennelly (Maryknoll: Orbis 1990), 63.
[2] Jon Sobrino, "Centralidad del reino de Dios en la teología de la liberación," in *Mysterium liberationis*, vol. I, eds. Ignacio Ellacuría and Jon Sobrino (San Salvador: UCA Editores, 1991), 477, translation my own.

L. M. Potter (✉)
University of St. Thomas, St. Paul, USA, MN
e-mail: laurel.marshall@bc.edu

© The Author(s), under exclusive license to Springer Nature Switzerland AG 2023
R. C. Barreto, V. Latinovic (eds.), *Decolonial Horizons*, Pathways for Ecumenical and Interreligious Dialogue,
https://doi.org/10.1007/978-3-031-44839-3_11

into the Christian theological imagination marked a turn to neighbor, to concrete communal and social reality, and to history and politics. For many of the Latin American faithful, liberation theology's call to social justice, to political struggle, and to the preferential option for the poor contrasted with their previous spiritual and ecclesial lives, which had been marked by "practices ordered to the salvation of souls, especially sacramental practices [...]. This intense ritual activity corresponded with a passivity to historical reality."[3] Commitment to the church's embrace of the world—defended by frequent references to *Gaudium et Spes* in the postconciliar documents of the Latin American Bishop's Conference (CELAM)—shone forth as a fundamental contribution of the first generations of Latin American liberation theology, a justified corrective to an ecclesial lifestyle dominated by ritual celebration that encouraged disengagement from society.

It would be difficult to argue that liturgical or sacramental theology was a primary focus for the first several decades of liberation theology. Though critiques of previous theologies of liturgy and sacrament mark many of the field's classic texts, diverse and constructive liturgical and sacramental reflections have long been lacking from liberationist traditions.[4] In his 1990 essay "*Sacramentos*," Víctor Codina attributes the lack of a well-articulated sacramental liberation theology to the fact that, according to liberation theology's own self-understanding as reflection on ecclesial praxis, "liberation theology will not be able to reflect on the sacraments before a new sacramental praxis is configured."[5] Interestingly, in practice, many changes to liturgical life and sacramental practice flourished in the first several decades of the ecclesial base community experience: rural catechists were formed to be *delegados* and *delegadas de la Palabra* in order to facilitate liturgies of the Word when a priest was unavailable, and com-

---

[3] Rodolfo Cardenal, *Vida, Pasión, y Muerte del Jesuita Rutilio Grande*, corrected and expanded edition (San Salvador: UCA Editores, 2020), 191, translation my own.

[4] Notable exceptions to this claim include Leonardo Boff's *The Sacraments of Life, the Life of the Sacraments*, originally published in 1983 in Portuguese, which describes the "sacramental imagination" through narrative accounts of "little-s" sacraments from Boff's own life before introducing the basics of conciliar sacramental theology (trans. John Drury, Washington, D.C.: Pastoral Press, 1987), and William T. Cavanaugh's *Torture and Eucharist: Theology, Politics, and the Body of Christ* (Malden, MA: Blackwell, 1998), wherein Cavanaugh proposes a "eucharistic counter-politics" capable of vindicating Christian hope in the face of the "anti-liturgy" of state torture.

[5] Víctor Codina, "Sacramentos," in *Mysterium Liberationis*, vol. II (San Salvador: UCA Editores, 2008), 268, translation my own.

munal reflection on lectionary readings in the liturgical space of the homily came to mark celebrations throughout Central and South America among ecclesial base communities (CEBs).[6] Brazilian biblicist Carlos Mesters systematized the practice of *lectura popular de la Biblia* among the CEBs,[7] and Ernesto Cardenal famously published the grassroots biblical reflections proclaimed in conversation-style homilies among his community in Solentiname, Nicaragua.[8] While Codina is hesitant to suggest that liberation theologians had little interest in liturgy and the sacraments—a hesitation likely due to the frequency and force of the Roman Catholic magisterial suspicion that liberation theology focused *only* on material, political praxis, and liberation[9]—it would be understandable if the novelty and relief of world-facing ecclesial concerns in the 1970s and 80s compared to the liturgical fundamentalism of Christian life in Latin America before this era contributed to the literature's focus on social and political ecclesial praxis. Whether a function of method and time or of cyclic theological priorities, the fact remains that liberation theologies have yet to develop a thoroughgoing, contemporary conversation around liturgical and sacramental theology.

Theologians began to point to the need for this conversation as early as the mid-1980s. In his pastoral experience, Leonardo Boff noted that "[…] the current rites speak little for themselves. They need to be explained. And a sign that has to be explained is not a sign."[10] He names this failure of signification "ritual mummification," referring to the apparent emptiness of normative liturgical grammar for the Latin American faithful. José

---

[6] In El Salvador, for example, by the mid-seventies, all five dioceses sponsored schools for catechists and leaders in other emerging pastoral roles. For more, see Peter Michael Sánchez, *Priest Under Fire: Padre David Rodríguez, the Catholic Church, and El Salvador's Revolutionary Movement* (Gainesville: University of Florida Press, 2015) and Cardenal, *Vida, Pasión, y Muerte del Jesuita Rutilio Grande*.

[7] For an English-language introduction to Mesters and his work, see Carlos Mesters, "The Use of the Bible in Christian Communities of the Common People," in *Liberation Theology: A Documentary History*, ed. Alfred T. Hennelly (Maryknoll, Orbis, 1995), pp. 14–28.

[8] Ernesto Cardenal, *The Gospel in Solentiname*, two volumes, trans. by Donald D. Walsh (Maryknoll: Orbis, 1976–82).

[9] This is one of the main concerns articulated in the Congregation for the Doctrine of the Faith's "Instruction on Certain Aspects of the 'Theology of Liberation'" (6 August 1984), Chapter VI, art. 4–5. Accessed 29 September 2022 at https://www.vatican.va/roman_curia/congregations/cfaith/documents/rc_con_cfaith_doc_19840806_theology-liberation_en.html

[10] Boff 17, translation my own.

María Castillo similarly believes that Catholic sacramental theology in Latin America suffers from a kind of symbolic dysfunction that occurs when the receiving community does not have the same meanings attached to a particular symbol as the issuing community. Castillo urges that this dysfunction, which leads to a divide between sacramental practice and Christian life, be addressed:

> [...] if there are people who do not consider worship to be the most preeminent and effective task that the Church may carry out in order to humanize our society and in order to reduce suffering in this world, then in this we have the clearest proof that Christian worship is not being celebrated how God commands and orders it [...] precisely because we want to be more radical and more effective in our liberating service to humanity; that's why we should be more demanding in our fidelity to Christian worship.[11]

That is, if Christian liturgy is not contributing to a humanizing praxis of churchgoers in the world, it is neither Christian nor liturgy; alternatively, if Christian praxis is not motivated out of the ritual celebration of the paschal mystery, participation in the Church's sacramental life, and in active hope of the eschaton, it cannot be said to be distinctively Christian (and the risk of falling into political ideology looms ever-greater).

These gaps between liturgical signification, worship, and Christian life in Latin America have not resolved themselves over the decades, though there is evidence that we are now at a time when liturgical and sacramental theology both (1) has new sacramental praxis available for reflection and (2) is sought by the very ecclesial communities and lived religious traditions that have served historically as *loci theologici* for Latin American liberation theologies. This chapter will take up the specific case of CEBs in El Salvador, who have various well-established liturgical practices, as well as interest in discussing the topic. On various occasions—such as in preparation for a national CEBs retreat in 2014, while coordinating with the archdiocese for the celebration of St. Óscar Romero's canonization in 2018, and during my own diagnostic research visits—Salvadoran CEBs members have expressed frustration at the scant liturgical and sacramental formation they have been able to access since the heyday of the diocesan

---

[11] José María Castillo, *Símbolos de Libertad: Teología de Los Sacramentos* (Salamanca: Ediciones Sígueme, 1981), 114.

lay formation programs in the 1970s.[12] Nevertheless, out of necessity, as the Salvadoran hierarchy has distanced itself from the CEBs, as new CEBs emerge on the margins of formal ecclesial structures, and as historic CEBs are pushed there, these communities have adapted their liturgical celebrations in creative though often non-normative ways in order to respond to their own celebratory needs.

While the celebratory styles of these communities of lay Catholics certainly represent a contribution to a liturgical liberation theology, it is important to note that both their praxis and analysis also have de(s)colonial characteristics. Whereas the first generations of liberation theologians used various critical economic theories to understand the causes behind the majority experiences of material poverty, the heirs of their reflections and pastoral activities today use a broader set of analytical tools to understand their realities of exclusion, marginalization, and oppression.[13] Without neglecting the inhumanity of large-scale, systematic material and economic poverty, members of the CEBs and other ecclesial communities reflect critically on gender inequality, the climate crisis, state and military violence, and the threatened life of Indigenous peoples in contemporary Latin America. This multifaceted analysis reflects an awareness among these communities of the colonial matrix of power, the enduring, intersecting webs of social, epistemic, and personal control levied against their ancestors and their communities today since colonization.[14] This study of the Salvadoran CEBs' liturgical praxis reflects a similarly multifaceted resistance to these colonial controls. After a few words about research methods, this chapter will describe three elements that stand out in

---

[12] I am grateful to the Brother Mercedes Ruiz Foundation (FUNDAHMER) and the national network of Salvadoran CEBs, who have shared with me their meeting minutes and reflections on different liturgical processes over the years.

[13] Liberation theology's so-called "socio-analytic mediation" is contrasted to other mediations used in Latin American theologies in Juan Carlos Scannone, *Theology of the People: The Pastoral and Theological Roots of Pope Francis* (Mahwah: Paulist Press, 2021), 11–12. I argue that an emergent decolonial mediation allows these different strains of Latin American theology to conspire together in resistance to coloniality, instead of competing for methodological priority, in Laurel Marshall Potter, "Yeast in the Dough: Marginal Ecclesial Communities in Contemporary El Salvador," *Ecclesiology* 18 (2022): 198–215.

[14] "Colonial matrix of power" as in the work of Aníbal Quijano, especially in "Coloniality and Modernity/Rationality," *Cultural Studies* 21, no.2–3 (2007): 168–178 and as expanded in Walter Mignolo, *Desobediencia epistémica: retórica de la modernidad, lógica de la colonialidad, y gramática de la descolonialidad* (Buenos Aires: Ediciones del Siglo, 2010), 12 and 79–80.

liturgies celebrated among CEBs in El Salvador for both their non-normative creativity with regard to Catholic liturgical rubrics as well as their resistance to different colonial controls.

QUALITATIVE RESEARCH FOR THEOLOGICAL STUDY

Though theology has always informally relied on accounts of the experiences and theological questions of the believing community, the formal use of qualitative research methods for assessing such experiences and questions is relatively emergent.[15] Especially for a Catholic church currently focused on the profound assumption of synodality as an ecclesial style, using the tools of the social sciences as part of the church's listening task is not outside the precedent set by the first generations of liberation theology. Ignacio Ellacuría defended the use of Marxist material-economic analysis in theological work, for example, by clarifying that sociological tools help understand reality more clearly and aid the theologian in making a judgment from the church's ongoing reception of revelation.[16] Since Ellacuría's time, however, methodological reflection on

---

[15] Robert Orsi is often cited as among the first to develop the category of "lived religion" in the field of religious studies, using different qualitative methods to research the experiences of believing communities in his works *The Madonna of 115th Street: Faith and Community in Italian Harlem, 1880–1950* (New Haven: Yale University Press, 1985) and *Thank You, St. Jude: Women's Devotion to the Patron Saint of Hopeless Causes* (New Haven: Yale University Press, 1998). In theology, the turn to qualitative and ethnographic methods has also grown from womanist and Latina scholars who have incorporated sources from the social sciences to describe the overlooked contexts where they identify God's presence: here I refer to M. Shawn Copeland's turn to narratives of enslaved and formerly enslaved women in *Enfleshing Freedom: Body, Race, and Being* (Minneapolis: Fortress Press, 2009), Nancy Pineda-Madrid's use of journalistic accounts of femicides in Ciudad Juárez in *Suffering + Salvation in Ciudad Juárez* (Minneapolis: Fortress Press, 2011), Natalia M. Imperatori-Lee's incorporation of literary narrative in *Cuéntame: Narrative in the Ecclesial Present* (Maryknoll: Orbis, 2018), and Nichole M. Flores's conversation with theatrical representations of the apparition of Our Lady of Guadalupe in *The Aesthetics of Solidarity: Our Lady of Guadalupe and American Democracy* (Washington D.C.: Georgetown University Press, 2021). Most recently, Susan Bigelow Reynolds has applied ethnographic methods to her study of ritual and ecclesiology in *People Get Ready: Ritual, Solidarity, and Lived Ecclesiology in Catholic Roxbury* (forthcoming from Fordham University Press, 2023).

[16] In response to the Congregation for the Doctrine of the Faith's 1984 "Instruction on Certain Aspects of the 'Theology of Liberation,'" Ellacuría identifies certain strains of Marxism as several of many sociopolitical tools that help theologians see reality clearly in order to make their particular theological judgment and Christian contribution. See Ignacio Ellacuría, "Estudio teológico-pastoral de la 'Instrucción sobre algunos aspectos de la teología de la liberación," *Revista Latinoamericana de Teología* 1, no. 2 (1984): 145–178.

qualitative and ethnographic methods has uncovered how these particular tools have been used to further reify colonialities of knowledge, being, and power.[17] In response, the field of "critical ethnography" has emerged to complicate the categories of objectivity and impartiality as criteria for scientifically rigorous qualitative study, with Douglas Foley and Angela Valenzuela characterizing it as "*the* site of philosophical and methodological revolt against positivism."[18] Jennifer Manning articulates a decolonial, feminist style of ethnography—an evolution of critical ethnography— which "enables us to open up space 'for the reconstruction and the restitution of silenced histories, repressed subjectivities, subalternized knowledge and languages' and emphasizes the need for the de-coloniality of power and knowledge."[19] Both critical ethnography's revolt against positivism and decolonial, feminist ethnography's insistence on dialogue with epistemic subalterns on their own terms supports an argument that these qualitative tools could be useful for research in theology, an explicitly and intentionally subjective field, especially among grassroots lay Catholics in El Salvador. In order, then, to "see" Salvadoran CEBs' liturgical celebrations in a helpful and accurate way for decolonial theological reflection, I considered both my own role as a researcher among these communities and different research methods that would be helpful in engaging CEBs members in participation and dialogue for the project.

Awareness of my own social positionality among the CEBs was a first critical dynamic to consider in designing and carrying out this study. There are many ways that I am different from the vast majority of CEBs members in a way that broadly affords me social privilege: I hold U.S. citizenship; I am a native English speaker; I have had consistent access to healthcare,

---

[17] For more on the decolonial critiques of classic ethnography and proposals for fields beyond theology, see Raminder Kaur and Victoria Louisa Klinkert, "Decolonizing Ethnographies," *HAU: Journal of Ethnographic Theory* 11, no. 1 (2021): 246–255, and subsequent articles in the "Currents" section of that issue, as well as Carolina Alonso Bejarano, Lucía López Juárez, Mirian A. Mijangos García, and Daniel M. Goldstein, *Decolonizing Ethnographies: Undocumented Immigrants and New Directions in Social Science* (Durham: Duke University Press, 2019).

[18] Douglas Foley and Angela Valenzuela, "Critical Ethnography: The Politics of Collaboration," in *The SAGE Handbook of Qualitative Research*, eds. Norman K. Denzin and Yvonna S. Lincoln, 3rd ed. (Thousand Oaks: SAGE Publications, 2005), 218, emphasis original.

[19] Jennifer Manning, "A decolonial, feminist ethnography: Empowerment, ethics, and epistemology," in *Empowering Methodologies in Organisational and Social Research*, eds, Emma Bell and Sunita Singh Sengupta (New Delhi: Routledge India, 2021), 45.

dignified housing, formal education, and protection from severe violence; and I have been racialized and enculturated into both whiteness and an awareness of coming from a part of the world that has undue influence and power on a global scale.[20] There are other ways that I am similar to or on the disadvantaged side of social norms compared to many CEBs members. In addition to identity, a second significant factor in evaluating my positionality *vis a vis* the CEBs are my long-term personal and professional relationships with CEBs members, particular communities, and the somewhat amorphous body of CEBs on a national level. These groups accompany and shape my ongoing professional discernment, and I worked for five years with FUNDAHMER, a Salvadoran nonprofit established by CEBs' lay leaders in the late 1990s. Additionally, several CEBs had already worked with me to create and evaluate qualitative theological research before this project began. My own personal understanding of Catholic spirituality and ecclesial life is fundamentally shaped by the CEBs; participation among these communities has been my longest-standing ecclesial habit. Whatever these groups and individual people think about me—and I about them—is conditioned, certainly, by the above-mentioned similarities and differences of identity and power, but it is also nuanced and challenged by years of personal encounter.

These long-standing relationships do not free me from the necessity of accounting for questions of identity or power as a researcher. Instead, I reflect on how these relationships condition the opportunities and limits of my research among the CEBs in particular ways. For example, I had little trouble recruiting participants in communities where FUNDAHMER works. I did, however, have a hard time getting buy-in from community members who are active in the community's liturgical life but who do not participate in, for example, the adult women's group that FUNDAHMER

---

[20] It should be noted that these characteristics do not necessarily afford me greater privilege in the context of the CEBs themselves. Developing rapport in a new community may be more difficult because of my physical presentation, national origin, and the community's subsequent expectations around my diet, language abilities, stamina for local conditions, or local and national background knowledge. Communities' distrust and/or racialized behavioral expectations of me are the result of long histories of imperialism, assistentialism, and paternalism, and represent part of the nuanced web of social and cultural dynamics that shape this kind of work.

accompanies. Alternatively, in communities that have separated from the National Network of CEBs or who work in relative isolation to other CEBs, it was easier for a relative outsider to approach and propose a meeting, as a kind of independent agent with a perceived disinterest in—or ignorance of—expanding the reach of the network. In these and other ways, my fundamental position of difference-in-relationship has allowed me perspectives and approaches to the CEBs and their liturgies that would be inaccessible to either a more decided outsider or a total insider. This insight informed the ongoing design of the project and shaped a priority to be aware of and make space for as many exchanges, debates, and perspectives as possible—including my own.[21]

The first six months of the study served as an extended period of participant observation at community events and liturgies, at regional and national meetings of CEBs representatives and members, and at social, cultural, and political events where the CEBs were involved. This extended observation revealed how communities I knew well had shifted during the pandemic and under the influence of a new national government. This phase also provided space for establishing working relationships with new-to-me communities over the course of several weekend visits and for visiting non-CEB ecclesial communities, such as an ecumenical community of families with disabled children in a rural town and an Anglican LGBTQ+ community in San Salvador. Beginning in July of the research year, the study shifted to two different processes. One was a short series of narrative-style focus group interviews, oriented to hearing the community's own telling of their liturgical history and hearing their reactions to selections from *Sacrosanctum Concilium* (SC), the Second Vatican Council's Constitution on the Sacred Liturgy. Whereas the participant observation phase collected mostly my perspective on the CEBs' liturgical celebrations, these group interview sessions allowed for dialogue and exchange between my own questions, the community's answers and further questions, and the chorus of their stories, memories, beliefs, and laments that

---

[21] My thinking on the topics of identity, positionality, power, and my own voice and opinions was especially shaped by Shulamit Reinharz's reflection as an outside researcher intimately involved in life on a kibbutz, in "Who Am I? The Need for a Variety of Selves in the Field," *Reflexivity & Voice*, edited by Rosanna Hertz (Thousand Oaks: SAGE Publications, 1997), 3–20.

these sessions provoked.[22] The second development was a participatory photography/photovoice process with 1–2 participants from a variety of communities throughout the country. The participants proposed and discussed themes for each month of the process, including "culture," "memory," "participation," "art," and "struggle," among others. A Salvadoran photographer supported this process, teaching participants some techniques for composing photographs and pointing out how those principles showed up in the images the group selected. This was an opportunity to hear directly from community members with almost no framing or introductions on my part. Participants took photos at liturgies where I was not present and interpreted the themes the group selected on their own, in ways I would not have come to myself. The result was a broad range of photos and images, all rooted in the general topic of "community liturgies," but ultimately encompassing many other aspects of community life.

Between these three research strategies—participant observation; narrative, focus group interviews; and a photovoice process—the CEBs' liturgies have proven to be a diverse, at times contradictory, but regular and relevant part of their life as Christians. While the process of transcribing, translating, and coding the liturgical database, interview transcripts, and the collection of photovoice participants' final images is still underway, I turn now to describing some elements of community liturgies as they have come up in our visits, conversations, and workshops.

---

[22] In designing the focus group aspect of this research, I relied on George Kamberelis and Greg Dimitriadis, "Focus Groups: Strategic Articulation of Pedagogy, Politics, and Inquiry," in *The SAGE Handbook of Qualitative Research*, 887–907. In this article, the authors recognize that focus groups can serve pedagogical, political, and research purposes, which certainly applied to my project. Often, communities had never heard of, much less read, *Sacrosanctum Concilium* before, so part of working with the document was teaching its significance and place in Catholic tradition. Additionally, the liturgical creativity of these communities is not unrelated to ecclesial politics; in the communities' photography exhibit about their liturgical celebrations, *lucha* (struggle) was one of eight themes that they chose to explain their liturgies. Thus, these workshops served multiple purposes beyond my own research ends and were not objective or disinterested in their potential educational or political effects.

Liturgical Motifs Among Salvadoran CEBs

During a 2021 diagnostic study in preparation for this project, a small sample of CEBs' liturgies served to establish a baseline of contemporary liturgical styles and to create a data collection worksheet to aid in note-taking during the participant observation phase. It was necessary to have some baseline for comparison, with room for extraordinary notes and additions, and the following nine elements of CEBs' liturgical celebrations stuck out as potentially useful for fruitful comparison: (1) a description of the physical space and artwork where the celebration took place, (2) the songs or hymns used during the celebration, (3) a description of the altar, (4) the selection of the readings, (5) the style and theme of the homily, (6) general topics of the prayers of intercession or other petitions, (7) notes on the eucharistic prayer and material, (8) the number and general demographic description of participants, and (9) notes about the presider(s). Over the course of the study, two more categories were added: (10) the entrance procession, and (11) the offertory. The remainder of this chapter turns to exploring three of these elements: the murals and artwork that adorn celebration spaces, the altars that communities construct for liturgy, and the communities' liturgical music.

Murals and Artwork in CEBs' Liturgical Celebrations

The physical spaces where the CEBs celebrate are adorned by community artwork, the most notable example being the public murals that adorn chapels, houses, and rural hermitages. Painting the walls of their worship spaces is an act of aesthetic resistance to the artistic choices of, for example, the Metropolitan Cathedral of San Salvador. The pure, clean, white walls of the Cathedral contrast with the walls of the CEBs' worship spaces, which are colorful, busy, and "*manchadas*"—literally, "stained." Communities describe the artwork in this way, in what I understand to be a tongue-in-cheek acknowledgment of how they feel their murals are viewed by the larger ecclesial community. Added to this perceived attitude is the fact that there *was* a mosaic-style mural on the front face of the National Cathedral called "*Armonía de mi pueblo*," designed by the Salvadoran artist Fernando Llort and installed by many working Salvadoran artists. This mural was taken down by Monsignor José Luís Escobar Alas, the current Archbishop, in 2012, with no clear reason given for the destruction.[23] Other rural communities tell of murals painted over by local priests as parishes take legal control of the land upon which worship spaces are built. Control of the aesthetic presentation of the chapel or hermitage shifts away from the community to the priest, who may visit a couple times a year. Given this archdiocesan and, increasingly, parochial tendency to erase murals from the walls of worship spaces, the CEBs prefer to use their walls as spaces dedicated to community memory and identity.

A figure who appears in nearly every CEBs mural is Monseñor Óscar Romero. Interestingly, many of the murals found in different communities were painted before Romero was canonized by the Roman Catholic church in 2018. As the slogan of his canonization celebration—"*Tu pueblo te hizo santo*"—affirmed, it was these grassroots, ecumenical, and poor churches, those who live at the intersections of so many margins, who preserved his memory and struggled for official recognition.[24] Mural art has been a significant part of this communal work of memory. Going to a liturgical celebration on Sunday and not seeing the parish priest is the norm in rural communities; not seeing Romero is unthinkable.

Just as Ignacio Ellacuría recognized that "With Monseñor Romero, God passed through El Salvador,"[25] the communities identify many heroes and martyrs—saints, in ecclesial dialect—who bring this same Spirit to be present in their history and current reality. Murals express this identification that communities make between Jesus, Romero, and other significant figures.

---

[23] More on this event in Rachel Heidenry, "Archbishop Orders Destruction of Salvadoran Mural," *Pulitzer Center*, January 6, 2012, https://pulitzercenter.org/stories/archbishop-orders-destruction-salvadoran-mural

[24] Michael E. Lee documents the tumultuous road to Romero's canonization in *Revolutionary Saint: The Theological Legacy of Óscar Romero* (Maryknoll: Orbis, 2018).

[25] This quote welcomes visitors to the "*Sala de los mártires*" at the Universidad Centroamericana José Simeón Cañas in San Salvador, a memorial space for Ellacuría and the seven others murdered on November 16, 1989, at the university by the Salvadoran armed forces. For Ignacio Ellacuría, Joaquín López y López, Elba Ramos, Celina Ramos, Ignacio Martín Baró, Juan Ramón Moreno, Amando López, and Segundo Montes, we say, "*¡Presentes!*"

11 TOWARD A DECOLONIAL LITURGICAL THEOLOGY   217

In one, various figures are depicted as if processing out from Jesus in his care. We find Romero; Bl. Rutilio Grande, SJ, in blue, martyred in 1977 and beatified by Rome in February 2022; Fr. Rafael Palacios, in green, a diocesan priest killed near San Salvador in June 1979: and Fr. Octavio Ortiz, in red, killed with four others in January 1979 while facilitating a youth retreat. They are surrounded by scenes of community life: an artisanal clay oven for baking bread, a cornfield, an adobe house with a red clay tile roof, Grandfather River—as people in this community refer to the Torola River—and brother fish, the sun, and the moon. The central message of this mural is clear: Jesus becomes incarnate in our reality, is fed by our tortillas, is warmed by our sun, and bathes in the same river as we do. In these murals, the communities represent their world and testify to the faith they express in this place. To a visitor, the murals give a warm welcome and announce where one has arrived.

The community that belongs to this mural is not the only one that has had conflict with the parish priest because of the images that they choose to adorn their chapel. The frame in the middle is of Fr. Octavio Ortiz, and this chapel was built on the land where he was born, donated by his family for collective use by the local community. Octavio's four brothers were also killed during the Salvadoran civil war (1980–1992), and his father, mother, and sisters sought refuge in San Salvador and in Honduras during the conflict. Afterward, his father, Don Alejandro, and his youngest sister, Anita, returned to continue pastoral work in the area. This particular framed image of Octavio was in the parish church in town until a new priest arrived and said that it was forbidden to display images of uncanonized figures inside of an ecclesial structure, and he took it down. Members of the community were as Mass that day, and they brought the frame back home. On the following anniversary of Octavio's martyrdom, they marched in procession to the town center carrying the image to ask for the priest to reconsider his decision; he refused. Since then, it has adorned the wall of the community's chapel, to which the priest does not have a key, despite his ongoing demands.

Altar Making in CEBs' Liturgical Celebrations

A second element of community liturgies to explore is the altar. The altar is the axis of the community celebration; everything else revolves around it. I begin with an altar that was built for the *pago de la tierra*, an agricultural ritual for planting celebrated by the Kakawira people in the northeastern part of the country.

Here, Nana (Grandmother) Chepa has built a Mayan altar according to the demands of the calendar. She tells that it is a reconstruction of the original world, and that this ceremony opens a path for re-establishing the original balance of the cosmos. A place-specific detail: beneath the flowers and fruit that can be seen in the photo, there is a square of four small planks of wood from the *quebracho* tree, on top of which has been built a cone, seen here, made of laurel wood. Nana Chepa explains that the altar is built in this way, just like houses in the local area are built. The four posts in the corners of an adobe house are made with *quebracho* trunks which, she says, is a feminine element because it is strong and can bear much weight. The roof beams that support the red clay tiles are made from laurel wood, masculine because of how sharp and straight they are. The flowers, the water, the fruit, the stones—all of the other elements, here made ritual and holy objects, are, at the same time, elements from this place's everyday life, fundamental for people's lives. The altar, then, is a little world, a micro-cosmos, and during the ceremony, all participants have the opportunity to interact with it.[26]

The CEBs' community celebrations are interreligious because they have learned to build altars from their *nanas* and *tatas*, from a source of knowledge that has filtered through to them from non-Biblical, non-Jesus sources. Jesus was not Kakawira, but the communities affirm that God has not been absent from Kakawira life.[27] As the traditions that have grown from testimony about Jesus continue to meet the spiritual traditions that have grown from the different peoples of what we call the Americas, communities have sought to preserve their wisdoms, weaving their theologies into Christian altars. Altar building is a living tradition among the CEBs.

---

[26] I should note here that Nana Chepa gave explicit permission for photos of this ceremony to be taken and shared. She explained that she wants the Kakawira spirituality and way of life to be known by future generations and believes that mixing ancient practices with modern ways of life is itself life-giving.

[27] The Roman Catholic bishops made a similar affirmation at the Second Vatican Council, writing: "From ancient times down to the present, there is found among various peoples a certain perception of that hidden power which hovers over the course of things and over the events of human history; at times some indeed have come to the recognition of a Supreme Being, or even of a Father. This perception and recognition penetrates their lives with a profound religious sense" (Second Vatican Council, "Declaration on the Relation of the Church to Non-Christian Religions, *Nostra Aetate*, October 28, 1965, sec. 2, https://www.vatican.va/archive/hist_councils/ii_vatican_council/documents/vat-ii_decl_19651028_nostra-aetate_en.html).

This altar comes from an anniversary celebration of a community that lives close to the Pacific coast, where many community members work in a shrimp farming cooperative. Some residents are originally from Cacaopera and have Kakawira heritage; they settled here upon returning from Honduras after the war. We see that here, they, too, have placed on the altar different elements that are fundamental for their lives: shrimp, beans, corn, seasonal fruits and vegetables, woven cloth, green branches, and fire. These are the first fruits of their world-place, a micro-cosmos. They also place photos of their martyrs on the altar. Hilario, the community's namesake, is there, along with Monseñor Romero, Padre Pedro, Bl. Rutilio Grande, Bl. Nelson Lemus, and Bl. Manuel

Solorzano. To *re-cordar*/re-member them, that is, to have them present again in our hearts and in body, is part of the re-balancing of the cosmos that this community seeks.[28] When we say in the Nicene creed, "we hope for the resurrection of the dead," we refer to these unjustly assassinated or otherwise prematurely killed figures. We yearn for the re-established world, balanced, just, in which these beloved companions and leaders are yet alive.

[28] In Spanish, "to remember" is *recordar*, coming from the Latin *cor* for heart, to re-heart. In English, to re-member evokes a reconstruction of a body. I prefer to nod to both languages, drawing on a diversity of roots and ways to describe the mystical presence of the communities' martyrs at their liturgical celebrations.

This altar is from a commemoration of a massacre that was committed in 1981. In March 2022, 41 years later, the community recognized this anniversary for the first time. Around the time of the more widely known massacre at El Mozote, in which the Salvadoran armed forces killed hundreds of unarmed civilians, many more extrajudicial killings and massacres of civil populations were committed in the surrounding communities on the armed forces' way through guerrilla territory. This is one of those cases. The site of the clandestine grave was exhumed last year, and, at long last, the single survivor, Don Santos, could bury his family members. This is a central act of Christian liturgy as lived in this particular place: Just as the believing community opposes the unjustified state murder of Jesus of Nazareth some two thousand years ago, so we oppose the unjustified state murder of these, our sisters and brothers, 41 years ago. We remember the names of those killed in the massacre at El Tablón, those whose names are on the altar—Patrocinia Luna, Epifania Luna, Julia Luna, Cristela Hernández, Margarito Luna, Juan Luna, Ricardo Luna, María Hernández—and we affirm that they are *presentes*.

Liturgical Song in the CEBs' Celebrations

A third element to explore is the CEBs' liturgical music. In number 39 of *Sacrosanctum Concilium*, sacred music is categorized as one of the liturgical elements that may be validly adapted to particular traditions and cultures, together with sacred art in general, as with murals, as seen above. These adaptations are considered by the document as a sort of first level of liturgical reform, a question of customs, able to be adapted "[w]ithin the limits set by the standard editions of the liturgical books."[29] These first-level adaptations contrast with the possibility that "[i]n some places and circumstances [...] an even more radical adaptation of the liturgy is needed."[30] However, it seems that for the CEBs of El Salvador, the adaptation of art and music is itself a process of profound inculturation and a theological contribution to the church and its liturgy. As the murals open space for communities to define and express themselves theologically, so grassroots hymns identify the communities and teach their faith.

---

[29] Austin Flannery, OP, ed. "Constitution on the Sacred Liturgy (*Sacrosanctum Concilium*)," in *Vatican Council II: Constitutions, Decrees, and Declarations* (Collegeville: Liturgical Press, 2014), 39, p. 132, hereafter "SC."
[30] SC 40.

The following song, which is used often during the eucharistic moment of community liturgies, is a good example of the profound and theological expression of the CEBs' liturgical music and song.

Si callara la voz del profeta, Las piedras hablarán. Si cerraran los pocos caminos, Mil veredas se abrirán.	If the voice of the prophet is silenced, The stones will speak. If the few inroads are closed, A thousand footpaths will open.
No es posible encerrar la verdad Al espacio que quieren dejar; Dios creo lo infinito del mundo Para ser siempre más	It's not possible to lock up the truth In the space where they want to leave it. God created the infinite of the world To always be greater
Es Jesús este pan de igualdad Venimos a comulgar Con la lucha del pueblo Que busca justicia y dignidad	Jesus is this bread of equality We come to commune With the struggle of a people Searching for justice and dignity
Comulgar es volverse un peligro Venimos a incomodar Con la fe y el compromiso Su reino va a llegar.	To commune is to become dangerous We come to provoke discomfort With faith and commitment God's reign will arrive.
El banquete de fiesta del reino Mucha gente rechazó Con los pobres, pecadores y enfermos, Jesucristo se quedó	Many people rejected The banquet festival of the reign. Jesus remained With the poor, with sinners, and the sick.
CORO	**CHORUS**
El poder construyo sobre arena, Con el tiempo va a caer, La unidad es la roca que el pueblo Puso para edificar	Power has built upon sand, With time it will fall. Unity is the rock that the people Set up for building.
CORO[a]	**CHORUS**

[a] "Pan de igualdad," in *Cantos del pueblo: Para animar la fe, la esperanza, y la lucha en comunidad*, eds. Equipo promotor ACOBAMOR (San Salvador: Talleres Gráficos UCA, 2021), 111

The community sings, "Jesus is this bread of equality/we come to commune/with the struggle of a people/searching for justice and dignity." They affirm the classic Catholic teaching that Jesus is truly present in the eucharistic material, and the weave together the reception of these blessed or consecrated elements with becoming like Jesus, struggling for equality, justice, and dignity in society. For the communities that sing this song, to celebrate the eucharistic moment is to "become dangerous [...] to provoke discomfort" for the status quo, and to prepare the arrival of the reign of God.

This second song is the *kyrie eleison* of the Campesina Mass, also sung frequently among communities in El Salvador.

Cristo, Cristo Jesús, identifícate con nosotros	Christ, Christ Jesus, identify with us.
Señor, Señor mi Dios, identifícate con nosotros,	Lord, Lord my God, identify with us. Christ, Christ Jesus, be in solidarity
Cristo, Cristo Jesús, solidarízate	Not with the oppressor class that squeezes and devours the community,
No con la clase opresora que exprime y devora la comunidad,	But rather with the oppressed, with my people who thirst for peace.
Sino con el oprimido, con el pueblo mío sediento de paz.[a]	

[a] "Pan de igualdad," in *Cantos del pueblo: Para animar la fe, la*

This hymn is not a translation of Latin to Spanish with a marimba thrown in for accompaniment. For those who sing this hymn, the plea that Christ have mercy on us is a plea that Christ identify and stand in solidarity with the poor. Here, the communities define and teach what divine mercy is, and it is not an impartial definition. In this way, liturgical music has served as a space for theological creativity and catechesis for the base of the church. When the magisterium categorizes music and art as a first-level kind of adaptation, the communities have taken advantage of that opening to sing the liturgy they desire.

Conclusion

After a brief exposure to some elements of Christian liturgy among ecclesial base communities in El Salvador, it is clear that the communities' liturgical praxis is ripe for dialogue with the theological tradition of the church and with their pastors. The liturgical elements described here push the boundaries of normative liturgical theology, but the CEBs' liturgical creativity and discernment leads, at least in some cases, to a celebration of Christian liturgy that re-members Christ and the christs of history, that offers strength for participants' Christian mission, and that opens community horizons toward the eschaton. As part of the church's reception of conciliar teaching, the CEBs' liturgical praxis calls for the ongoing, systematic articulation of a liturgical/sacramental liberation theology, in which participation in the liturgical life of the universal Church nourishes local churches' active hope in the reign of God.

The community's liturgies are also coherent with the increasingly decolonial mediation of their social analysis. Their murals, altars, and songs speak specifically to a praxis of decolonial *being* and creative expression, a re-membering of history that affirms divine activity on behalf of the poor and marginalized outside the enduring walls of colonial religious power. Here, the non-normative liturgical practices of the Salvadoran CEBs claim that the divine is present beyond the guarantees of the normative rubrics of the Catholic magisterium, and participants bet in a real way on their belief that the God of Christianity is on the side of the *damnés* of history.

CHAPTER 12

Toward Decolonizing Penitential Rites: A Diasporic and Ecumenical Exploration of Worship on (Still) Colonized Land

Kristine Suna-Koro

Decolonizing Christian worship is a matter of theological, liturgical, ethical, and pastoral exigency in the present socio-historical era of postcoloniality. As the Western colonial modernity became a global colonial design,[1] postcoloniality—or its convoluted, metastasizing, and shapeshifting twilight which we currently indwell—manifests in a myriad of diverse ways across the planet in broader societies and faith communities alike. In the United States of America where I, as a diasporic Latvian-American theologian, currently live and work, the question of decolonization cannot be meaningfully addressed without first confronting the widespread oblivion and indifference among the so-called mainstream/mainline North

[1] Walter D. Mignolo, *Local Histories/Global Designs: Coloniality, Subaltern Knowledges, and Border Thinking* (Princeton: Princeton University Press, 2012).

K. Suna-Koro (✉)
Xavier University, Cincinnati, OH, USA
e-mail: sunakorok@xavier.edu

© The Author(s), under exclusive license to Springer Nature Switzerland AG 2023
R. C. Barreto, V. Latinovic (eds.), *Decolonial Horizons*, Pathways for Ecumenical and Interreligious Dialogue,
https://doi.org/10.1007/978-3-031-44839-3_12

American Christian churches about their own histories and legacies as instruments and conduits of colonial conquest of Indigenous nations and their land. It is not feasible to address here the whole "legion" of issues at the intersection of Christian worship and decolonization. Hence, my goal in this chapter is to probe the decolonial potential of liturgical confession and repentance through exploring the so-called Penitential rites of public communal worship.

As a *Lutheran* Latvian-American theologian, I can attest that Lutherans usually insist that they take repentance seriously. After all, if one only recalls the momentous events of 1517 when Martin Luther posted his "95 Theses," it all begins with repentance. Thesis #1 hammers home the centrality of repentance—understood here as way more dynamic, existential, and inherently soteriological transformation rather than a mere moralistic and transactional ritual or even an isolated sacrament: "Our Lord and Master Jesus Christ, in saying 'Do penance[...]', wanted the entire life of the faithful to be one of penitence."[2]

---

[2] Martin Luther, "95 Theses" or "Disputation for the Clarifying the Power of Indulgences," *The Annotated Luther: The Roots of Reform, Vol. 1* (Volume and section ed. Timothy J. Wengert; Minneapolis: Fortress Press, 2015), 34. Here Luther is still using the formulaic Matt 14:17 Vulgate translation *poenitentiam agite* for the much richer and holistic Greek term *metanoeite*. Luther and later Lutherans will expand on the nexus of transformations that *metanoeite* entails—change of mind, change of life, reorientation of values and yes, also repentance and penance. Luther also adds in Thesis #2 that repentance/penitence in the specific context of the complex and the contentious dispute about indulgences "cannot be understood as referring to sacramental Penance, that is, confession and satisfaction as administered by the clergy," ibidem. Luther also insists that the expanded penance cannot be limited "solely to inner penitence—indeed such inner penitence is nothing unless it outwardly produces various mortifications of the flesh," ibidem, 35. The inner penitence in this case would refer to the element of contrition in the standard medieval pattern of sacramental penance (*contritio cordis, confessio oris, satisfactio operis*). In his "Sermon on the Sacrament of Penance" (1519), Luther elaborates on the connection but also on the distinction between penitence/repentance and the Sacrament of Penance as it was understood and practiced at the time, see *The Annotated Luther: The Roots of Reform, Vol. 1*, 188–201. Luther's early sacramental theology entertained the understanding of Penance as a sacrament as did the early Lutheran confessional writings such as the Augsburg Confession and the Apology to the Augsburg Confession. Later theological, liturgical, and ecclesiastical developments, however, settled on affirming only Baptism and Eucharist as "proper" sacraments for the Lutheran and other Protestant traditions.

In this essay, by "repentance" I mean what Luther—and many others on the cusp of early modernity—in his context conceptualized as "penitence," namely, *metanoia*: the complex nexus of contrition, confession, absolution, satisfaction, and reconciliation. By the more specific term "Penitential rites," I mean the scripted, institutionalized/official, and commonly used patterns or orders of confession and absolution in ordinary Sunday public worship in North-Atlantic Christian communities of faith representing Lutheran, Anglican/Episcopal, and Roman Catholic traditions.

This essay was researched and written in my home office and my university campus in Cincinnati, Ohio. Both my house and my university are located on the conquered homelands of the Indigenous/Native Peoples/First Nations/Indian tribal nations of the Algonquian speaking peoples of Delaware, Miami, and Shawnee.[3]

Why Do the Liturgical Practices of Penitence/Confession (Still) Matter? Working Assumptions and Aspirations

The first question that needs to be asked is why one would explore these traditions of worship in the first place? As an immigrant, I find myself indwelling the crossroads of several traditions. Here I am exploring the Penitential rites of communal worship of the three traditions I'm currently most embedded in: I am a theologian and pastor of the Latvian Evangelical Lutheran Church in America. Moreover, I also often worship in Anglican/Episcopalian communities—courtesy of my migratory life and a deeply influential educational sojourn in Great Britain during the early years of my educational and pastoral path. And I earn my daily bread by teaching theology at a Catholic Jesuit university in the American Midwest.

There is another, far more important, reason beyond the liturgical trifecta of my diasporic life for exploring these traditions. Despite the notable institutional diminishment of mainstream/mainline Christian institutionalized traditions which are predominantly comprised by White North Americans and which are sometimes called "liturgical traditions," these

---

[3] I include this information as a respectful land acknowledgment based on locally available information for Cincinnati, OH, USA. There is no single uniform way of referring to the various Indigenous peoples in North America, see, for example, Stephanie Perdew, "On Native Land," *The Christian Century*, November 2022, 54–57.

communities of faith still have considerable membership and impact on local and translocal societies. How these communities of faith worship, therefore, can make not just a figurative but also a material difference today. How their worship forms or malforms their spiritualities, their values, their subjectivities, and their agency in both interpersonal and sociopolitical arenas, therefore, constitutes a salient decolonial concern for our moment in history. The present reflections do not pretend to offer some meta-liturgical analysis for all times and all places. They are rather embedded in and speak out of the current socio-historical moment in dialogue with liturgical traditions and decolonial imaginaries.

The key focus of these reflections is two-pronged: First, to explore which patterns and structures in the cluster of Penitential rites for public communal worship can be mobilized to potentially assist decolonial transformations in liturgical assemblies—alongside recognizing some key impediments for such potential transformations. And second, to briefly highlight some problematic elements in dominant models of Absolution/Forgiveness as an ongoing challenge for decolonizing Penitential rites in the environment of the Indigenous land dispossession. These explorations inescapably begin with an examination of not just individual but also ecclesiastical conscience.

Sarah Augustine, for example, invites a question that no Christian community in North America should take lightly:

> As a church, do we stand where we say we do? Many of us believe that we and our institutions stand with the oppressed. In reality, the church as a body collectively benefits from harming the most vulnerable people. Engaging in repair will mean turning away from this violence by risking our own security to challenge the powers that threaten us all.[4]

Augustine counsels a path that Christians can undoubtedly recognize: "[…] I call on the church to acknowledge wrongdoing and begin the process of seeking repair in relationships with Indigenous Peoples."[5] In other words, the decolonial repair begins with a movement of repentance. In liturgical context, this is where Penitential rites may contribute to decolonial repair.

---

[4] Sarah Augustine, *The Land is Not Empty: Following Jesus in Dismantling the Doctrine of Discovery* (Harrisonburg, VA: Herald Press, 2021), 208.
[5] Ibidem, 210.

A COMPOSITION OF PLACE: THE CONTEXT OF EXPLORING CHRISTIAN WORSHIP ON STOLEN LANDS[6]

The broader context of this exploration is the still widespread oblivion and indifference in North American Christian churches (Mainline and Evangelical, White, Black, Latinx/Hispanic, and Asian American alike) regarding their own histories and legacies as instruments and conduits of colonial conquest of Indigenous nations and their land. Even if denominational statements on the Doctrine of Discovery and Land Acknowledgments are issued, how many regular church members even know that they exist, let alone ponder what implications they might have for their own local liturgical assemblies? As the Potawatomi Christian author Kaitlin Curtice has put it, notably in the present tense,

> Settler colonial Christianity puts itself at the center of everything as the sole power […] settler colonial Christianity is a religion that takes, that demeans the earth and the oppressed, and that holds people in these systems without regard of how Jesus treated people. So to be part of a colonizing religion, I have to constantly ask, Who am I following?[7]

The immediate context for my reflections is the renewed attention to the tragic North American histories of colonization and genocidal violence as the discoveries of unmarked burial grounds of Indigenous children at the "Indian boarding schools" in 2021 once again have called attention to cultural imperialism, territorial dispossession, and enduring intergenerational trauma of Native nations in Canada and the United States.[8] Pope Francis' meeting with Canada's Métis Nation and Inuit People in Rome in March–April 2022[9] and his subsequent "penitential pilgrimage" to Canada

---

[6] With "composition of place" I'm referring here to a key concept in Ignatian/Jesuit spirituality—*compositio loci*—which emphasizes the awareness of the context and our embeddedness in concrete historical, cultural, emotional, and interpersonal realities.

[7] Kaitlin B. Curtice, *Native: Identity, Belonging, and Rediscovering God* (Grand Rapids: Brazos, 2020), 35–36.

[8] U.S. Department of the Interior, "Department of the Interior Releases Investigative Report," May 5, 2022. Online: https://www.doi.gov/pressreleases/department-interior-releases-investigative-report-outlines-next-steps-federal-indian. Volume 1 of the Report is available here: https://www.bia.gov/sites/default/files/dup/inline-files/bsi_investigative_report_may_2022_508.pdf

[9] Salvatore Cernuzio, "Canada's Indigenous Delegations: 'Pope Francis listened to our pain'," March 28, 2022. Vatican: https://www.vaticannews.va/en/pope/news/2022-03/pope-francis-canada-indigenous-delegations-audience-interview.html. Accessed 6.20.2022.

in July 2022[10] brought much needed attention to the dispossessions of colonial violence still endured by the Indigenous peoples as "the Doctrine of Discovery is not a historical concept but a current juggernaut."[11]

Worship is at the heart of Christian life. Worship does not happen in a historical, cultural, and moral vacuum. No matter which liturgical rites are being performed by whatever Christian denomination, worship happens in a particular place. The often fully unacknowledged fact is that for Christian churches in the Americas, most worship takes place on conquered, unceded, and unacknowledged Indigenous land. From decolonial perspectives, this is the most basic and most indispensable liturgical and ecclesiological fact for the faith which gravitates around the incarnate Word who becomes flesh at a particular historical time and in a particular geocultural location.

This fact, I propose, is the incarnational gateway which the emerging American liturgical theologies would be wise not to dismiss as too simplistic or merely political. After all, all individual and communal prayers, supplications, intercessions, doxologies and adorations originate from people who are standing, sitting, or kneeling somewhere. Every "somewhere" in the Americas remains variably infused by the specters of the coloniality of power, being, and knowledge. Patty Krawec reminds, "Decolonizing is not another word for antiracism or anti-oppression; it is not just another way of saying diversity and inclusion."[12] It rather means "returning the land to the people from whom it was taken. We could be the most antiracist society on earth, but as long as our institutions rely on stolen land and the displacement of Indigenous people, the United States will remain a colonial state."[13] Some hopeful strides have been made, including here in Ohio when a United Methodist community in 2021 returned three acres of sacred land, including the historic Wyandot Mission Church, to the Wyandotte Nation of Oklahoma. Yet such specific and materially relevant acts of repentance or conversion—indeed, acts of *metanoia*—albeit with

---

[10] Pope Francis, "General Audience," Wednesday, 3 August 2022. Vatican: https://www.vatican.va/content/francesco/en/audiences/2022/documents/20220803-udienza-generale.html. Accessed 9.28.2022.

[11] Augustine, *The Land is Not Empty*, 87.

[12] Patti Krawec, "Can these stones live?" *The Christian Century*, September 2022, 49.

[13] Ibidem, 49.

limited impact for restitution due to the magnitude of ongoing colonial systems of power, are sporadic.[14]

Decolonization for Christian worship assemblies—whatever else it may mean—means at least a recognition that a "delinking" from both the privilege of oblivion or even willful ignorance about our own ecclesiastical histories now deserves to be acknowledged as a *spiritual* and *moral* exigency.[15]

Underneath the Church Floor: Toward Decolonizing the Primordial Worship Space

It all really begins with a seemingly simple question: where do we worship as a liturgical assembly? In a typical liturgical theology, when one talks about "worship space," it usually means a church or a chapel. It signals, virtually by default, some permanently or temporarily appointed location which is set apart or formally consecrated for communal rites of worship or individual practices of devotion. Yet what I mean by "worship space" in the context of these reflections is a more primordial spatial reality. It is the slice of the planet which holds and literally grounds all those carefully crafted and adorned sanctuaries: it is the land on which all such sanctuaries inevitably stand. The foundational and primordial worship space is actually underneath the church floor.

For Christian assemblies of worship, land is where such delinking needs to begin as "land is our first relationship, and it is the first relationship that we need to restore" since "colonialism has disconnected us from land, severed us from that first relationship—often through violence."[16] In this case, the "us" who are severed from the right relationship with the land include, asymmetrically, both the Indigenous peoples and all sorts of settler communities, including relatively recent immigrants such as my own diasporic Latvian American community.

---

[14] Mark Caudill, "Sacred Native American lands returned to Wyandotte Nation by United Methodists." September 21, 2019. Website: https://www.mansfieldnewsjournal.com/story/news/2019/09/21/sacred-native-american-lands-returned-united-methodists/2386770001/. Accessed 6.12.2022.

[15] Walter D. Mignolo, "Delinking: The rhetoric of modernity, the logic of coloniality and the grammar of de-coloniality," *Cultural Studies* 21, no. 2–3 (2007): 449–514 and also his recent *The Politics of Decolonial Investigations* (Duke University Press, 2021), 1–81 among his other publications.

[16] Krawec, "Can these stones live?", 47.

The present state of affairs reveals a chronic condition of unfaithfulness to the "dangerous memory" of the Gospel: namely, in the words of Johann Baptist Metz, to the memory of life, suffering, death, and resurrection of Jesus Christ in solidarity with the vanquished, the victimized, the disempowered, and the dispossessed. As a result, what obtains, from a decolonial point of view, is what Metz called "false consciousness of our past and an opiate for our present"[17]—theologically, ecclesially, liturgically, and ethically. Moreover, memories of suffering, as Metz rightly insists, "make demands on us" and "make the present unsafe."[18]

Decolonial transformation of Christian ecclesial communities in North America is neither feasible nor consequential without a dialectic of repentance and reconciliation in the worship assemblies originating from any settler colonialist and immigrant lineages, be they Roman Catholic, Protestant, nondenominational, or postdenominational. But what do and what can the so-called liturgical traditions in the ecclesiastical spectrum of denominations offer? The decolonial liturgical theologian Claudio Carvalhaes has recently noted that in postcolonial contexts and for decolonial intentions we cannot avoid "ask[ing] about worship books. Can we still use them? Can the denominational books of prayers bring something good?"[19]

It is with this question in mind, I proceed to explore the scripted rituals of public communal worship for confession and absolution. The working assumption remains that despite the undeniable embeddedness of these traditions in various and enduring legacies of colonialism, they still can potentially function as "resources and tools for transformation."[20]

---

[17] Johann Baptist Metz, *Faith in History and Society: Toward a Fundamental Practical Theology* (New York: Seabury, 1980), 109.
[18] Ibidem, 109, 200.
[19] Claudio Carvalhaes, "A Decolonial Prayer," in *Decolonial Christianities: Latinx and Latin American Perspectives*, edited by Raimundo Barreto and Roberto Sirvent (Palgrave Macmillan, 2019), 275.
[20] Raimundo Barreto and Roberto Sirvent, "Introduction," in *Decolonial Christianities,* 11.

What Do (Some) Lutherans, Roman Catholics, and Episcopalians Say When They Confess and Repent?

I have surveyed Penitential/Confession rites of my own church in America and in the homeland as well as of the Evangelical Lutheran Church in America (ELCA), Roman Catholic Church (RCC), and the Episcopal Church in the USA (ECUSA). Here I present a summary of the key official Penitential/Confession rites. One caveat is mandated before I proceed. This exploration does not involve experimental rites currently under review during the trial use, where such experimental rites are denominationally endorsed and permissible for public communal worship. As is often the case in vital and rejuvenated liturgical spaces and communities, worship assemblies, and leaders often find creative ways of blending scripted rites with astonishing variety of locally resonant and relevant liturgical performances. It is not, however, the case everywhere. As I will show below, some traditions allow for a wider spectrum of local liturgical improvisation while others do not.

Key Elements of the Latvian Evangelical Lutheran Penitential Rites

The 1992 *Dziesmu grāmata* (*Hymnal for Latvians in the Homeland and Abroad*) contains the most widely practiced Eucharistic rites for Sunday worship as well as the Service of the Word in the worldwide Latvian Lutheran diaspora. Up until a few years ago, it was also the standard rite for Lutherans in the homeland.

There are two Penitential rites to choose from for "Confession and Absolution" (*Grēksūdze un Absolūcija*).[21] Penitential rite 1 A traditionally is positioned right after *Introitus* and *Gloria Patri* at the beginning of the service. Penitential rite 1 A *may* include an appropriate hymn verse and the presider *may* opt for a short (hopefully) *Bikts runa*—penitential mini-homily alongside appropriate Scriptural verses. The prayer of Confession follows. There are two options for this prayer. One is a traditional prayer beginning with "I, poor sinner ..." which by and large follows the form

---

[21] *Dziesmu grāmata latviešiem tēvzemē un svešumā* (LELBA Latvian Evangelical Lutheran Church Abroad and Latvian Evangelical Church in America, 1992), 4–8, 13–20.

which in the North American context is still in use in the Lutheran Church-Missouri Synod (LCMS) tradition.[22]

As for Penitential Rite 1 B, it follows directly after the opening hymn by a short responsorial dialog between the presider and the assembly using verses from *Psalm 121* which is then followed by the Latvian translation of the traditional Collect for Purity ("Almighty God, to whom all hearts are open and all desires known …"). A brief invocation using 1 John 1:8–9 follows after which there is an option for silence. There is also a prayer using *Rom 7:19* supplemented by the traditional Lutheran acknowledgment of our bondage to sin and the inability to free ourselves followed by the petition for forgiveness. In conclusion, the presider declares God's forgiveness which is then followed by *Gloria Patri* and an expanded *Kyrie*. The rite concludes with a sung responsorial *Gloria in excelsis*. Penitential Rite 1B bears a very strong North American diasporic imprint and borrows some patterns from Evangelical Lutheran Church in America (ELCA) so-called "Green Book" (Lutheran Book of Worship, LBW).

Key Elements of the Roman Catholic Penitential Rites

In comparison to the Latvian Lutheran rite, the current version of the Roman Missal entails three forms for the Penitential Act in mass. Form A is the already well-known classic *Confiteor* rite. Form B is the very brief invocation for mercy ("Have mercy on us, O Lord …"). Both A and B forms are followed by *Kyrie* while the popular Form C is itself patterned on *Kyrie* with added invocations in responsorial format. There is an alternative substitution of the Penitential Act forms with the Sprinkling Rite.[23] Of course, the Absolution, strictly speaking, is not present in the Roman mass as the Penitential Act does not equal the sacrament of Penance and Reconciliation. That involves private sacramental confession.

---

[22] I have already addressed some of the aspects of this tradition in my article on confession and reconciliation "Confession of Sin and the 'Sinned-Against': An Inquiry from a Lutheran Perspective," *Liturgy* 3, no. 1 (2019): 21–29. Texts in both English and Latvian are available and analyzed to greater detail in the article.

[23] Website: https://www.catholicbishops.ie/wp-content/uploads/2011/02/Order-of-Mass.pdf. Accessed 9.15.2022.

Key Elements of the Episcopalian (ECUSA) Penitential Rites

Like Latvian Lutherans and Roman Catholics, American Episcopalians frame their ordinary Sunday worship in accordance to scripted Penitential rites of public worship. The *Book of Common Prayer* (BCP)[24] offers two Penitential Orders which can be used either for separate services of repentance as well as two orders for Confession of Sin for Eucharistic Rites One and Two. In the Penitential Orders, there are appointed verses from the Scripture and the core prayers are prescribed in the rite following the well-known generalized and abstract pattern with the familiar catch-all petitions of "we have not loved you [God] with our whole heart" and "we have not loved our neighbors as ourselves." As far as room for flexibility, specificity, and contextuality is concerned, we need to look for the instructional text in italics: there is an optional space for a homily if the Penitential Orders are used as separate services. In this setting, there is also space to conclude the service "with suitable prayers" which again allows for some more specific focus on the sins being confessed depending on the liturgical and pastoral choices of worship leaders.

The brief orders for the Confession of Sin in both Eucharistic Rites One and Two do not offer any flexibility beyond the choice of two scripted prayers of confession in Rite One while Rite Two offers the same generalized prayer of confession from the Rite Two Penitential Order.

Key Elements of the Evangelical Lutheran Church in America (ELCA) Penitential Rites

To complete the brief survey, I am most intrigued—for the reasons to be addressed in the next section below—by the Penitential rites of the ELCA. *The Evangelical Lutheran Worship of ELCA* (2006) presents the most flexible ritual framework for ordinary Sunday worship among the options reviewed so far. All 10 Settings for the Holy Communion prescribe a scripted rite of Confession and Forgiveness. The shape of the Penitential rites generally follows the traditions already outlined above. However, the prayers for Preparation and Confession are accompanied by

---

[24] All references to the Book of Common Prayer (BCP) are to the 1982 edition of *Prayer Book and Hymnal Containing the Book of Common Prayer and the Hymnal 1982 According to the Use of The Episcopal Church*. This publication includes the 1979 *The Book of Common Prayer and Administration of the Sacraments and Other Rites and Ceremonies of the Church* (New York: The Church Hymnal Corporation, 1986).

the rubrics (i.e., instructions) in italics which inconspicuously yet repeatedly indicate that, "the presiding minister may lead one of the following or another prayer of preparation" or "another confession." Absolution can be announced "with these or similar words."[25] There is an analogous flexibility in the stand-alone rite of Corporate Confession and Forgiveness.[26]

DECOLONIZING MAINLINE PENITENTIAL RITES: PITFALLS AND PROMISES

There are clearly recognizable liturgical, theological, historical, and cultural differences in the scripted Penitential rites of all these traditions of worship. At the same time, despite differences, all surveyed rites for public communal Sunday worship are characterized by ahistoricity and acontextuality of the liturgical language and theological imaginaries of sin, confession, and absolution.

From decolonial perspectives, it registers as an intractable pitfall if the prayers of Confession as well as the forms of Absolution are the same regardless of when the assembly is worshipping in terms of the liturgical Church Year, or in terms of pastoral context, or in terms of wider sociocultural context and its moral exigencies. As I have pointed out elsewhere, the words being said by those who have sinned and by those sinned-against are exactly the same—and that is the case for the words of Absolution as well. This, as I have argued, is deeply problematic on moral, pastoral, and liturgical levels even apart from explicitly decolonial considerations.[27] The key soteriological and theo-ethical functions of repentance and its ritual expressions in Penitential rites of communal worship are to acknowledge wrongdoing and to reconcile with God and fellow creation in the context of specific postbaptismal sins. In the Western Christian traditions, ontological challenges of the condition of "original sin" are primarily addressed already in the sacrament of Baptism.

The dominance of ahistorical and acontextual dimensions of repentance in the Western tradition reflects and reinforces the individualistic

---

[25] *Evangelical Lutheran Worship* (Minneapolis: Augsburg Fortress, 2006), 94–96. The rite of Confession and Forgiveness can be substituted with the rite of Thanksgiving for Baptism, 97.

[26] Ibidem, 238–242.

[27] Please see my articles "Confession of Sin and the 'Sinned-Against': An Inquiry from a Lutheran Perspective," and "Liturgy and Lament: Postcolonial Reflections from the Midst of a Global Refugee Crisis," *Liturgy* 34, no.2 (2019): 31–40.

and deceptively apolitical theologies of sin. Ahistoricity and acontextuality have dominated Western Christian hamartiologies at the expense of social and structural dimensions of sin. How fruitful is the path to repentance on autopilot when the rites provide no opportunity to verbally confess *specific* sins in a local and historically concrete context? As long as these hamartiologies continue to dominate, the process of robust decolonization of Penitential rites can hardly materialize. A simultaneous and long overdue decolonization of the dominant Christian hamartiologies is also needed at a more foundational level of theological imagination and pastoral practice.

What about the promises? The diasporic 1992 Latvian Lutheran rite 1A still allows for the optional Penitential mini-homily before the prayers of Confession. Such option exists in BCP, too. Such options provide space and opportunity for the presiding minister to focus the attention of the worshipping community on specific realities and manifestations of sin before the actual prayer of Confession is said by the whole assembly. This could be, at least indirectly, a fruitful moment (yet not often used in practice) of reflection, solidarity, and exhortation to increase the awareness of communal and personal inscription in the colonial violence.

A tentative yet promising avenue is discreetly present in ELCA rites. There is some (inconspicuous) room for flexibility. It may potentially bring the necessary specificity, historicity, and contextuality to Penitential rites. Under prophetic pastoral and theological leadership, as I have witnessed in ELCA Sunday worship on some occasions, both Prayers of Preparation and Confession can be locally shaped to resonate with communal and individual sinful legacies and present realities such as racism, sexism, homophobia, economic dispossession, and—very slowly and very rarely—also with the systemic legacies of colonialism.

On Newness and Repetition

Joining hands with Vatican II vision of *Sacrosanctum Concilium* toward active and fully conscious participation in worship—at least as an aspiration that shouldn't be scorned even if it remains an idealistic proposition—I submit that the path of decolonizing Penitential rites and communal Sunday worship starts with profound questioning of conventional liturgical routines in the so-called liturgical traditions. It begins with delinking from the false universals of liturgical ahistoricity and acontextuality as well as false equivalencies of guilt and responsibility in theologies of sin and respective liturgical scripts of Confession and Absolution. In the absence of decolonized imaginary of repentance churches will continue to obliviously or deliberately practice what Metz memorably described as a "eulogistic evasion of what really matters."[28]

In Metzian terms, decolonization of repentance—in theology, in liturgy, and in ecclesiology—will indeed make the present unsafe. At the same time, it may also make it potentially more truthful, more liberating and more open to reconciliation and repair. It will certainly render worship spaces and worshipping assemblies more ambivalent about themselves as spaces for revelation and salvation.

Liturgically speaking, new and much more contextual—historically, pastorally, ecologically, socio-culturally, and ethically—Penitential rites are needed to meaningfully ritualize the overlapping terrains of individual and social sin. The histories and legacies of colonial conquests and stolen Indigenous lands fall into both of these categories of sin. I do not propose to simply discard the traditional forms of Confession and Absolution. It is rather a matter of, first, examining, challenging, and potentially reforming the dominant theological and liturgical imaginary which—at least in the mainline Protestant and Roman Catholic traditions—often privileges historical longevity and the so-called historical "authenticity" of rites over pastoral relevance. Decolonization in this context means *adding* new rites that explicitly engage and intersect with both liturgical histories as well as histories and legacies of sin. It is also a matter of offering denominational endorsements to develop and use such contextual rites to directly address the realities of communal and structural sin. It means offering theological, spiritual, and pastoral guidance on how to discern our individual accountability for such structural sins as spiritual preparation for decolonizing worship. Such initiatives would be most welcome—while also being most challenging—for those liturgical traditions with the longest historical pedigrees of tightly scripted public communal worship where the denominational identity is directly connected with the use of expressly defined ritual forms (Roman Catholics, Anglicans/Episcopalians, most Lutherans).

Furthermore, I would like to underscore that there is an important distinction between on one hand holding various "extraordinary" services (such as one-time commemorations, thanksgivings, dedication of plaques,

---

[28] Metz argues that "Hence we must take care not to let our prayers turn into a eulogistic evasion of what really matters, serving merely to lift the apathy from our souls and our indifference and lack of sympathy towards other people's suffering," in Karl Rahner and Johann B. Metz. *The Courage to Pray* (New York: Crossroad, 1981), 20.

chapels, and memorials) involving various types of repentance for political and cultural violence against the Indigenous nations, and on the other hand having ordinary Penitential rites in public common worship which are performed on any regular Sunday. Such practice stretches beyond Land Acknowledgments on denominational or congregational websites or reciting them before (i.e., outside) the worship service and other church events. Without doubt, these gestures of repentance and desired reconciliation are important. They are also incredibly tricky and can result in hurtful experiences even when grounded in good intentions.[29]

The key for a decolonization of worship that might "stick" on a personal and systemic level is to re-evaluate and adjust the *ordinary* forms which are widely used for regular communal Sunday worship. That is where the spiritual senses of worshippers are shaped and nurtured in much less spectacular, but in more enduring and resilient ways. Repetition, as liturgical scholarship emphasizes, is a distinctively liturgical virtue.[30]

Grace cannot be limited to extraordinary moments and locations alone to facilitate the demanding and unsafe labor of contrition and confession toward what Roman Catholic theology of repentance still describes as "satisfaction"—namely, to "repair the harm" and "remedy all the disorders sin has caused."[31]

The element of satisfaction—apart from the historical debacle of indulgences—should not be dismissed. Even Martin Luther hastened to clarify that the "best kind of satisfaction is to sin no more and to do all possible good toward your neighbor, whether enemy of friend. This kind of satisfaction is rarely mentioned. We think to pay for everything simply through assigned prayers."[32]

---

[29] See Becca Whitla's insightful article "The Theological Challenge of Territorial Acknowledgments in Liturgy," *Worship* 96 (January 2022):55–75.

[30] To mention just one representative argument of scholarly consensus on the role of repetition in liturgical formation of Christians, E. Byron Anderson summarizes that "Sunday by Sunday, year by year, our liturgical practices are writing an affective, physical, and imaginal argument in our bodies through which we come to know ourselves, our world, and God. Ritual repetition trains our bodies such that the habits of liturgical gesture and action as well as ethical living become natural," "Liturgy: Writing Faith in the Body," *Liturgical Ministry* 20 (Fall 2011): 174.

[31] *Catechism of the Catholic Church*. Second edition. Article 1459. Website: https://www.vatican.va/archive/ENG0015/__P4D.HTM. Accessed 9.2.2022.

[32] Luther, "Sermon on the Sacrament of Penance," *The Annotated Luther: The Roots of Reform, Vol. 1*, 200.

And, Finally, the Absolution: Some Further Questions

But what about the Absolution/Forgiveness? Scripted Penitential rites for public worship ordinarily end with some kind of clergy-facilitated Absolution/Forgiveness which either declares, or invokes, or announces, or prays for God's forgiveness. But if reconciliation not only with God but also with "our neighbor" (as BCP puts it in the invitation to Confession) is the ultimate goal of repentance, then we need to ask if decolonizing the Absolution means to hold space for some form of Absolution/Forgiveness by the sinned-against neighbors? Is it not rather presumptuous that contrition, confession, and absolution can be ritually transacted and communicated within the detached safety of the rite without providing appropriate liturgical space for the voices of the sinned-against to be invited and heard in Penitential rites *if* such voices are able and willing to participate in certain circumstances?

As a Lutheran, I wonder if decolonizing the soteriological bravado of the conventional Lutheran formulas of Absolution should entail a modulation toward the subtle Anglican/Episcopalian ambivalence of declaration *of* prayer *for* forgiveness in their Penitential rites? Or perhaps it is time for a new theological reflection on the necessity for a stronger emphasis on open-ended supplication in some penitential contexts—such as coming to grips with the histories and legacies of colonialism in North America and elsewhere—that aligns more closely with the liturgical comportment of the Roman Catholic Penitential Act? All three forms (A, B, C) conclude with the priest announcing forgiveness in a vocative sense: "*May* almighty God have mercy on us, forgive us our sins, and bring us to everlasting life."[33]

Decolonization calls for rites which are incarnational enough, liquid enough, sensitive enough, and spacious enough to accommodate a decolonizing dialectic of repentance in ordinary common worship to incorporate specific actualities and legacies of social sins to be brought to light before God and before those who were/are sinned-against. A glimpse of what is involved in such a dialectic of repentance can be found in what Pope Francis finally acknowledged in his April 2022 meeting with the representatives of the First Nations of Canada in the aftermath of the

---

[33] Website: https://www.catholicbridge.com/catholic/catholic-mass-full-text.php. Accessed 10.27.2022. Italics added for emphasis.

unmarked Indigenous children's burial ground discoveries. Francis remarked that he feels indignation and shame as he asked first, "God's forgiveness." But immediately after that he went on to say that "I want to say to you with all my heart: I am very sorry. And I join [...] Canadian bishops in asking your pardon."[34] In July 2022, Francis embarked on "penitential pilgrimage" to Canada to, again, ask for forgiveness on his journey of remembrance. Undoubtedly, the long colonial debacle between imperial Christianity and the Native nations in North America is far from resolved, let alone reconciled. But Francis' acknowledgment that praying for God's forgiveness alone is not enough for a meaningful reconciliation is a step toward decolonization of repentance. Asking for pardon from those sinned-against is nonnegotiable even if such pardon *cannot* and *must not* be presumed or expected by default. Furthermore, the process of decolonizing repentance - which should not be confused with any kind of panacea or premature closure - must also include, where applicable, public acknowledgment of communal responsibility of whole church bodies and theological traditions in colonial conquests. As far as the Roman Catholic church is concerned, on March 30, 2023, the Dicasteries for Culture and Education and for Promoting Integral Human Development issued the "Joint Statement" repudiating the "concepts" associated with the Doctrine of Discovery.[35] Despite Vatican's prolonged reluctance to officially repudiate this notorious body of theopolitical teachings as well as the evasive caveats about the distinctions between proper "doctrine" and allegedly *ad hoc* manipulations of the papal bulls for political purposes, and the long-running casuistry of "abrogation" vs. "repudiation," the statement finally recognizes the Roman church's complicity in the sinister policies of colonialism.

How to ritualize this double-pronged dynamic repentance and forgiveness (vis-a-vis God/sinned-against) not only on extraordinary occasions but rather in the repetitive ordinary rites of public worship looms large as one of the preeminent contemporary challenges of decolonizing liturgy

---

[34] Pope Francis, "Meeting with Representatives of Indigenous Peoples of Canada, Address of His Holiness Pope Francis," Vatican, April 1, 2022. Website: https://www.vatican.va/content/francesco/en/speeches/2022/april/documents/20220401-popoli-indigeni-canada.html. Accessed 6.17.2022.

[35] The Dicasteries for Culture and Education and for Promoting Integral Human Development "Joint Statement," March 30, 2023. Online source: https://press.vatican.va/content/salastampa/en/bollettino/pubblico/2023/03/30/230330b.html.

under the auspices of institutionalized ecclesial communities. Mignolo remarked that "decoloniality focuses on changing the terms of the conversation and not just its content."[36] If so, then the decolonization of repentance for the liturgical traditions will need to begin with a momentous re-thinking not only of the liturgical *ordo* but primarily of the theology underlying the Penitential rites. Decolonial re-thinking pushes beyond mere tinkering at the fringes by slightly changing this or that particular word, phrase, or gesture. In the spirit of 2 Corinthians 5:17–20, decolonization is rooted in a "new creation." New ways of living, believing, knowing, and worshipping can only spring from being "in Christ."

To sum up, the most radical decolonial challenge concerns the scope and form, and ultimately, the very theology of Absolution. Who in the Christian assemblies of faith and worship has the theological, spiritual, and ethical authority to declare or proclaim God's forgiveness in which particular contexts and for which particular sins—and on what grounds? These questions, obviously, go well beyond the turf of liturgical theology and analysis of rites. All things considered, Penitential rites, performed in and upon the primordial space of worship—the land underneath our sanctuary floors or directly under our feet—can serve as a fruitful gateway toward decolonizing liturgy.

Conclusion

The primordial planetary worship space under the feet of all Christians in North America is the unceded Indigenous nations' lands which makes Christian worship materially possible. Decolonization in this context requires an intentional conversion as delinking from the ongoing ontologies of colonial conquest. Decolonizing Penitential rites for public common worship today calls for a broad and contextual re-scripting of these rites and for adaptive ritual performances. Scripted Penitential rites ought to be flexed and dilated to open them up for a potentially more efficacious dialectic of repentance for postcolonial Christians to participate in even if they are not the original authors of those sinful realities. Authorizing local and decentralized re-scripting of Penitential rites could facilitate a methodological deliverance from attachment to ahistorical and acontextual abstractions of sin for which no one really feels either sorry or responsible for, or, worse, which may effectively re-traumatize the victims and

---

[36] Mignolo, *The Politics of Decolonial Investigations*, 332.

survivors of socio-culturally entrenched systemic sins. Such re-scripting does not demand mere deduction but rather a multiplication of ritual forms for Penitential rites.

The decolonial journey for North American churches is unimaginable without contrition and confession. That is to say, without becoming repentantly ambivalent about our relationship with the underlying (literally) liturgical space—the land on which our sanctuaries stand in which we gather, pray, lament, confess, proclaim, adore, mourn, and praise God. Repentant ambivalence about worshipping on colonized land as the foundational liturgical space is engendered by, as a minimum, contrite openness to the call for interpersonal and social *metanoia*. It is the basic spiritual and liturgical precondition for the theology and praxis of decolonial repair toward a "satisfaction" in the sense Luther advocated for. Kaitlin Curtice has argued that "[i]t is not solely the job of the oppressed to break apart toxic systems: the privileged must partner with the oppressed and come together with their own tools to fix what is broken."[37] Decolonized Penitential rites, although not a panacea, is one such potentially efficacious tool to transform the pernicious privilege of oblivion.

---

[37] Curtice, *Native*, 135.

CHAPTER 13

Decolonizing Churches and the Right to the Sacrament

Dale T. Irvin

Churches by the inner logic of grace that compels them are called to be places of freedom. As such they are to be interstitial experiences manifesting what Homi K. Bhabha calls the "third space."[1] Kristine Suna-Koro in her book, *In Counterpoint: Diaspora, Postcoloniality, and Sacramental Theology*, has pointed toward the transforming possibilities that emerge when the ecclesia through its sacramental imaginary is reconceptualized as

---

[1] Homi K. Bhabha, *The Location of Culture* (New York: Routledge, 1994), 55–5 footnotes in 6 and elsewhere capitalizes the term. Others use the lowercase "third space." Edward W. Soja, who develops the concept further along Bhabha's lines of cultural production, terms it "Thirdspace," as one word. See Edward W. Soja, *Thirdspace: Journeys to Los Angeles and Other Real-and-Imagined Places* (Oxford: Blackwell Publishing: 1996).

D. T. Irvin (✉)
The New School of Biblical Theology, Orlando, FL, USA

© The Author(s), under exclusive license to Springer Nature Switzerland AG 2023
R. C. Barreto, V. Latinovic (eds.), *Decolonial Horizons*, Pathways for Ecumenical and Interreligious Dialogue,
https://doi.org/10.1007/978-3-031-44839-3_13

third space.[2] The Eucharist in particular as a decolonized "semiotic event" is reconfigured as "[…] a hybrid sacramental mystery of non-hegemonic convergence and synergy of divine, human, and nonhuman agencies […]" that is open to all.[3] Building on her work, and in dialogue with Edward Soja and Henri Lefebvre regarding "the right to the city," I will make the case in this chapter for "the right to the sacrament" that extends beyond the ecclesia. In agreement with Suna-Koro, I will conclude that a decolonized sacramental imaginary is not ecclesiocentric, but what Letty Russell termed "oikocentric."[4]

Third Space

The concept of the third space has found its way into a range of disciplines and fields of theoretical work over the last several decades. Sociologist Ray Oldenburg is often credited with having coined the term "third place" in his 1989 publication, *The Great Good Place*, to name locations in urban life such as clubs, cafes, libraries, and even public parks where community

---

[2] Kristine Suna-Koro, *In Counterpoint: Diaspora, Postcoloniality, and Sacramental Theology* (Eugene, OR: Cascade Books, 2017). Suna-Koro has not been alone in developing the notion of the church as third space. Wonhee Anne Joh, *Heart of the Cross* (Louisville: Westminster John Knox Press, 2006) drew upon the concept throughout her book, linking it in a postcolonial framework with the critical Korean concept of *jeong*, which is variously translated into English as love, eros, compassion, relationality, or mutuality. Christopher Richard Baker, *The Hybrid Church in the City: Third Space Thinking* (New York: Ashgate, 2007/London and New York: Routledge, 2016), develops the concept in the context of postmodern urban experience in England. Kirsten van der Ham, "A Familiar Book in a (Un)Familiar Context: A Comparative Qualitative Study on Bible Usage of Indonesian Congregations in the Netherlands," *Journal of World Christianity* 12, No. 2 (fall 2022), 218–250, esp. 231–232 has applied the concept to churches formed from among Indonesian migrants now living in the Netherlands. Joining Suna-Koro in developing the concept of church as third space in practical theology is Sarah Travis, *Decolonizing Preaching: The Pulpit as Postcolonial Space* (Eugene, OR: Cascade Books, 2014). Yohan Go, "Envisioning a Gospel-Driven Korean Methodist Ecclesiology: A Constructive Homiletical Theological Proposal" (PhD diss., Boston University, 2022), https://hdl.handle.net/2144/44827, has more recently drawn upon Joh and Travis to develop the notion of third space for decolonizing Korean churches through preaching.
[3] Suna-Korao, *In Counterpoint*, 286.
[4] Letty M. Russell, (Louisville: Westminster/John Knox Press, 1993), 89.

formation takes place.[5] "Third places" in his theoretical framework are alongside "first place" (the home) and "second places" (work locations). The concept took a much more critical turn in postcolonial theory as "place" gave way to "space," and notions of hybridity and interstitiality took hold. In most instances, the critical postcolonial concept of the third space can be traced along a genealogical trajectory that goes back one way or another to the work of Homi K. Bhabha, especially his book *The Location of Culture* that was published in 1994.[6]

Culture for Bhabha is not just a set of abstractions or concepts that float above our heads.[7] Culture is spatial. It is material. It has location—hence the title of his book. The spatial, material, worldly character of culture does not mean it is not representational. Quite the opposite is in fact the case. The representational aspects of culture are a function of its materiality, or its worldliness. All cultural forms, all symbolic representations, have in some sense a material, or spatial character. They can be located somewhere. They come from some place even if they end up in another place. Historians like to track their journey back through time and space. They go looking to see where someone got this idea or that practice and are delighted when they find what can reasonably be attributed to being called the "source" in an earlier time or another place. In doing so, historians often end up looking for (and thereby constructing) stable meanings that arc across time in a transcendent manner, a practice that Michel Foucault has criticized in his archeological investigations of knowledge, arguing instead for radical ruptures in historical experience.[8]

---

[5] Ray Oldenburg, The Great Good Place: Cafés, Coffee shops, Community centers, Beauty Parlors, General Stores, Bars, Hangouts, and How They Get You through the Day (New York: Paragon House, 1989). Regarding credit for coining the term, see Stuart M. Butler and Carmen Diaz, "'Third Places' as Community Builders," Brookings Institution, Wednesday, September 14, 2016, online at https://www.brookings.edu/blog/upfront/2016/09/14/third-places-as-community-builders/

[6] Homi K. Bhabha, *The Location of Culture* (New York: Routledge, 1994).

[7] See Roger M. Keesing, "Theories of Culture," *Annual Review of Anthropology* 3 (October 1974): 73–97; and idem, "Theories of Culture Revisited," in Robert Borofsky, ed., *Assessing Cultural Anthropology* (New York: McGraw-Hill, Inc., 1994), 301–310.

[8] See Michel Foucault, *The Archaeology of Knowledge* (London: Routledge, 1972); and Hubert L. Dreyfus and Paul Rabinow, *Michel Foucault: Beyond Structuralism and Hermeneutics* (Chicago: University of Chicago Press, 1983).

It is the meaning of these representations that gets dislodged in Bhabha's work, thereby avoiding the construction of a transcendent arc but not ignoring the connections. It is not so much a matter of ruptures as it is a matter of doublings, of multiplicities for Bhabha. Cultures extend over time. They occupy time and space. But this is not to say that they are static. On the contrary, cultures are dynamic processes. New meanings arise from within as expressions of the dynamic process, doing so interactively with the wider built environment. The same object, activity, or experience can have one meaning at one time and then within the same culture assume a different meaning at another time. The multiplicity of meanings according to Bhabha is constitutive of culture. Otherness, in other words, is not an external phenomenon, but is internal to culture, opening up possibilities for difference, change, or we might say theologically, transformation or even transcendence from within.

Bhabha is most interested in investigating these processes in locations that can be termed intersections or meeting places where one or more cultures come into interaction, and where there are imbalances of power. In this regard, he has repeatedly turned to the multiple colonial contexts of inequality in the modern era to locate the third spaces that open up there. The notion of third space for him is a moving one, one that refuses to sit still to be investigated properly. It is the site of an encounter, a crossroads, a transit lounge, and even a refugee camp. Always it is a space of liminality and change. Bhabha often calls them interstices, but it would be misleading if we thought of them as simply spaces in between. These interstices are not gaps but encounters. They are not places of emptiness, but places of openness.[9] They are more like the spaces of intersection and overlap in Venn diagrams, spaces of multiplicity, spaces where more than one thing is going on, spaces on contingency and contradictions, spaces where different and even incommensurable meanings and practices are taking place.

Third space for Bhabha is a linguistic event. It is a place of translation and interpretation, where one thing becomes another. Language is not something apart from the material world. Language participates in the materiality of the world for him, even as it escapes reduction to material causes or production. Language and cultures can both be located without being confined. This is the province of metaphor for Bhabha. Metaphors,

---

[9] Homi K. Bhabha, "In the Cave of Making: Thoughts on Third Space," in Karin Ikas and Gerhard Wagner, eds., *Communicating in the Third Space* (New York: Routledge, 2009), xi.

in which one thing becomes another (I am already thinking of the doctrine of "transubstantiation") are possible as figures of speech only because they are constitutive of culture and the material world through and through.

In his "Preface" to *Communicating in the Third Space*, Bhabha writes:

> To hold, in common, a concept like third space is to begin to see that thinking and writing are acts of translation. Third space, for me, is unthinkable outside the locality of cultural translation.[10]

He goes on to say that it was a form of local knowledge that resulted from a mis-translation of the biblical term for the Holy Spirit by Christian missionaries in Northern India in the early nineteenth century that first led him to the concept of third space. Considering this story from Northern India alongside a host of others up through recent truth and reconciliation commissions, Bhabhi writes:

> What struck me with some force was the emergence of a dialogical site—a moment of enunciation, identification, negotiation—that was suddenly divested of its mastery or sovereignty in the midst of a markedly asymmetrical and unequal engagement of forces. In an intercultural site of enunciation, at the intersection of different languages jousting for authority, a translational space of negotiation opens up through the process of dialogue.[11]

Bhabha's concept draws heavily upon linguistic theory. In an essay first published in 1988 as "The Commitment to Theory"[12] that was reprinted in revised form as "Cultural Diversity and Cultural Difference,"[13] he wrote:

> The linguistic difference that informs any cultural performance is dramatized in the common semiotic account of the disjuncture between the subject of a proposition (*énoncé*) [what is said] and the subject of enunciation [the one who is speaking the words in a specific context], which is not represented in the statement but which is the acknowledgment of its discursive embeddedness and address, its cultural positionality, its reference to a present time and a specific space. The pact of interpretation is never simply an

[10] Bhabha, "In the Cave of Making," ix.
[11] Bhabha, "In the Cave of Making," x.
[12] Homi K. Bhabha, "Commitment to Theory," *New Formations* 5 (Summer 1988), 5–23.
[13] Homi K. Bhabha, H. K. Bhabha, "Cultural Diversity and Cultural Differences," *The Post-Colonial Studies Reader*, ed. B. Ashcroft et al., Routledge, New York, 2006, p. 156.

act of communication between the I and the You designated in the statement. The production of meaning requires that these two places be mobilized in the passage through a Third Space, which represents both the general conditions of language and the specific implication of the utterance in a performative and institutional strategy of which it cannot 'in itself' be conscious. What this unconscious relation introduces is an ambivalence in the act of interpretation.[14]

Bhabha's concept of third space emerges from a linguistic analysis, but it encompasses the full range of binaries and splits that one encounters in social and cultural life. As such it is closely related to his notion of hybridity, which he employs to understand the emergence of new transcultural forms in colonial contexts.[15] Both in turn are embedded in a larger theoretical decolonizing project regarding postcolonial culture and difference. Third spaces are not usually found at the centers of colonial power, but at the margins. When they are found at the centers of colonial power, they have the effect of turning the center into a margin, or creating a space of marginality right at the center. Third spaces are often paradoxical in this regard, for in turning the center into a margin, they introduce borders from within, thereby opening the center to its own crossings.

Third spaces for Bhabha are more than just places of ambivalence in interpretation. Their ambivalence opens them up to something more. Third spaces are borderlands and places of marginalization from which new possibilities emerge. There are multitiered places and spaces where multiple encounters of differences are taking place at the same time. No one is ever just one thing in these spaces. Nothing is ever simple. "Thirdspace is a meeting point, a hybrid place, where one can move beyond the existing borders," writes the urban social geographer Edward W. Soja. "It is also a place of the marginal women and men, where old connections can be disturbed and new ones emerge."[16] Soja writes:

[14] Bhabha, "Commitment to Theory," 20; *The Location of Culture*, 53.
[15] See Antony Easthope, "Bhabha, Hybridity and Identity," *Textual Practice* 12, no. 2 (1998), 341–348. For a closely argued historical study of this phenomenon in the colonial context of African American enslavement, see Mechal Sobel, *The World They Made Together: Black and White Values in Eighteenth-Century Virginia* (Princeton: Princeton University Press, 1987).
[16] Edward W. Soja, "Thirdspace: Toward a New Consciousness of Space and Spatiality," in Karin Ikas and Gerhard Wagner, eds., *Communicating in the Third Space* (New York: Routledge, 2009), 49–61; and idem, *Postmodern Geographies: The Reassertion of Space in Critical Social Theory* (Brooklyn: Verso Books, 2011), 56.

Everything comes together in Thirdspace: subjectivity and objectivity, the abstract and the concrete, the real and the imagined, the knowable and the unimaginable, the repetitive and the differential, structure and agency, mind and body, consciousness and the unconscious, the disciplined and the transdisciplinary, everyday lie and unending history.[17]

Third spaces are spaces of radical openness. They are spaces in which the universe opens up to becoming something new, something different. Bhabha calls them spaces that are "beyond," spaces in which we "dwell 'in the beyond,'" spaces where human beings can *"touch the future on its hither side."*[18] They are what Levinas might term spaces of transcendence in our midst, places that are "transcendent to the point of absence."[19] In this regard they are critical spaces, spaces where the current way of living, the current arrangements of power in the world, can be criticized. Soja writes, "A Thirdspace consciousness is the precondition to building a community of resistance to all forms of hegemonic power."[20]

Third spaces are spaces where doubling takes place, where one encounters ambiguous signs that lie between the familiar and the unknown, where the familiar becomes unknown and the unknown becomes familiar. They are, in other words, spaces of simultaneous dwelling and crossing, or crossing and dwelling. They are spaces, says Bhabha of the "uncanny," or as he prefers to translate the term from Freud in German, the "unhoming."[21] Third spaces are places where one is "unhomed," where the familiar is transformed into the strange and the strange is made familiar. They are spaces where one's self becomes another. "The Third Space," Bhabha

[17] Soja, "Thirdspace," 54.
[18] Bhabha, *The Location of Culture*, 7, emphasis original.
[19] Levinas, God. Death and Time, 224.
[20] Soja, "Thirdspace," 56.
[21] Bhabha, *The Location of Culture*, 13; see also Dale T. Irvin, "Theology, Migration, and the Homecoming," in Elaine Padilla and Peter C. Phan, eds., *Theology of Migration in the Abrahamic Religions* (New York: Palgrave Macmillan, 2014), 7–25. Freud's essay, *Das Unheimlich*, was originally published in German in 1919. The standard English translation of the title has been *The Uncanny*. Freud, however, argues for the etymological meaning of "Unheimlich" at the beginning of his essay, interpreting it over against "Heimlich." Freud notes that the word has also come to mean in German that which is eerie, but then goes on to argue: "I can say in advance that both these courses lead to the same conclusion—that the uncanny [Unheimlich] is that species of the frightening that goes back to what was once well known and has long been familiar." It is the experience of the familiar becoming unfamiliar, or of one becoming "unhomed." See Sigmund Freud, *The Uncanny*, David McLintock, gras. (New York: Penguin Putnam Inc., 2003), 124.

writes, "is a challenge to the limits of the self in the act of reaching out to what is liminal in the historic experience, and in the cultural representation, of other peoples, times, languages, texts."[22] In an extended passage in *The Location of Culture*, he elaborates:

> The intervention of the Third Space of enunciation, which makes the structure of meaning and reference an ambivalent process, destroys this mirror of representation in which cultural knowledge is customarily revealed as an integrated, open, expanding code. Such an intervention quite properly challenges our sense of the historical identity of culture as a homogenizing, unifying force, authenticated by the originary Past, kept alive in the national condition of the People. [...] It is only when we understand that all cultural statements and systems are constructed in this contradictory and ambivalent space of enunciation, that we begin to understand why hierarchical claims to an inherent originality or 'purity' of culture are untenable [...]. It is that Third Space, though unrepresentable in itself, which constitutes the discursive conditions of enunciation that ensure that the meaning and symbols of culture have no primordial unity or fixity; that even the same signs can be appropriated, translated, rehistoricized, and read anew.[23]

THIRD SPACE AND THE SACRED

I think Bhabha is talking about processes that are fundamentally religious. He does not have to use the language of religious studies overtly to be pointing us in this direction. I think he is describing what religions of the world often call the "unveiling," "revelation," or even "conversion."

Third space is the space of crossing and dwelling, where foreign lands become homelands (migration) and home lands become foreign lands (again, the uncanny, the "unhomely" and "unhoming").[24] Third space is an ambivalent space of enunciation. As such it is a weak space, the space of

---

[22] Bhabha, "In the Cave of Making," xiii.
[23] Bhabha, The Location of Culture, 54–55.
[24] Here I am echoing the description of Christians found in the *Letter to Diognetus* (190–200 CE), 5.5, Joseph B. Lightfoot and J. R. Harmer, eds., *The Apostolic Fathers* (London: Macmillan and Co., 1891), 505.

13 DECOLONIZING CHURCHES AND THE RIGHT TO THE SACRAMENT 255

an "event" in John Caputo's terms.[25] Caputo links this with his own conception of the divine as the weakest principle in the universe. It is an interstitial space, a space "in between" that is not empty, but full. It is a space of transformation and conversion, where one thing becomes another. It is a space that connects the seen and the unseen, what is and what is not (or not yet). Third space is the space of simultaneous coming and going. The third space is a space of immanent transcendence, or transcendent immanence. It is that which is unrepresentable in itself but is the ground of representation. One is reminded of St. Augustine's quip, that if you comprehend it, it is not God.[26] The ancients in the Christian movement called it the "mystery," and the manner of representation that it grounds a "sacrament."

I cited Edward Soja earlier not only because he has helped develop the concept of the third space. Soja was a social geographer who studied cities.[27] He recognized the manner in which temples and their accompanying ceremonial activities were key components in the emergence of cities some 10,000 years ago in human experience. Even in ancient locations that generally lacked explicit temples or identifiable religious monuments, such as the Harappan Civilization in the Indus Valley that emerged around 3000 BCE and flourished from 2500 BCE to 1900 BCE, there is extensive archeological evidence for priests performing rituals, including sacrifices, and for ceremonial beliefs and practices that engage the unseen world of spiritual beings.[28]

---

[25] John D. Caputo, *The Weakness of God: A Theology of the Event* (Bloomington: University of Indiana Press, 2006), 9, writes: "The name of God is the name of an event transpiring in being's restless heart, creating confusion in the house of being, forcing being into motion, mutation, transformation, reversal. The name of God is the name of what can happen to being, of what being would become, of what rising up from below being pushes being beyond itself, outside itself, as being's hope, being's desire. The name of God is being's aspiration, its inspiration, its assertion, for God is not being or a being, but a ghostly quasi-being, a very holy spirit."

[26] Edmund Hill, ed., The Works of Saint Augustine. A Translation for the 21st Century. Sermons, III/4 (New York: New City Press, 1992), 220.

[27] See for instance Soja, Thirdspace: Journeys to Los Angeles and Other Real-and-Imagined Places.

[28] See Gregory L. Possehl, *The Indus Civilization: A Contemporary Perspective* (Plymouth, UK: AltaMira Press, 2002), esp. Chapter 8, "Indus Religion," 141–156; and Jane R. McIntosh, *The Ancient Indus Valley: New Perspectives* (Santa Barbara: ABC Clio, Inc., 2008), esp. Chapter 9, "Religion and Ideology," 275–300. McIntosh argues that the Great Bath in the city of Mohenjo-daro was a specifically religious building, but this is the only one in the Harappan Civilization that she identifies is such a way.

While no two cities on earth have ever been exactly the same, they share features of spatial design that incorporate cosmological symbols that express collective belief systems. Soja notes that despite what appears at times to be chaotic or disorganized urban forms, even in the ancient world,

> the built environment was not simply a random construction. From the very start, then, urban space was designed and produced as a self-conscious expression of local and territorial culture, a materialized "symbolic zone" to use Iain Chamber's term, in which the real and the imagined commingled to comprehend, define, and ceremonialize a much-enlarged scale of social relations and community [...].[29]

Liliana Gómez and Walter Van Herek in the introduction to their edited volume, *The Sacred in the City*, are more explicit in their analysis of the manner in which the built environment, ancient and contemporary, is sacred space. They argue that the sacred is diffused throughout the urban experience, in no small part due to the fact that human beings have the capacity to imagine and believe in what cannot be seen. This is a critical insight for understanding the manner in which the sacred is more than institutional religion. The sacred cannot be reduced to its theistic forms and expressions, for there are non-theistic forms and expressions of this dimension.[30] They prefer the term "the sacred" over "religion" as a means of liberating this dimension that Rudolf Otto called "the holy" from its institutional captivity.[31] While religion is often limited to specific institutions, the sacred is more diffused throughout the built environment.

Here it is important to note what R. Scott Appleby calls the "ambivalence of the sacred."[32] Appleby follows the Christian systemic theologian Paul Tillich, who argued for the fundamental ambiguity of the sacred that appears phenomenologically in human history as both the divine and the

---

[29] Edward W. Soja, *Postmetropolis: Critical Studies of Cities and Regions* (New York: Wiley-Blackwell, 2000), 34.

[30] Liliana Gómez and Walter Van Herck, "Framing the Sacred in the City: An Introduction," *The Sacred in the City*, Liliana Gómez and Walter Van Herck, eds. (London and New York: Continuum International Publishing Group, 2021), 1–12.

[31] Rudolf Otto, *The Idea of the Holy: An Inquiry into the Non-Rational Factor in the Idea of the Divine and Its Relation to the Rational*, John W. Harvey, trans. (London: Oxford University Press, 1926).

[32] R. Scott Appleby, *The Ambivalence of the Sacred: Religion, Violence, and Reconciliation* (Lanham, MD: Rowman & Littlefield Publishers, 2000).

demonic.[33] Following Otto's depiction of the mystery of the sacred or the holy as always both terrifying (*tremendum*) and compelling (*fascinosum*), Tillich argued that the ground of being out of which the holy emerges in human experience is an abyss that is the source of both the divine and the demonic. Tillich continues:

> Such a concept of the holy opens large sections of the history of religion to theological understanding, by explaining the ambiguity of the concept of holiness at every religious level. Holiness cannot become actual except through holy "objects." But holy objects are not holy in and of themselves. They are holy only by negating themselves in pointing to the divine of which they are the mediums. If they establish themselves as holy, they become demonic. They still are "holy," but their holiness is antidivine.[34]

Tillich goes on to argue that a nation that sees itself as inherently holy and not just a medium for the holy becomes demonic. The same can be applied to religious institutions, which see themselves as inherently holy. Having noted this, it is important to clarify that while religion has often been complicit in the project of colonization, the sacred ultimately cannot be colonized.[35]

This is also not to argue that the sacred is all-encompassing. It does not mean there are not also aspects, experiences, or dimensions of the built environment that are "profane," to use Émile Durkheim's terminology.[36] I would argue here, however, that the boundary between the sacred and the profane that Durkheim sought to establish is far more permeable and fluid than he acknowledged. Third spaces are those times and places where the sacred and profane become indistinguishable, where the ambivalence between them opens up to new possibilities. Suna-Koro follows this line of thinking to make the argument that the Chalcedonian understanding of Christ as fully human and fully divine makes Christ and not just the sacraments a third space. Central to Bhabha's understanding of a third space is that it is a place where unequal powers converge, without the power

---

[33] Paul Tillich, "The Demonic: A Contribution to the Interpretation of History," in *The Interpretation of History* (New York: Charles Scribner's Sons, 1936), 77–123.

[34] Paul Tillich, Systematic *Theology, vol 1: Reason and Revelation, Being and God* (Chicago: University of Chicago Press, 1951), 216.

[35] Gómez and Van Herek, "Framing the Sacred in the City," 4.

[36] See Émile Durkheim, *The Elementary Forms of Religious Life*, trans. by Carol Cosman (Oxford: Oxford University Press, 2002 [1912 original]), 36–38.

imbalance continuing. Concerning the Chalcedonian "concurrence," Suna-Koro writes:

> But this is a Third Space of reconciled relationality, a borderland between a suffocating union of absorption and a grinding tension of allergic difference. Jesus Christ embodies the hybrid Third Space in which Divinity givers without forcing to take, and assumes to transfigure, not assimilate without residue or consent.[37]

"Christ, as the hybrid hypostatic union of Third Space, is also a theopolitics incarnate and sacramentalized," she writes. Following Anselm Min, she argues that the hypostatic union is the sacrament of divine solidarity with suffering and injustice.[38] Suffering and injustice are, of course, found within the church, but they are not only found there. They are outside the church as well. The movement in a third space has to flow in either direction, from church to world and from world to church. This means that the potential and actual third spaces of sacramental solidarity cannot be confined within the built environments of the walls of the sanctuary of the Christian church, within the built pool of a baptismal font, or behind the built environment of an altar. In the wider built environment, all third spaces are sacramental, if not fully sacraments in the classical theological sense.

The Western or Latin theological tradition has tended not only to confine the sacraments to ecclesial spaces, but has limited their number (7 for Roman Catholics, 2 for Protestants). In effect the church colonized the sacred and held it captive within its ecclesial practices. A considerable body of recent theology, often drawing upon Eastern Orthodox theological resources, has sought to free the sacramental imagination from its exclusively ecclesial location. The Orthodox theologian John Chryssavgis has provided one of the most thorough articulations of this broader sacramental understanding in his recent book *Creation as Sacrament: Reflections on Ecology and Spirituality*. Chryssavgis is admittedly addressing the broader global ecological crisis that we are now experiencing, which guides his arguments. In doing so, he situates the human person, or humanity as a whole, within the context of creation, the world that was built by God. He writes for instance:

---

[37] Suna-Koro, *In Counterpoint*, 248.
[38] Suna-Koro, *In Counterpoint*, 250.

When we discern the sacramental principle in the world—the presence of God in every person and every place—then we can rejoice and celebrate the fullness of life and the joy of creation.[39]

In his chapter in an edited volume on eco-theology that was published in 2000 Chryssavgis has one passing reference to the built environment being capable of sacramental meaning. He writes:

Just as the Spirit is the "air" that the whole world breathes, so too the earth is the "ground" which we all share. Were God not present in the density of a city, or in the beauty of a forest, or in the sand of a desert, then God would not be present in heaven either. So if, indeed, there exists today a vision that is able to transcend—perhaps transform—all national and denominational tensions, it may well be that of our environment understood as sacrament of the Spirit. The breath of the Spirit brings out the sacramentality of nature and bestows on it the fragrance of resurrection.[40]

Noting that the sacred is present in the density of a city, Chryssavgis immediately leaves it to return to the argument for "the sacramentality of nature." I take "nature" for him to mean what he also calls "creation," the cosmos, an environment that God built. I want to linger in the human settlement, the village, or the city, the environment that humanity has built and inhabits, what the Greeks called the *oikoumenē* or the part of the earth in which humans built their houses, to locate the sacramental, the sacraments, and third spaces more explicitly. Sacraments entail human labor, the human-built environment, which reaches its greatest density in urban experiences. Sacraments, third spaces, are spaces of grace, found in the collective reality of our built environments. They belong to the city, not just to the church. Some of these are offered by ecclesial communities and have an explicit Christian mark or identity to them. Others do not. In either case, as third spaces, they cannot be closed, they cannot be colonized, otherwise they cease to be fully sacramental.

---

[39] John Chryssavgis, Creation as Sacrament: Reflections on Ecology and Spirituality (London: T & T Clark, 2019), 93.

[40] John Chryssavgis, "The World of the Icon and Creation" in *Christianity and Ecology: Seeking the Well-Being of Earth and Humans*, ed. Dieter T. Hessel and Rosemary Radford Ruether (Boston: Harvard University Press, 2000), 91.

The Right to the City and the Right to the Sacraments

One of Edward W. Soja's most passionate commitments was to making cities places of greater justice. In doing so, he drew upon Henri Lefebvre's notion of "the right to the city."[41] Cities are collective human enterprises that emerge from the collaborative work of people holding different interests, skills, and conceptions of their purpose. They emerge from surplus production and in turn help to accelerate those processes that create surpluses. The notion of "the right to the city" means that both the intellectual and material resources that are produced by the collaborations that build cities belong to all people who live in the city, not just some. David Harvey summarizes Lefebvre's concept succinctly:

> The right to the city is far more than the individual liberty to access urban resources: it is a right to change ourselves by changing the city. It is, moreover, a common rather than an individual right since this transformation inevitably depends upon the exercise of a collective power to reshape the processes of urbanization. The freedom to make and remake our cities and ourselves is, I want to argue, one of the most precious yet most neglected of our human rights.[42]

As the webpage for the organization, "Global Platform for the Right to the City," states:

> The Right to the City is the right of all inhabitants, present and future, permanent and temporary, to inhabit, use, occupy, produce, govern and enjoy just, inclusive, safe and sustainable cities, villages and human settlements, defined as commons essential to a full and decent life.[43]

Soja extends this concept in the spatial direction of a new regionalism and internationalism. In doing so, he allows us to see the right to the city to be

---

[41] See Henri Lefebvre, "The Right to the City," chapter 14 in *Writings on Cities*, translated and edited by Eleonore Kofman and Elizabeth Lebas (New York: Wiley-Blackwell, 1996), 147–159.

[42] David Harvey, "The Right to the City," *New Left Review* 53 (Sept/Oct 2008), 23.

[43] GPR2C "Know More" webpage, online at https://www.right2city.org/the-right-to-the-city/, accessed June 4, 2022.

a universal human right, without abandoning the importance of space and place.[44]

I am arguing here first that the sacred extends beyond the specifically Christian experience in our human built environments.[45] The Christian sacramental experience participates in a wider ecology or economy of the sacred in our built environments. This is not to argue that Christians should be compelled to participate in the wider sacramental economy of human life and production. I also leave aside the question of whether other religious actors and communions or communities ought to open their spiritual doors to Christians and others who are not directly engaged in their life. Acknowledging the commonality of the sacred and not being compelled to participate in the sacred experiences of others are not incompatible. But this means that the economy of the sacred goes in both directions. The sacraments that the church offers are derived from the same world of human production and meaning. As such they do not belong only to the church, but are open to the city and to the world. The right to the city and the right to the sacrament are two sides of the same reality. Harvey argues, "The question of what kind of city we want cannot be divorced from that of what kind of social ties, relationship to nature, lifestyles, technologies and aesthetic values we desire."[46] This applies to religious, spiritual, or faith-based communities as much as it does to any other component of the complex urban ecology.

What does this look like in theological terms? Arguing that baptism must only be by water in the name of the Trinity or Jesus Only ignores Aloysius Pieris' argument for the double baptism of Jesus himself. Acknowledging that Jesus was baptized in water by John, Pieris writes:

> The Baptizer preached bad news about the coming judgment, but Jesus, whom he baptized, had good news to give about imminent liberation. The precursor was conferring baptism of water on converts. The beloved Son

---

[44] Edward W. Soja, *Seeking Spatial Justice* (Minneapolis: University of Minnesota Press, 2010), 65–67.

[45] This obviously puts me in opposition to what has been termed "Christian exclusivism," and on the side of either inclusivist or pluralist perspectives, both of which I can affirm. These basic perspectives and their various nuanced alternatives are set forth succinctly in Alan Race and Paul M. Hedges, eds. *Christian Approaches to Other Faiths* (London: SCM Press, 2008). My own perspective lines up most closely with that of Peter C Phan, *The Joy of Religious Pluralism: A Personal Journey* (Maryknoll: Orbis Books, 2017).

[46] Harvey, "The Right to the City," 23.

would rather have the baptism of the cross conferred on himself for the conversion of the world. The one would question the belief that salvation came simply by membership in the chosen community and ask for individual conversion, but the other would change the people so converted into a community of love.[47]

Restricting the eucharist to those who have been baptized in the church ignores Jesus' own practice. The event that has come to be called "the Last Supper" came to dominate early Christian sacramental imagination, but it was not the only eucharistic theology that we find in the first century. The Didache does not refer to the Jerusalem tradition in explaining the eucharist, but refers to the open-air meals that took place in Galilee. In John 6:11 at one of those open-air meals, Jesus took the loaves, gave thanks (εὐχαριστήσας), and distributed them to all of those who were seated, a number that the Gospel writer puts at 5000. There is no reference to anyone asking for baptismal certificates.

Restricting ordination to those who have had hands properly laid upon them by a bishop or by others in the church forgets the instructions of Hippolytus of Rome in chapter 9 of *The Apostolic Tradition* that someone who has suffered for their faith need not have hands laid on them for the office of deacon or elder as they have already been ordained by their confession. Baptism, eucharist, and ministry are far more complex than even the most engaged ecumenical theological conversations of the past century recognized them as being.[48]

I opened this essay with a plea that we seek to decolonize the sacraments. I have sought to do so by moving them into the third space of the sacred in the city. I close this chapter with a plea that we decolonize an ecclesiocentric understanding of the location of the sacraments, and in the words of Letty Russell, take up an *oikocentric* view that situates them in the world. She explains:

> The shift from an *ecclesiocentric* to a *theocentric* and, for some, to an *oikocentric* perspective means that the church becomes more modest in its claims to be the medium of God's action and instead sees itself as a sign or instrument

---

[47] Aloysius Pieris, *An Asian Theology of Liberation* (Maryknoll: Orbis Books, 1988), 48.
[48] I am of course referencing the Faith and Order Commission, *Baptism, Eucharist and Ministry: Paper #111* (Geneva: World Council of Churches, 1982) and the subsequent discussion in the ecumenical world, which has now been greatly eclipsed in contemporary discussions of ecclesiology.

of the *action, which is taking place in and through all parts of the groaning universe.*[49]

I don't argue that churches should cease their sacramental practices. Decolonizing the sacraments of the church requires opening them to the world, and opening the vision of the church itself to seeing the sacraments not just in the world that God has created, but in the built and living world that human beings have created. Decolonizing the sacraments allows for seeing the sacramental realities that are found in the built human environments, in communities outside the church, in the city itself, and in all nations and peoples.

I have found a recent ally in this regard in a forthcoming book by the ecclesiologist Fred R. Anderson. Anderson is best known as a liturgical theologian whose works are published in a number of our hymnals.[50] He was for several decades before his retirement the senior pastor of Madison Avenue Presbyterian Church in New York City. He is best known in Presbyterian church circles for advocating the restoration of the weekly eucharist in worship and for his high sacramental liturgical practices. Anderson's new book is titled *Why Did Jesus Die and What Does That Have to Do with Me?: A Biblical and Sacramental Understanding of Atonement*. In its pages, he makes the argument as a working pastor that the atonement only makes sense when it is performed sacramentally, and not preached dogmatically. He emphasizes the meaning of "at-one-ment," which is about (com)union and not substitution. In the final chapter of the book, Anderson turns his attention specifically to baptism and eucharist. Regarding the latter, he notes that Christ died for all. Why are not all then welcomed to the table, he asks? He writes:

> In his life, Jesus welcomed all who would come to him. Excluding no one, he welcomed the outcast, the marginalized, the poor, the sick, the suffering—all of whom the religious establishment had designated sinner. He bound them into community within himself, eating and drinking with them. Even Judas was at that first table. How then, can anyone claiming to minister in Christ's name turn another away who comes in faith?

---

[49] Letty M. Russell, *Church in the Round: Feminist Interpretations of the Church* (Louisville: Westminster/John Knox Press, 1993), 89.

[50] See Fred R. Anderson, *Singing Psalms of Joy and Praise* (Louisville: Westminster Press, 1986); and idem, *Singing God's Psalms: Metrical Psalms and Reflections for Each Sunday in the Church Year* (Grand Rapids: Wm. B. Eerdmans Publishing Co., 2016).

Anderson goes on to argue that "the sacraments are means of grace, not discipline." To deny the sacrament to any person, he writes, "... is not only a distortion of the sacrament; it is an abuse of the gift and extraordinary privilege of pastoral ministry."

> Being a steward of the mysteries of God—one of the ancient terms for those the church ordains to the ministry of word and sacrament—does not mean we have been set aside to defend the Risen Lord from those who would try to abuse him. He is quite able to do that for himself if need be. More likely, he is welcoming the abuser, forgiving, and beginning that person's transformation. Dare we stand in the way of that? We must remember that the Eucharist is not a reward for having lived saintly lives, but medicine for our mortality—food to nurture us more deeply into faithfulness.[51]

Anderson does not minimize the importance of the sacraments. He does not advocate abandoning their distinctive practice. He does argue that all are to be welcomed to the table, whether or not they are members of the church. I call it a decolonizing turn from the disciplinary practices of the modern colonial to the ancient understanding of the mystery of grace made manifest in our presence. The right to the city is the right to the sacrament. All are welcomed.

---

[51] Fred R. Anderson, *Why Did Jesus Die and What Does That Have to Do with Me? A Biblical and Sacramental Understanding of Atonement* (Eugene, OR: Wipf & Stock, 2022), 237.

Index[1]

A
Abya Yala, 190
African church, 87n27, 182
Anti-imperial, 91n44
Anti-racist, 167
Anzaldúa, Gloria, 6n10, 7, 25, 28, 98
Authoritarianism, 94
Autochthonous, 12, 192
Autonomy/autonomous, 24, 91, 92, 189

B
Baptismal, 174, 175, 258, 262
Bias, 125n19
Binary, 90, 98, 252
Birth, 7, 81, 91, 93, 150
Black Lives Matter, 171, 180

C
Capitalism, 43, 44, 67, 81, 82, 97, 191, 199
Caribbean, 1, 5n8, 20, 24, 24n23, 25, 31, 32n54, 33, 94, 187
Catholic, Catholicism, 11, 15, 59, 92, 103, 103n4, 113, 115, 116, 144, 147, 149, 152–157, 159, 162, 168–171, 169n12, 173–175, 179, 184, 208–212, 210n15, 214n22, 224, 226
CELAM, 93, 110, 206
Christianity, 4, 8–11, 21, 47, 48, 67–70, 72, 90–96, 102–107, 103n4, 110, 115, 121–139, 143–162, 167, 171, 181, 185, 187, 187n10, 189, 193, 195–198, 205, 226, 231, 243

---

[1] Note: Page numbers followed by 'n' refer to notes.

Christology, 189n15
Church of the poor, 93, 135
Colonial, 3–6, 4n4, 9, 10, 12, 13,
    21–23, 27, 28, 32, 32n54, 33,
    42–44, 57, 57n7, 58, 60–63,
    61n16, 62n22, 68, 70, 71,
    79–82, 81n5, 85, 88, 90, 97, 98,
    102–104, 118, 122, 123, 127,
    129, 130n38, 132–136, 133n49,
    139, 145–147, 157, 162, 167,
    172, 182, 188–190, 193,
    195–199, 209, 209n14, 210,
    226–228, 231–233, 239, 240,
    243, 244, 250, 252, 252n15, 264
Colonialism, coloniality, 4–6, 5n8, 9,
    11, 12, 20–35, 43–46, 43n18,
    51, 57, 60, 61, 63, 66, 68, 71,
    74, 81, 81n5, 82, 92, 97, 98,
    101, 103–105, 114, 121, 122,
    123n8, 124, 129, 131–133, 136,
    139, 144–147, 163, 166, 167,
    169–171, 187, 189, 191, 197,
    200, 209n13, 211, 232–234,
    239, 242
Community, 4, 9, 10, 23n17, 24–27,
    37–53, 64, 65, 69, 71, 73, 81,
    82, 89, 96, 109, 110, 112–114,
    116, 118, 119, 123–125, 131,
    132, 135–137, 139, 145, 157,
    169, 171, 172, 179, 188, 191,
    193, 196, 206–227, 210n15,
    212n20, 214n22, 222n28, 229,
    230, 232–235, 239, 244, 248,
    253, 256, 259, 261–263
Conciliar, Conciliarism, 92n48
Confession, 160, 174, 228–230,
    228n2, 234–242, 236n22,
    238n25, 245, 262
Conflict, 9, 20, 41, 49, 70, 85,
    103n4, 218
Conquest, 13, 20, 29, 32, 33, 97,
    228, 231, 240, 244

Contextualize, 65, 174
Creativity, 6, 23n17, 25, 98, 117, 120,
    210, 214n22, 225
Culture, 6n10, 8, 9, 11, 23n17, 25,
    28, 34, 52, 61–63, 65, 66, 70,
    73, 74, 80, 88, 90, 92, 97, 99,
    102, 104–106, 108, 111, 113,
    116, 118, 119, 125, 128, 137,
    138, 184, 192, 193, 197, 214,
    223, 249–252, 254, 256

D
Dangerous memory, 234
De-colonial, de-colonize, 1–16,
    20–35, 58, 66–73, 75, 80, 83,
    90–99, 121–139, 143–162,
    183–201, 205–245, 247–264
Delgado, Teresa, 124n14
Democratization, 195
Diaspora, 1, 9, 10, 20–35, 58–60, 62,
    68, 68n42, 70, 94, 157, 235
Dictatorship, 94
Dussel, Enrique, 4, 4n5, 8, 8n17, 9,
    11, 33, 90, 125, 135, 135n58,
    137, 139, 144

E
Eastern Orthodoxy, 258
Ecclesiology, 2–4, 8, 12, 15, 163, 168,
    172, 176n41, 179, 180, 182,
    197, 240, 262n48
Ecumenical, ecumenism, 10, 11, 15,
    79–99, 80n1, 159, 160, 162,
    184, 213, 216, 227–245,
    262, 262n48
Ellacuría, Ignacio, 210n16, 216n25
Epistemology, 11, 81,
    121–125, 195–197
Eurocentric, 5, 9, 11, 12, 134,
    143–162, 171

Europe, 4, 8, 39, 43, 44, 46, 103, 106, 143, 144, 146–148, 150, 152, 156–158, 161, 162, 170, 175, 190

F
Francis, Pope, 11, 15, 101–120, 231, 242, 243

G
Gender, 2, 30, 64, 74, 95, 97, 98, 167, 209
Genocide, 4, 66
Global South, 12, 90, 92, 93, 95, 144–147, 162, 189
Grassroot, 94, 96, 127, 132, 135–137, 139, 207, 211, 216, 223

H
Hierarchy, 4, 5, 15, 21, 72, 144, 147, 209
Hispanic, 27, 28, 165, 231

I
Identity, 2, 9, 24, 27–29, 45, 47, 66, 67, 69–71, 88, 89, 93, 98, 99, 108, 114, 115, 117, 118, 138, 152, 154, 156, 158, 167, 187, 191, 195, 197, 212, 213n21, 216, 240, 254, 259
Imagination, 24, 27, 187, 187n10, 189, 190, 195, 198, 200, 206, 239, 258, 262
Imprisonments, 94
Inconsistencies, 184
Independence, 7, 104, 121, 122, 123n8
Indigenization, 126, 130
Indigenous, 3n3, 4, 5, 5n6, 11, 13, 32n54, 56, 57, 60, 61, 65–70, 68n42, 72–74, 82, 89, 90, 95–99, 123, 125, 126, 128, 129, 131, 135–138, 136n62, 145, 184, 186, 190, 194, 196, 198, 209, 228–233, 229n3, 240, 241, 243, 244
Inequality, 2, 26, 167, 209, 250
International Missionary Council (IMC), 85

K
Korea, 84, 102
Kwok Pui-lan, 31

L
Latin, Latinx, 5, 7, 14, 41, 42, 97, 103n4, 148, 150, 151, 157, 158, 158n28, 162, 183–201, 222n28, 225, 231, 258
Lee, Michael E., 216n24
LGBTQ+, 213
Liberation theologies, 10, 13, 15, 92n49, 97, 205–210, 209n13, 225
Luther, Martin, 146n4, 158–161, 228, 228n2, 229, 241, 245

M
Marginalized, 10, 24n23, 74, 95, 184, 226, 263
Marxist, 145, 210
Materiality, 249, 250
Medieval, 179n49, 228n2
Memory, 6, 10, 13, 14, 69, 71, 72, 80, 138, 138n69, 173, 213, 214, 216, 234
Metaphors, 48, 250
Metz, Johann Baptist, 234, 240, 240n28

Mignolo, Walter, 6, 7, 21, 25, 28, 33, 81, 97, 132, 133n49, 233n15, 244
Migration, 9, 10, 23–29, 44–46, 58, 62, 118, 137–139, 157, 254
Mission, missionaries, 11, 14, 32n55, 79, 80n1, 83–89, 93, 102–105, 108–113, 118, 119, 124n12, 125, 129, 132, 133, 137, 138, 167, 169, 170, 172, 182, 185, 190, 193, 194, 225, 251
Multicultural, 27, 28, 52

N

Nationalism, 50, 132, 138, 192, 199, 200
Neoliberalism, 2, 96

O

Oppression and Marginalization, 2, 10, 11, 26, 45, 60–63, 68n42, 69, 70, 81, 98, 127, 167, 170, 185, 209, 252
Ordination, 262
Orthodox, Orthodoxy, 148, 193, 258

P

Patriarchy, 66, 67, 81, 82, 182
Paul VI, Pope, 119
Peripheries, 11, 25, 74, 104, 112
Political theology, 47, 47n28
Postcoloniality, 227
Presbyterian Church, 263
Protestant, Protestantism, 80, 83, 84, 103n6, 129, 144, 147, 155–159, 161, 162, 165, 234, 240, 258
Puerto Rico, 1, 9, 20, 20n2, 21, 28, 32n54, 124n14

Q

Queer, 6n10, 97

R

Racism, 4n4, 10, 12, 39, 43n18, 51, 52, 60, 63, 66, 67, 97, 163, 166, 167, 169–175, 177, 182, 191, 239
Remembrance, 243

S

Second Vatican Council, 104, 220n27
Secularism, 105
Sexuality, 30, 74, 97, 98
Social justice, 70, 206
Solidarity, 25, 27, 92–94, 96, 133, 138, 225, 234, 239, 258
Spanish, 2, 3n2, 5n6, 20, 28, 32n54, 33, 56, 68, 189n15, 192, 198, 222n28, 225
Synodality, 75, 210

T

Thomas, M. M., 88
Tillich, Paul, 256, 257
Tolerance, 155, 162
Totalitarian, 189
Tradition, 2, 13, 15, 34, 48, 52, 65–70, 73, 88, 90, 102, 106, 107, 107n19, 113–116, 116n55, 119, 126n21, 152, 153, 157, 161, 178–180, 192, 193, 196, 206, 208, 220, 223, 225, 229, 230, 234–240, 236n22, 244, 258, 262
Transgender, 67

W
World Christianity, 10, 11, 90–96, 121–139, 193, 198
World Council of Churches (WCC), 80n1, 85, 86, 86n26, 87n27, 89, 262n48
World Missionary Conference, 83, 84
World War I, 85, 132

Y
Yoruba, 130, 138